DIRECTORY OF COMMONWEALTH LAW SCHOOLS 2003/2004

T0333857

Cavendish
Publishing
Limited

London • Sydney • Portland, Oregon

ON BEHALF OF THE
COMMONWEALTH LEGAL EDUCATION ASSOCIATION

DIRECTORY OF COMMONWEALTH LAW SCHOOLS 2003/2004

Edited by
Professor John Hatchard
General-Secretary, CLEA

Cavendish
Publishing
Limited

London • Sydney • Portland, Oregon

ON BEHALF OF THE
COMMONWEALTH LEGAL EDUCATION ASSOCIATION

First edition first published in Great Britain 2003 by
Cavendish Publishing Limited, The Glass House,
Wharton Street, London WC1X 9PX, United Kingdom
Telephone: + 44 (0)20 7278 8000   Facsimile: + 44 (0)20 7278 8080
Email: info@cavendishpublishing.com
Website: www.cavendishpublishing.com

Published in the United States by Cavendish Publishing
c/o International Specialized Book Services,
5804 NE Hassalo Street, Portland,
Oregon 97213-3644, USA

Published in Australia by Cavendish Publishing (Australia) Pty Ltd
3/303 Barrenjoey Road, Newport, NSW 2106, Australia

British Library Cataloguing in Publication Data
Directory of Commonwealth Law Schools 2003–2004
1 Law Schools – Commonwealth countries – Directories
I Commonwealth Legal Education Association

340'0711'0171241

Library of Congress Cataloguing in Publication Data
Data available

ISBN 1-85941-758-2

1 3 5 7 9 10 8 6 4 2

Printed and bound in Great Britain

To all those who have contributed to the work of the Commonwealth Legal Education Association over its first 30 years

FOREWORD

The Commonwealth Legal Education Association (CLEA) is proud to present its 2003/2004 *Directory of Commonwealth Law Schools* which has been compiled and edited by the General-Secretary of the CLEA, Professor John Hatchard. The previous editions published in 1996 and 1999 proved invaluable to law teachers, law students and legal practitioners throughout the Commonwealth and beyond.

Despite the fact that we are into the 21st century and in the midst of the information technology revolution, the need for the directory in book form is still essential because many Commonwealth law schools are in developing countries, where electronic access is not always available or reliable. In this era of the global village law, the directory provides Commonwealth law teachers, and those in non-Commonwealth countries wishing to network with colleagues throughout the Commonwealth, with a ready source of valuable information.

The events of 11 September 2001 have graphically illustrated how globalisation has impacted on the new world order. While structural adjustment programmes have continued to threaten the national economies of developing countries and the developed world has continued to retreat behind tariff walls and agricultural subsidies, a new danger has arisen. The clarion call to defeat 'global terrorism' in all its guises has led to a rolling back of human rights gains in many countries – developed and developing. As a result it is crucial that law schools in the Commonwealth and elsewhere produce young lawyers who are alive to these dangers and suitably equipped to assist their countries in devising suitable responses. This is particularly true of law schools in developing countries that are still in transition from dictatorship to democracy. Every effort must be made to ensure that the human rights gains made are not reversed under the guise of defeating terrorism. An important method of educating law students about these dangers and how to deal with them is to draw upon the richness of talent that exists in law schools across the Commonwealth.

The CLEA tries to respond to the need for contact amongst Commonwealth law schools by publishing the directory and other works of interest for law teachers, law students and legal practitioners. To this end I would encourage all users of the directory who are not institutional or individual members of the CLEA, but who qualify for membership, to enrol as members of the organisation. By so doing we can work together to respond to the challenges of the new world order and improve the quality of legal education throughout the Commonwealth.

The editor has had to rely on the regional representatives of the CLEA to provide the information that is contained in the directory. While every attempt has been made to be as inclusive and accurate as possible, inevitably there will be some omissions and inaccuracies. Should this be the case we request affected parties to provide us with the relevant information as soon as possible so that it may be included in the next edition of the directory. Such information may be sent to: Professor John Hatchard, General-Secretary, Commonwealth Legal Education Association, c/o Legal and Constitutional Affairs Division, Commonwealth Secretariat, Marlborough House, Pall Mall, London SW1Y 5HX, UK.

Once again, on behalf of the CLEA and the many Commonwealth law teachers and law students we represent, I would like to express our sincere appreciation to Cavendish Publishing for publishing the third edition of the directory.

Professor David McQuoid-Mason
President, CLEA
University of Natal
Durban
South Africa

CONTENTS

INTRODUCTION

The publication of the third edition of the CLEA's *Directory of Commonwealth Law Schools* marks another significant step towards the Association's aim of developing the definitive work on Commonwealth legal education and legal studies.

For some the 'Commonwealth' still has negative connotations: not least because of its links with Britain's imperial past; its seeming ineffectiveness in dealing with modern day political problems within and between its Member States; and the importance of other international and regional groupings such as the United Nations, the African Union and the European Union. Much of this criticism is misplaced and is the result of a misunderstanding of the nature of the organisation itself. Yet this negativity has also affected many law teachers and legal practitioners, who seemingly regard Commonwealth legal studies as having little or nothing to offer.

In this they are quite wrong. As this book hopefully demonstrates, the use of Commonwealth jurisprudence in law teaching and in legal research is intellectually stimulating and of great practical value as well as providing law students with an invaluable added dimension to their studies. A bonus here is that the material is almost always in English, most of the 54 Commonwealth member countries enjoy a shared legal tradition, and much of the material is readily available on the internet! If proof was needed of the vibrancy and significance of Commonwealth jurisprudence, it is to be found in the judgments of apex courts around the Commonwealth in which comparative Commonwealth jurisprudence is regularly cited and applied.

The value of comparative Commonwealth jurisprudence was well demonstrated at the 1995 CLEA conference in Durban, South Africa. At a session on the 'new South Africa' one speaker detailed the enormous challenges facing the South African Constitutional Court in interpreting the complex fundamental rights provisions of the new South African Constitution. Participants from India then dominated the discussion and gently pointed out that the Indian Supreme Court had resolved many of these constitutional issues years ago! It is worth noting that the South African Constitutional Court has always made good use of Indian (as well as other Commonwealth) jurisprudence in their own judgments.

The book is divided into four sections:

- Section 1 is a much expanded section providing full details on the CLEA and its wide range of programmes.
- Section 2 is an entirely new section that provides a background to the Commonwealth and brings together Commonwealth documentation that is of most interest and relevance to law teachers and legal practitioners.
- Section 3 contains a directory of Commonwealth law schools. Each individual country entry provides readers with an overview of legal education in that country as well as details of every known law school. As legal education in the Caribbean and South Pacific is undertaken on a regional basis, a combined entry for each region is provided. Thanks to the assistance of members of the CLEA Executive Committee in particular, we have been able to include considerably more information than ever before about Commonwealth law schools, their research centres and publications.
- Section 4 is also entirely new and lists specialist law journals of, and research

centres attached to, Commonwealth law schools. The list is intended to assist law teachers develop better links with those with like interests elsewhere in the Commonwealth, and to find new avenues for publishing their research.

A note of thanks

In 2001, the Association celebrated its 30th anniversary. It is salutary to recall that its creation and development has been through the initiative and contribution of relatively few individuals. In the early days, three in particular stand out: Lakshman Singhvi and the late Tom Kellock, (neither of whom was a law teacher), and Tom Colchester (who served for many years as General-Secretary and was not even a lawyer). In later years the Association has also been well served by its senior office holders (all law teachers), such as William Twining, James Read, Yash Ghai, Madhava Menon and David McQuoid-Mason; by Margaret Rogers and Jill Cottrell (both of whom served as General-Secretary); and Jeremy Pope (the long time Hon Treasurer of the Association). Members of the CLEA Executive Committee have also played, and continue to play, a crucial role in supporting and developing the Association's work.

The Association is also deeply indebted to the two bodies that have sustained it for many years. Firstly, the Commonwealth Foundation, which has provided, and continues to provide, invaluable financial support. Secondly, the Legal and Constitutional Affairs Division of the Commonwealth Secretariat which, under successive Directors who have served as Hon Treasurers, has provided not merely a home for the Association but enormous assistance in so many ways.

I think it fitting, therefore, that this directory is dedicated to all those who have contributed so much to the first 30 years of the Association.

John Hatchard
General-Secretary, CLEA
September 2002

SECTION 1
ABOUT THE CLEA

ABOUT THE CLEA

The Commonwealth Legal Education Association (CLEA) fosters and promotes high standards of legal education in the Commonwealth. It was founded in December 1971 at a meeting in Marlborough House, London and has had its headquarters there ever since, courtesy of the Legal and Constitutional Affairs Division.

The CLEA is recognised as a Charity by the UK Charity Commissioners and receives funding from the Commonwealth Foundation as well as from other sources.

It is a Commonwealth-wide body with regional Chapters in South Asia, Southern Africa, West Africa and the Caribbean together with several national Chapters and committees. The day to day running of the Association is in the hands of the General-Secretary.

Membership is open to individuals, schools of law and other institutions concerned with legal education and research. Full details of current membership rates and benefits of membership are found in *Commonwealth Legal Education*, the newsletter of the Association or can be obtained from the CLEA General-Secretary.

Applications for membership and other information may be addressed to Professor John Hatchard, General-Secretary, Commonwealth Legal Education Association, c/o Legal and Constitutional Affairs Division, Commonwealth Secretariat, Marlborough House, Pall Mall, London SW1Y 5HX, UK (Tel: +44 207 7476415; Fax: +44 207 7476406; email: clea@commonwealth.int; website: www.ukcle.ac.uk/clea).

LEGAL EDUCATION IN THE COMMONWEALTH: THE WAY AHEAD

The programmes of the CLEA

In 1994 in his inaugural address, the then President of the CLEA, Professor NR Madhava Menon, drew attention to the need to make legal education socially relevant and professionally useful – for law schools to prepare themselves for the demands of the profession in the context of the information revolution and other global challenges, and to support continuing legal education and distance learning programmes. He also drew attention to the need for a fresh look at law curricula and teaching methods.

In response to this, the CLEA General Meeting in Durban, South Africa, in 1995 approved the following themes as the basis for the development by the Association of a programme of action designed to achieve sustainable improvement in legal education throughout the Commonwealth.

Developing human resources
- Training of law teachers.
- Development of and support for research.

Developing non-human resources
- Improving library facilities, including establishing a minimum holdings list for Commonwealth law schools.
- Developing the use of electronically produced data.

Curriculum development
- Exchanging information and experiences of degree structures: eg, the modular debate; identification and development of new areas for the provision of courses relevant to Commonwealth countries such as law and development; commercial law; law and privatisation.
- Exchanging information and experiences on the development of courses incorporating a comparative law approach.
- Strengthening external and distance learning programmes.

Professional training
- Reviewing the role of the law school: eg, the development of integrated programmes.
- Strengthening links between law schools and vocational training institutions.
- Addressing the needs of vocational training institutions.

Strengthening links between Commonwealth law schools
- Facilitating exchange of faculty members.
- Facilitating research collaboration.
- Encouraging the exchange of information.

In consequence, a three-year plan of action (1997–99) was devised, which provided the basis for the activities of the Association. At the CLEA General Meeting in Adelaide in April 2000, members approved a new plan of action for the period 2000–03. The original five themes were retained and a sixth added:

Strengthening clinical legal education and law clinics in the Commonwealth

Current CLEA programmes

Publications and research

- *Commonwealth Legal Education* is published three times a year and contains news and views about law and legal education developments in the Commonwealth.
- *Journal of Commonwealth Law and Legal Education* (biannually).
- *Directory of Commonwealth Law Schools* (published biennially).
- A variety of books on law and legal education in the Commonwealth.
- The Association's website (www.ukcle.ac.uk/clea) provides access information on the CLEA and legal education in the Commonwealth as well as a wide range of Commonwealth legal materials, model curricula and some publications.

In 2001 Cavendish Publishing became the official publishers of the CLEA.

Conferences

The Association organises regular international and regional conferences and seminars. Recently, it has organised/co-sponsored conferences on topics such as law and development, human rights and just and honest government as well as on legal education. Venues have included Australia, Nigeria, Cayman Islands, the UK, Jamaica, Sri Lanka and Malaysia.

Commonwealth Law Lecture series

This is a unique series that takes place on a Commonwealth-wide basis. Lectures are given by leading legal academics and judges. The collected lectures will be published in early 2003.

Curriculum development

The Association is committed to developing new curricula that reflect both the importance of Commonwealth jurisprudence and the need for law schools in the Commonwealth (and beyond) to equip their students to meet the demands of the 21st century lawyer:

- Human rights for the Commonwealth.
- Transnational crime/anti-terrorism law.
- Environmental justice (in preparation).
- Labour law (in preparation).

Strengthening law schools

- Providing training and materials for the teaching of a course on international co-operation to combat crime.
- Establishing the Commonwealth Legal Education Research Centre in Cameroon.

Strengthening the Harare Commonwealth Principles

- The Association works with the Commonwealth and three other Commonwealth professional organisations – Commonwealth Magistrates' and Judges' Association, Commonwealth Lawyers' Association and Commonwealth Parliamentary Association – on the development of the Latimer House Guidelines for the Commonwealth.
- The Association supports the work of the Commonwealth Human Rights Initiative.

Activities for law students

- Commonwealth law students' mooting competition.
- Commonwealth law students' essay competition.

Full details of these activities are provided below.

CLEA OFFICERS 2003

President

David McQuoid-Mason
University of Natal, Howard College of Law, Durban 4001, South Africa
Tel: +27 31 2602487; Fax: +27 31 2602559
email: Mcquoidm@nu.ac.za

Vice Presidents

Joe Silva
Sri Lanka Law College, 244 Hulftsdorp Street, Colombo 12, Sri Lanka
Tel: +94 1 323759; Fax: +94 1 436040
email: locwal@slt.lk

Peter Slinn
Centre for International Studies and Diplomacy, School of Oriental and African Studies, Thornhaugh Street, London WC1 0XG, UK
Tel: +44 207 8984840; Fax: +44 207 8984839
email: ps1@soas.ac.uk

Keith Sobion
Council of Legal Education, Norman Manley Law School, PO Box 231, Mona Campus, Kingston 7, Jamaica
Tel: +1876 9271899; 9271235; Fax: +1876 9771012
email: nmls1@hotmail.com

Honorary Treasurer

Dianne Stafford
Legal and Constitutional Affairs Division, Commonwealth Secretariat, Marlborough House, Pall Mall, London SW1Y 5HX, UK
Tel: +44 207 7476410; Fax: +44 207 7476406
email: d.stafford@commonwealth.int

General-Secretary

John Hatchard
Commonwealth Legal Education Association, c/o Legal and Constitutional Affairs Division, Commonwealth Secretariat, Marlborough House, Pall Mall, London SW1Y 5HX, UK
Tel: +44 207 7476415; Fax: +44 207 7476406
email: clea@commonwealth.int

EXECUTIVE COMMITTEE MEMBERS 2003

Australasia

Ros Macdonald
Queensland University of Technology, Faculty of Law, GPO Box 2434, Brisbane,
Queensland 4001, Australia
Tel: +61 7 38642707; Fax: +61 7 38642222; 38641152
email: r.macdonald@qut.edu.au

Europe

Selina Goulbourne
Law Department, School of Social Science and Law, University of Greenwich,
Maritime Campus, 30 Park Row, London SE10 9LS, UK
Tel: +44 208 3318727; Fax: +44 208 3318473
email: s.goulbourne@gre.ac.uk

East and Central Africa

Lillian Tibatemwa-Ekirikubinza
Faculty of Law, Makerere University, PO Box 7062, Kampala, Uganda
Tel: +256 41 542284; Fax: +256 41 255879; 554297
email: ltibatemwa@muklaw.bushnet.net

The Caribbean

Keith Sobion
Council of Legal Education, Norman Manley Law School, PO Box 231, Mona Campus,
Kingston 7, Jamaica
Tel: +1876 9271899; 9271235; Fax: +1876 9771012
email: nmls1@hotmail.com

Southern Africa

David McQuoid-Mason
University of Natal, Howard College of Law, Durban 4001, South Africa
Tel: +27 31 2602487; Fax: +27 31 2602559
email: Mcquoidm@nu.ac.za

South Asia

Joe Silva
Sri Lanka Law College, 244 Hulftsdorp Street, Colombo 12, Sri Lanka
Tel: +94 1 323759; Fax: +94 1 436040
email: locwal@slt.lk

West Africa

Seth Bimpong-Buta
Ghana School of Law, PO Box 179, Accra, Ghana
Tel: +233 21 664822; 663246; 664775; Fax: +233 21 778185
email: sethbb@hotmail.com

North America

Jeff Berryman
Faculty of Law, University of Windsor, Ontario N9B 3P4, Canada
Tel: +1 519 2533000 ext 2965; Fax: +1 519 9737064
email: jberrym@uwindsor.ca

Ad hoc members

Jeremy Cooper
School of Law, University of Middlesex, The Burroughs, London NW4 4BT, UK
email: jeremycooper1@hotmail.com (responsible for the CLEA website)

Alexis Goh
Faculty of Law, University of Western Sydney, Entrance #1 off Hackett Drive, 35
Stirling Highway, Crawley, WA 6009, Australia
email: a.goh@uws.edu.au (responsible for the Commonwealth Law Lecture series)

Country representatives

The Association has a network of country representatives. Details of these appear
under the appropriate country entry in the directory.

CONSTITUTION OF THE CLEA

1 Name

The name of this organisation is the Commonwealth Legal Education Association,
hereinafter referred to as the Association.

2 Object and powers

The object of the Association is to advance education by fostering and promoting high
standards of Legal Education in all Commonwealth countries. In furtherance of the said
objects but not further or otherwise the Association shall have the following powers:

(a) to encourage the provision of the facilities required to achieve high standards of
legal education and research in all Commonwealth countries;

(b) to promote, maintain and strengthen contacts and co-operation between
individuals, institutions, organisations and associations interested in legal
education and research in Commonwealth countries;

(c) to assist existing organisations concerned with legal education and research in
Commonwealth countries and to foster the establishment of such bodies in
appropriate circumstances;

(d) to disseminate information and literature concerning legal education and research;

(e) to promote and conduct research in the field of legal education;
(f) to maintain registers and publish directories of teachers of law and others concerned with legal education and research in the Commonwealth;
(g) to publish a journal of legal education;
(h) to facilitate the exchange of students and researchers in the field of law;
(i) to facilitate exchange of legal materials among institutions concerned with legal education and research;
(j) to promote better understanding and closer collaboration between all branches of the legal profession in the Commonwealth;
(k) to foster and promote programmes of continuing legal education;
(I) to organise specialised, regional and general conferences of law teachers and others concerned with legal education and research;
(m) to do anything that is conducive or incidental to these objects.

3   Membership

(1) All applications for membership of the Association shall be made to and shall be dealt with by the Executive Committee.
(2) The Executive Committee shall admit to membership such institutions, organisations, associations or any of their constituent parts and such individuals as it may in its discretion think fit.
Without limiting in any way the powers of the Executive Committee under clause 3(2), the following shall be eligible for membership:
(a) any institution, organisation or association interested in legal education or research;
(b) any organisation or association of teachers of law;
(c) any individual who is or has been a law teacher, legal researcher, practising lawyer, judge, magistrate, law officer or a person otherwise concerned with legal education or research.
(3) The subscription for all classes of membership shall be determined by the Executive Committee from time to time.

4   General Meetings

A General Meeting of the members of the Association shall ordinarily be held at least once every year at such time (not being more than 18 months after the holding of the preceding General Meeting) and at such place as the Executive Committee shall determine.

At such General Meeting, the business shall include the election of the Executive Committee, the appointment of an auditor, the consideration of an annual report of the work done by or under the auspices of the Committee and of the audited accounts, and the transaction of other matters as may from time to time be necessary.

5   Executive Committee

(1) The affairs of the Association shall be managed by an Executive Committee. Subject to the general directions of a General Meeting, the Executive Committee may take any action on behalf of the Association which, in its opinion, will further the objects of the Association.
(2) The members of the Executive Committee shall be elected at the General Meeting of the Association in accordance with clause 4 above. The Committee shall, so far

as is practicable, be broadly representative of the Commonwealth as a whole and shall consist of not less than six and not more than 10 persons.

(3) Election to the Executive Committee shall be for four years but members shall be eligible for re-election.

(4) In addition to the members so elected, the Executive Committee may co-opt up to three further members being full members of the Association whether individuals or representative or a combination of both who shall serve until the conclusion of the next General Meeting after individual co-option PROVIDED THAT the number of the co-opted members shall not exceed one-third of the total membership of the Executive Committee at the time of co-option. Co-opted members shall be entitled to vote at meetings of the Executive Committee.

(5) Any casual vacancy in the Executive Committee may be filled by the Committee and any person appointed to fill such a casual vacancy shall hold office until the conclusion of the next General Meeting of the Association and shall be eligible for election at that meeting.

(6) The Executive Committee shall appoint and fix the remuneration of the General-Secretary and of all other staff not being members of the Committee as may in their opinion be necessary.

(7) The Executive Committee may make by-laws and regulations within the frame-work of this Constitution for the furtherance of the objects of the Association.

6   Amendment of the Constitution

A General Meeting may amend this Constitution by a two-thirds majority of those present and voting in accordance with the by-laws and regulations PROVIDED that no alteration shall be made which would have the effect of causing the Association to cease to be a charity at law.

7   Dissolution

If the Executive Committee by a simple majority decide at any time that on the ground of expense or otherwise, it is necessary or advisable to dissolve the Association, it shall call a meeting of all members of the Association who have the power to vote, of which meeting not less than 21 days' notice (stating the terms of the Resolution to be proposed thereat) shall be given. If such decision shall be confirmed by a simple two-thirds majority of those present and voting at such meeting, the Executive Committee shall have power to dispose of any assets held by or on behalf of the Association. Any assets remaining after the satisfaction of any proper debts and liabilities shall be given or transferred to such other charitable institution or institutions having objects similar to the objects of the Association as the Executive Committee may determine.

SOUTH ASIA CHAPTER OF THE CLEA

President

Joe Silva
Sri Lanka Law College, 244 Hulftsdorp Street, Colombo 12, Sri Lanka
Tel: +94 1 323759; Fax: +94 1 436040
email: locwal@slt.lk

Country representatives

Pakistan

Mir Aurangzeb
University Law College, Khojak Road, PO Box 75, Quetta, Balochistan 87300, Pakistan
Fax: +92 81 826492
email: miraurangzeb@yahoo.com

India

S Sivakumar
Kerala Law Academy (email: sivku98@hotmail.com) and A Raghunadha Reddy, Sri Krishnadevaraya University, Faculty of Law, Anantapur, Andhra Pradesh 515003, India
email: raghu_sku@yahoo.com

Roving CLEA representative for South Asia

Lakshman Marasinghe
email: lmarasi@hotmail.com

CONSTITUTION OF THE CLEA (SOUTH ASIA CHAPTER)

Preamble

Whereas the Commonwealth Legal Education Association (CLEA) Constitution contemplates the formation of National or Regional Chapters of the Association,

And whereas the Asian participants of the CLEA Conference at Bangalore (1993) unanimously resolved to constitute such a Regional Chapter for South Asian countries in the Commonwealth,

THIS CONSTITUTION was adopted at Maharshi Dayanand University, Rohtak in February 1994, and approved by the Executive Committee of the CLEA at the University of Warwick in July 1994.

1   Name

The name of the Association is the Commonwealth Legal Education Association (Asia Chapter) hereinafter referred to as the CLEA (Asia).

2   Objects

(i)   The objects of the Association shall be the same as those of the CLEA in their application to the Asian region.

(ii) In particular, the objects include promotion of high standards of legal education in the region, facilitating academic and professional exchanges and organising conferences, workshops and study tours in the region.

3   Membership

(i)   The Association will have four types of membership – institutional, individual, associate and honorary.

(ii) All institutional and individual members of the CLEA will automatically be members of the respective categories of the CLEA (Asia).

(iii) Teachers, researchers and practitioners of law working in countries of the region can be admitted according to rules framed for the purpose as associate members.

(iv) The Executive Committee may on invitation admit members of the legal profession as Honorary Members.

(v) The office-bearers of the CLEA from the region will be *ex-officio* members of the CLEA (Asia).

(vi) The subscription for associate membership shall be determined by the Executive Committee.

(vii) The Executive Committee shall admit applicants for Associate membership and invite persons for honorary membership and its decision in this regard shall be final.

4 General Meetings

(i) A general meeting of the members of the Association shall ordinarily be held at least once every year at such time and at such place as the Executive Committee shall determine.

(ii) The General Meeting shall consider and pass resolutions on the activities of the Association, consider and approve budget proposals, audited statement of accounts of the Association and generally guide the work of the Association.

5 Executive Committee

(i) The affairs of the Association shall be managed by an Executive Committee. Subject to the general directions of a General Meeting, the Executive Committee may take any action on behalf of the Association, which in its opinion, will further the objects of the Association.

(ii) The members of the Executive Committee shall consist of a minimum of five and a maximum of ten persons as constituted at the General Meeting and as prescribed hereunder:

(a) President to be elected from among members of the CLEA belonging to the region;

(b) Secretary elected from among members of the CLEA (Asia);

(c) a Joint Secretary elected from among members of the CLEA (Asia);

(d) Treasurer elected from among members of the CLEA (Asia);

(e) a minimum of two and a maximum of three members elected from among members of the CLEA (Asia) representing as many countries of the region as possible.

(iii) Election to the Executive Committee shall be for three years.

(iv) In addition to the members so elected the Executive Committee may co-opt up to three further members, being full members of the Association. Co-opted members shall be entitled to vote at meetings of the Executive Committee. The *ex-officio* members also have the same status as the co-opted members.

(v) Any casual vacancy in the Executive Committee may be filled by the Committee and any person so appointed to fill such a casual vacancy shall hold office until the conclusion of the next General Meeting of the Association and shall be eligible for election at that meeting.

(vi) The Executive Committee may make by-laws and regulations within the framework of this Constitution for the furtherance of the objects of the Association.

6   Amendments of the Constitution

A General Meeting may amend this Constitution by a two-thirds majority of those present and voting in accordance with the by-laws and regulations.

SOUTHERN AFRICA CHAPTER OF THE CLEA

President

Phillip Iya
University of Fort Hare, Private Bag X1314, Alice 5700, South Africa
Tel: +27 40 6022122; Fax: +27 40 6532334
email: philiya@hotmail.com

CONSTITUTION OF THE CLEA (SOUTHERN AFRICA CHAPTER)

1   Name

The name of the Association is the Commonwealth Legal Education Association (Southern Africa Chapter) hereinafter referred to as the CLEA (Southern Africa).

2   Objects

2.1   The objects of the CLEA (Southern Africa) shall be the same as those of the CLEA in their application to the Southern Africa region.

2.2   In particular, the objects include promotion of high standards of legal education in the region, facilitating academic and professional exchanges and organising conferences, workshops and study tours in the region.

3   Membership

3.1   CLEA (Southern Africa) shall have four kinds of membership: institutional, individual, associate and honorary.

3.2   All institutional and individual members of the CLEA in the Southern African region shall automatically be members of the respective categories of the CLEA (Southern Africa).

3.3   Teachers, researchers and practitioners of law working in the Commonwealth countries of the Southern Africa region may be admitted as associate members of the CLEA (Southern Africa) according to the regulations regarding associate membership.

3.4   The Executive Committee of the CLEA (Southern Africa) may on invitation admit members of the legal profession as honorary members.

3.5   The office bearers of the CLEA from the Southern African region shall be *ex officio* members of the CLEA (Southern Africa).

3.6   The subscriptions payable by the different categories of membership shall be determined by the Executive Committee of the CLEA (Southern Africa).

3.7 The Executive Committee shall have the power to admit applicants as associate members and to invite persons to become honorary members.

4   General Meetings

4.1 A General Meeting of the members of the CLEA (Southern Africa) shall ordinarily be held at least once every 18 months at the same time as the proceedings of the Southern African Society of University Law Teachers (SULT), and shall be held at the same venue as the SULT conferences.

4.2 A General Meeting shall consider and pass resolutions on the activities of the CLEA (Southern Africa), consider and approve budget proposals and audited statements of account, and generally guide the work of the CLEA (Southern Africa).

5   Executive Committee

5.1 The affairs of the CLEA (Southern Africa) shall be managed by an Executive Committee. Subject to the general directions of a General Meeting, the Executive Committee may take any action on behalf of the CLEA (Southern Africa) which in its opinion will further the objects of the CLEA (Southern Africa).

5.2 The members of the Executive Committee shall consist of a minimum of five and a maximum of 10 persons elected at a General Meeting and as prescribed hereunder:

5.2.1 A President elected from among members of the CLEA (Southern Africa).

5.2.2 A Secretary elected from among members of the CLEA (Southern Africa).

5.2.3 A Joint Secretary elected from among members of the CLEA (Southern Africa).

5.2.4 A Treasurer elected from among members of the CLEA (Southern Africa).

5.2.5 A minimum of three and a maximum of six members elected from among members of the CLEA (Southern Africa) representing as many of the Commonwealth countries of the Southern African region as possible.

5.3 Election of the Executive Committee shall be for a period of three years.

5.4 The Executive Committee may co-opt up to three further members from among members (including *ex officio* members) of the CLEA (Southern Africa). Such co-opted members shall be entitled to vote at meetings of the Executive Committee.

5.5 Any casual vacancy on the Executive Committee may be filled by the Committee and any person so appointed to fill such a vacancy shall hold office until the conclusion of the next General Meeting of the CLEA (Southern Africa) and shall be eligible for election at that meeting.

5.6 The Executive Committee may make regulations within the framework of this Constitution for the furtherance of the objects of the CLEA (Southern Africa).

6   Financial arrangements

6.1 Funds collected or raised by subscription shall be deposited in the name of the CLEA (Southern Africa) in a bank account at the same bank as that used by SULT, or in the name of the CLEA (Southern Africa) in a coded account at a university approved by the Executive Committee.

6.2 The Secretary or Joint Secretary and Treasurer or President shall jointly operate the accounts of the CLEA (Southern Africa) according to the directions of the Executive Committee.

7 Dissolution

7.1 On dissolution of the CLEA (Southern Africa) its bank accounts shall be closed and any funds remaining shall be submitted to the Commonwealth Legal Education Association.

8 Amendments to the Constitution

8.1 A General Meeting may amend this Constitution by a two-thirds majority of those present and voting in accordance with the regulations.

WEST AFRICA CHAPTER OF THE CLEA

President

Seth Bimpong-Buta
Ghana School of Law, PO Box 179, Accra, Ghana
Tel: +233 21 664822; 663246; 664775; Fax: +233 21 778185
email: sethbb@hotmail.com

Country representatives

Cameroon

Samgena Galega
University of Buea, Department of Law, Faculty of Social and Management Sciences, PO Box 63, Buea, Cameroon (email: dr_sdgalega@yahoo.com)

Nigeria

Toyin Doherty
Nigerian Law School, PMB 170, Garki Bwari, Abuja, Federal Capital Territory, Nigeria (Fax: +234 9 5231570; 5231571)

[The Constitution of this Chapter follows closely that of the Southern African Chapter and is not reproduced here. If required, a copy can be obtained from the President of the Chapter.]

CARIBBEAN CHAPTER OF THE CLEA

President

Keith Sobion
Council of Legal Education, Norman Manley Law School, PO Box 231, Mona Campus, Kingston 7, Jamaica
Tel: +1876 9271899; 9271235; Fax: +1876 9271012
email: nmls1@hotmail.com

[The Constitution of this Chapter follows closely that of the Southern African Chapter and is not reproduced here. If required, a copy can be obtained from the President of the Chapter.]

ACTIVITIES OF THE CLEA

Curriculum Development Programme

The Association is developing new curricula that reflect both the importance of Commonwealth jurisprudence and the need for law schools in the Commonwealth (and beyond) to equip their students to meet the demands of the 21st century lawyer. Recognising that in many Commonwealth law schools resources are extremely limited, the curricula also include relevant materials for use with the course. The courses and materials are available on the CLEA website (www.ukcle.ac.uk/clea) or on CD-Rom and are updated periodically.

Transnational crime and terrorism

The development of this course is a response to the need for legal expertise in combating transnational crime and 'terrorism' at the international, regional and national levels. This is particularly so given the terms of the UN Security Council Resolution 1373 of 28 September 2001, which calls upon all States to adopt further measures in accordance with the relevant provisions of international law, including international standards of human rights, to prevent terrorism and to strengthen international co-operation in combating terrorism. These include: working towards universal implementation of the numerous international and regional conventions in place to address terrorism and organised crime; strengthening of national, regional and international legal frameworks to combat terrorism and organised crime in a comprehensive manner; and increased efforts to prevent the use and abuse of the financial services sector by money launderers and the like.

Law teachers must remain abreast of these developments both in terms of their teaching and their research. The CLEA has developed a curriculum and a training programme on transnational crime in association with the Commonwealth Secretariat, Criminal Law Unit. This deals with the key issues of anti-money laundering laws, mutual assistance, extradition and proceeds of crime.

Three 'training the trainer' workshops have been held on the curriculum: in Barbados in 1999 (for the Caribbean region), in 2001 in Accra, Ghana (for the West Africa region) and in Lusaka, Zambia in April 2002 (for the Southern and Eastern African regions). A fourth training workshop for the Asia-Pacific region is planned for 2003. The CLEA expects that law schools in these regions will introduce the course as soon as possible.

Human rights curriculum

This model curriculum is designed to assist law schools and others institutions develop courses on human rights for their undergraduate students. The materials included in the curriculum pay particular attention to, and include a significant amount of material on, the contribution made by the Commonwealth and Commonwealth countries to the protection and promotion of human rights.

The model curriculum is available through the CLEA website (www.ukcle.ac.uk/clea) and contains key Commonwealth human rights materials (and links to other relevant materials).

Environmental justice

This course is in preparation.

Labour law

This course is in preparation.

CLEA Publications Programme

The publication programme is a significant part of the activities of the Association. The official publishers for the CLEA are Cavendish Publishing.

Periodicals

Commonwealth Legal Education

Commonwealth Legal Education is the newsletter of the Association. It appears three times a year under the editorship of the General-Secretary and contains a range of information on the activities of the Association, legal developments in the Commonwealth and news from Commonwealth law schools. It is sent to all the CLEA members as well as to all known law schools and law libraries in the Commonwealth.

Journal of Commonwealth Law and Legal Education

At the CLEA conference in Adelaide in April 2000 it was agreed that the Association would publish a fully refereed journal devoted to developments in law and legal education in the Commonwealth. The first issue of the Association's new journal was published in January 2002 with Gary Slapper and Matthew Weait (both of the Open University, UK) as the general editors.

The patrons of the journal are:

> The Rt Hon the Lord Woolf, The Lord Chief Justice of England and Wales
> The Rt Hon the Baroness Boothroyd

Honorary editors include:

> Justice Noel Anderson (Court of Appeal, New Zealand)
> Justice Austin L Davis (Justice of Supreme Court, The Bahamas)
> The Lord Lester of Herne Hill, QC
> Professor Patrick McAuslan, MBE (Birkbeck College, University of London)
> Judge Richard May (United Nations)
> Geoffrey Robertson QC
> The Rt Hon the Lord Justice Sedley
> Professor William Twining (University College London, University of London)

Books

1   *Facing Complexity: Law and Development in the 21st Century* (eds A Perry-Kessaris and J Hatchard) (2003, Cavendish Publishing).
     This volume, in honour of Peter Slinn, contains edited papers from the June 2001 CLEA co-sponsored conference on 'Law and Development in the 21st Century: The Challenge of Globalisation'.

2   *CLEA Directory of Commonwealth Law Schools 2003/2004.*
3   *CLEA Directory of Commonwealth Law Schools 1999/2000.*
4   *CLEA Directory of Commonwealth Law Schools 1996/1997.*
5   *Parliamentary Supremacy and Judicial Independence: A Commonwealth Approach* (eds J Hatchard and P Slinn) (1999, Cavendish Publishing).
     This contains the proceedings from the Latimer House Colloquium. Copies are available free of charge to all the CLEA members.
6   *Legal Education: 2000 and Beyond* (papers from the 1998 CLEA conference in Ocho Rios, Jamaica).
7   *Learning Lawyers' Skills* (N Gold, K Mackie and W Twining) (1989, Butterworths).
8   *Access to Legal Education and the Legal Profession* (R Dhavan, N Kibble and W Twining) (1989, Butterworths).
9   *Human Rights Today* (ed V Carter) (2003, forthcoming).
     This contains proceedings from the CLEA co-sponsored Cayman Islands Colloquium.
10   *Current Legal Issues in the Commonwealth* (ed A Goh) (2003, forthcoming).
     This book contains the lectures given in the first Commonwealth Law Lecture series 2001–02.

CD-Rom publications

The Association has launched an initiative to use CD-Roms to enable it to send materials quickly and cheaply to all law schools in the Commonwealth. The CD-Roms are available free of charge to all the CLEA members. The first two publications in the series are:

1   *Legal Education and The Administration of Justice in West Africa* (ed J Hatchard, 2001).
     This contains edited papers from the November 2000 CLEA conference in Abuja, Nigeria.
2   *Curriculum Development for the 21st Century* (2002).
     This contains papers from the December 2001 CLEA conference in Colombo, Sri Lanka.

CLEA website (www.ukcle.ac.uk/clea)

The Association's website contains a wealth of information about the Association and legal education in the Commonwealth. It also has a variety of useful links. The website is maintained by the UK Centre for Legal Education at the University of Warwick.

CLEA conferences and meetings 2000–02

Innovation in Legal Education: Challenging the Future
April 2000, Adelaide, Australia

Legal Education and the Administration of Justice in West Africa
November 2000, Abuja, Nigeria (the first West Africa CLEA conference)

Conference on the Legal Deterrents to Coups
January 2001, London, UK (co-hosted with King's College, London and the British Institute of International and Comparative Law)

Law and Development in the 21st Century: The Challenge of Globalisation
June 2001, Cumberland Lodge, UK (co-hosted with the British Institute of International and Comparative Law and the School of Oriental and African Studies)

Human Rights Today Caribbean Symposium
September 2001, Cayman Islands (co-hosted with the Cayman Islands Government)

Curriculum Development for the 21st Century: With Particular Reference to Globalisation and International Human Rights
December 2001, Colombo, Sri Lanka

Workshops on International Co-operation in Combating Crime
Barbados (2000), Accra, Ghana (2001), Lusaka, Zambia (2002) (co-organised with the Criminal Law Unit, Commonwealth Secretariat)

Current CLEA projects

Commonwealth Law Lecture series

The Association organises the Commonwealth Law Lecture series. The object of the series is to provide a forum in which to create greater awareness of, and provoke discussion on, current legal developments in the Commonwealth generally or in a particular Commonwealth country or region.

A key feature of the series is that lectures take place on a Commonwealth-wide basis and are given by high profile legal personalities. During the first series (2001–02) lectures were held in Australia, Botswana, Canada, Ghana, Singapore, South Africa, Sri Lanka, Uganda and the UK. The lectures will be published in early 2003.

For details of the second series contact: Alexis Goh, University of Western Sydney, Australia (email: a.goh@uws.edu.au).

Commonwealth Legal Education Research Centre

The CLEA is supporting the University of Buea, Cameroon in establishing the Commonwealth Legal Education Research Centre (CLERC). This is in response to the acute shortage of legal materials in the country. The Centre is a non-profit making organisation that has as its principal goal the furtherance and development of legal education in Cameroon. It serves as a research centre for law students, legal academics/scholars, practitioners and judges.

Further details can be obtained from the Director of CLERC, Samgena Galega, University of Buea, Cameroon (email: dr_sdgalega@yahoo.com).

Roman-Dutch Law Group

The Group provides a forum for the exchange of views and materials on Roman-Dutch law for Commonwealth law teachers. For details contact Joe Silva, Sri Lanka Law College, Sri Lanka (email: locwal@slt.lk).

Medico-Legal Project

Based at the University of Natal, Durban, this project enables law teachers from Commonwealth African universities to develop materials on medico-legal issues for use in their own jurisdictions. For details contact: David McQuoid-Mason (email: mcquoidm@nu.ac.uk).

Latimer House Monitoring Process

The *Latimer House Guidelines on Parliamentary Supremacy and Judicial Independence* were adopted at a colloquium sponsored by four Commonwealth Associations, including the CLEA. The Monitoring Process provides information (and comment) relating to recent developments in the Commonwealth that impact (favourably or otherwise) on the Guidelines. 'Monitoring' information already appears in *Commonwealth Legal Education*. The Guidelines themselves appear below (p 24).

THE CLEA AND LAW STUDENTS

Commonwealth law students' mooting competition

The organising and running of this major international competition is now a well established part of the activities of the Association. In recent years, the competition has been staged in Vancouver, Kuala Lumpur and Colombo. In 2003 it will be held in Melbourne, Australia.

The rules of the competition appear below. Further details are available from the CLEA moot co-ordinator Ros Macdonald, Queensland University of Technology, Australia (email: r.macdonald.qut.edu.au).

Commonwealth mooting competition official rules

Organisation

The Commonwealth mooting competition (the Competition) will be organised jointly by the CLEA, the Commonwealth moot co-ordinator and a mooting committee appointed by the organising body of the host nation (the Mooting Committee).

Eligibility

The Mooting Committee, after consultation with the CLEA, will decide on the regions in the Commonwealth for the purposes of the Competition. Regional organisers appointed by the Mooting Committee will select regional teams in a manner the regional organisers decide after consultation with the Mooting Committee. One team from each region may participate in the competition.

Membership of teams

Each team will consist of two counsel and, if the participating region so wishes, a reserve, each of whom:

(i) on the date of selection of the team, is a *bona fide* law student at an institution in the region that he or she represents; and
(ii) on the date of the start of the Competition has not been admitted to the unrestricted practice of law in any jurisdiction.

The names of the two counsel and the reserve must be given to the Commonwealth moot co-ordinator and the Mooting Committee at least one month before the start of the Competition.

Assistance

Teams may not have any outside assistance in the preparation or presentation of their cases other than general guidance on the issues involved and research sources.

The problem

(i) The problem must involve issues of international or Commonwealth interest, and must be concerned solely with a point or points of law.
(ii) It will be set by the Mooting Committee and approved by the CLEA.
(iii) A copy of the problem will be sent to the regional organisers at least two months before the commencement of the Competition. The same problem will be used throughout the Competition.
(iv) Any ambiguities arising out of the problem must be pointed out to the Commonwealth moot co-ordinator and the Mooting Committee before the Competition begins. The Mooting Committee may then resolve the ambiguities at its absolute discretion.
(v) Teams are expected to prepare arguments for both the appellant and the respondent.

The competition

(i) Each team will moot twice in the first round (the General Round), once as appellant and once as respondent. If necessary, byes will be awarded by lot. Each team will be awarded individual and team marks at the end of each moot.
(ii) The four teams with the highest points total will moot in the second round. The teams with the two highest points will moot against each other and the teams with the third and fourth highest points will moot against each other. The teams with the highest and third highest marks will appear for the appellant in the second round. The two teams with the highest points total from the second round will moot in the third and final round. The team with the highest marks will appear for the appellant.
(iii) The marks awarded in each of the three rounds will be published.
(iv) The mooter with the highest total of individual points from the General Round will be awarded the best mooter prize.
(v) The winning team in the third round of the Competition will be awarded the Commonwealth mooting competition trophy, which it may retain until the next Competition.

Judges

(i) Each General Round Moot will be held before a panel of three judges appointed by the Mooting Committee.

(ii) One of the judges of a Moot in the General Round of the Competition may be the Commonwealth moot co-ordinator or his or her nominee.

(iii) Each second round Moot will be held before three appellate court judges (or equivalent), none of whom may be working or resident in a region represented in the Moot unless both competing teams agree. The most senior judge will be the presiding judge.

(iv) The third round Moot (the Final) will be held before three appellate court judges (or equivalent), none of whom may be working or resident in a region represented in the Moot unless both competing teams agree. The most senior judge will be the presiding judge.

Substitute of counsel by reserve

A reserve may only substitute for a designated counsel in a moot when that counsel is ill or otherwise unable to participate. The Commonwealth moot co-ordinator must consent to the substitution before the moot.

Moot procedure

(i) Each team may cite a total of 12 authorities (whether cases, books or articles) for both appellant and respondent. Each list of authorities must have written on it in a prominent place, the team's region, the names of the members, whether it is an appellant or respondent's list and the date. Each team must send their lists of authorities by either facsimile or email to the Commonwealth moot co-ordinator at least two weeks before the commencement of the moot. The copies will be distributed to the judges, together with the moot problem.

(ii) Each team is to give a final list of authorities to be cited as appellant and respondent to the Commonwealth moot co-ordinator by 5 pm on the day before the start of the Competition. The Commonwealth moot co-ordinator will distribute the lists to all teams on the evening before the start of the Competition. Any later amendments to lists of authorities may be made only after consultation with the Commonwealth moot co-ordinator.

(iii) Each team must send their outlines of argument as appellant and respondent by either facsimile or email to the Commonwealth moot co-ordinator at least two weeks before the start of the moot. The copies will be distributed to the judges, together with the moot problem. Each outline of argument must have written on it in a prominent place, the team's region, counsel's name, whether counsel appears as senior or junior counsel, whether counsel appears for the appellant or respondent and the date.

(iv) Each team is to give its final outlines of argument as appellant and respondent to the Commonwealth moot co-ordinator by 5 pm on the day before the start of the Competition. The Commonwealth moot co-ordinator will distribute the outlines of argument to all teams on the evening before the start of the Competition. Any later amendments to outlines of argument may only be made after consultation with the Commonwealth moot co-ordinator.

(v) Counsel must wear business dress during each moot.

(vi)   At the beginning of every moot, each team must hand up to the Bench a folder containing:
    (a)   counsels' names;
    (b)   copies of counsels' written outlines of argument to be followed during the Moot;
    (c)   a list of authorities to be relied on during the Moot;
    (d)   photocopies of the relevant material from all authorities and other materials referred to in argument (eg, legislation); and
    (e)   an index, or some other means (tabs, etc) for finding relevant material.
(vii) Counsel will be heard in the following order:
    (a)   senior counsel for the appellant;
    (b)   junior counsel for the appellant;
    (c)   senior counsel for the respondent;
    (d)   junior counsel of the respondent;
    (e)   senior counsel for the appellant may then exercise a right of reply, during which no new arguments may be raised.
(viii) Any judge may interrupt counsel at any time to ask a question.
(ix)   Each counsel has 20 minutes to make submissions. This time limit does not include questions and answers.
(x)   The right of reply is limited to five minutes.
(xi)   The judges may adjourn to consider their decision at the conclusion of the moot.

Adjudication

(i)   Each judge must complete an individual marking sheet for each participant in a moot.
(ii) The presiding judge will average the marks awarded by each judge, transpose them to the moot marking sheet and announce which team has won for the purposes of the Competition.
(iii) The winning team is the team that has the highest total marks. The winning team will not necessarily be the team for which judgment is given on the law.

Scouting

Counsel, a reserve or any persons affiliated with a team, must not attend any moot other than one in which his or her team is participating while that team is still competing.

Disputes

Any dispute about the Competition must be referred to the Commonwealth moot co-ordinator. Before making a decision about a dispute, the Commonwealth moot co-ordinator may consult the mooting committee. A decision made by the Commonwealth moot co-ordinator about a dispute concerning the Competition is final.

Commonwealth law students' essay competition

In recent years, the CLEA has held three student essay competitions. The most recent was held in 2000–01 on the topic 'What Role Should Commonwealth Law Students and Law Schools Play to Meet the Challenges of the New Millenium?'. The joint winners came from Sri Lanka and Nigeria.

The next competition is scheduled for 2003 and is open to all undergraduate students studying law in the Commonwealth. Full details will appear in *Commonwealth Legal Education.*

PROMOTING JUST AND HONEST GOVERNMENT AND HUMAN RIGHTS

Latimer House Guidelines for the Commonwealth

[Guidelines on good practice governing relations between the executive, parliament and the judiciary in the promotion of good governance, the rule of law and human rights to ensure the effective implementation of the Harare Principles.]

Background

A Joint Colloquium on 'Parliamentary Supremacy and Judicial Independence towards a Commonwealth Model' was held at Latimer House, United Kingdom, from 15–19 June 1998. The Colloquium was sponsored by the Commonwealth Legal Education Association, Commonwealth Lawyers' Association, the Commonwealth Magistrates' and Judges' Association and the Commonwealth Parliamentary Association.

The overall object of the Colloquium was to adopt draft Guidelines on good practice governing relations between the Executive, Parliament and the Judiciary in the promotion of good governance, the rule of law and human rights to ensure the effective implementation of the Harare Principles.

Over 60 participants attended, representing 20 Commonwealth countries and three overseas territories. These included senior judges, parliamentarians and legal academics from around the Commonwealth. The outcome was the adoption of the Latimer House Guidelines (LHG).

In 1999 Commonwealth Law Ministers at their Meeting in Port of Spain, Trinidad referred the Guidelines to Senior Officials of Law Ministries (SOLM) for study and a report. At their November 2001 meeting in London, Senior Officials considered the Guidelines. Their report states:

> Senior officials noted that the principles of good governance and judicial independence had been clearly endorsed by Commonwealth Heads of Government and welcomed the general thrust of the declaration of the Guidelines. On the issue of judicial appointment mechanisms and the control of funds for judicial purposes, Senior Officials agreed that the Guidelines needed revision. A revised text should stress the importance of ensuring that any appointment mechanisms should be widely accepted as guaranteeing the quality of those selected and that the resources provided for the judiciary should be adequate and protected from misuse. With such revisions the Guidelines could be laid before [Commonwealth Law] Ministers for approval.

Following consultations with members of the judiciary and legal professions throughout the Commonwealth, refinements were agreed to Chapter II of the

Guidelines. The following represents the amended version of the Guidelines together with some explanatory notes.

Preamble

RECALLING the renewed commitment at the 1997 Commonwealth Heads of Government Meeting at Edinburgh to the Harare Principles and the Millbrook Commonwealth Action Programme and, in particular, the pledge in paragraph 9 of the Harare Declaration to work for the protection and promotion of the fundamental political values of the Commonwealth:

- democracy;
- democratic processes and institutions which reflect national circumstances, the rule of law and the independence of the judiciary;
- just and honest government;
- fundamental human rights, including equal rights and opportunities for all citizens regardless of race, colour, creed or political belief;
- equality for women, so that they may exercise their full and equal rights.

Representatives of the Commonwealth Parliamentary Association, the Commonwealth Magistrates' and Judges' Association, the Commonwealth Lawyers' Association and the Commonwealth Legal Education Association meeting at Latimer House in the United Kingdom from 15–19 June 1998.

HAVE RESOLVED to adopt the following Principles and Guidelines and propose them for consideration by the Commonwealth Heads of Government Meeting and for effective implementation by member countries of the Commonwealth.

Principles

The successful implementation of these Guidelines calls for a commitment, made in the utmost good faith, of the relevant national institutions, in particular the executive, parliament and the judiciary, to the essential principles of good governance, fundamental human rights and the rule of law, including the independence of the judiciary, so that the legitimate aspirations of all the peoples of the Commonwealth should be met.

Each institution must exercise responsibility and restraint in the exercise of power within its own constitutional sphere so as not to encroach on the legitimate discharge of constitutional functions by the other institutions.

It is recognised that the special circumstances of small and/or under-resourced jurisdictions may require adaptation of these Guidelines.

It is recognised that redress of gender imbalance is essential to accomplish full and equal rights in society and to achieve true human rights.[1] Merit and the capacity to

---

1   The final paragraph does not refer expressly to other forms of discrimination, eg, on ethnic or religious grounds. There are a number of approaches to the redress of existing imbalances, such as selection based on 'merit with bias', ie, where, eg, if two applicants are of equal merit, the bias should be to appoint a woman where there exists a gender imbalance.

perform public office regardless of disability should be the criteria of eligibility for appointment or election.

Guidelines

Parliament and the judiciary

1   The legislative function is the primary responsibility of parliament as the elected body representing the people. Judges may[2] be constructive and purposive in the interpretation of legislation, but must not usurp Parliament's legislative function. Courts should have the power to declare legislation to be unconstitutional and of no legal effect. However, there may be circumstances where the appropriate remedy would be for the court to declare the incompatibility of a statute with the Constitution, leaving it to the legislature to take remedial legislative measures.

2   Commonwealth parliaments should take speedy and effective steps to implement their countries' international human rights obligations by enacting appropriate human rights legislation. Special legislation (such as equal opportunity laws) is required to extend the protection of fundamental rights to the private sphere. Where domestic incorporation has not occurred, international instruments should be applied to aid interpretation.

3   Judges should adopt a generous and purposive approach in interpreting a Bill of Rights. This is particularly important in countries which are in the process of building democratic traditions. Judges have a vital part to play in developing and maintaining a vibrant human rights environment throughout the Commonwealth.

4   International law and, in particular, human rights jurisprudence can greatly assist domestic courts in interpreting a Bill of Rights. It also can help expand the scope of a Bill of Rights, making it more meaningful and effective.

5   While dialogue between the judiciary and the government may be desirable or appropriate, in no circumstances should such dialogue compromise judicial independence.

6   People should have easy and unhindered access to courts, particularly to enforce their fundamental rights. Any existing procedural obstacles to access to justice should be removed.

7   People should also be made aware of, and have access to, other important foras for human rights dispute resolution, particularly Human Rights Commissions, Offices of the Ombudsman and mechanisms for alternative dispute resolution.

8   Everyone, especially judges, parliamentarians and lawyers, should have access to human rights education.

Preserving judicial independence

1   Judicial appointments
    Jurisdictions should have an appropriate independent process in place for judicial appointments. Where no independent system already exists, appointments should be made by a judicial services commission (established by the Constitution

---

2   It has been suggested that judges 'shall' have a duty to adopt a constructive and purposive approach to the interpretation of legislation, particularly in a human rights context.

or by statute) or by an appropriate officer of State acting on the recommendation of such a commission.[3]

The appointment process, whether or not involving an appropriately constituted and representative judicial services commission, should be designed to guarantee the quality and independence of mind of those selected for appointment at all levels of the judiciary.

Judicial appointments to all levels of the judiciary should be made on merit with appropriate provision for the progressive removal of gender imbalance and of other historic factors of discrimination.

Judicial appointments should normally be permanent; whilst in some jurisdictions, contract appointments may be inevitable, such appointments should be subject to appropriate security of tenure.[4]

Judicial vacancies should be advertised.

2   Funding

Sufficient and sustainable funding should be provided to enable the judiciary to perform its functions to the highest standards. Such funds, once voted for the judiciary by the legislature, should be protected from alienation or misuse. The allocation or withholding of funding should not be used as a means of exercising improper control over the judiciary.[5]

Appropriate salaries and benefits, supporting staff, resources and equipment are essential to the proper functioning of the judiciary.

As a matter of principle, judicial salaries and benefits should be set by an independent body and their value should be maintained.

3   Training[6]

A culture of judicial education should be developed.

Training should be organised, systematic and ongoing and under the control of an adequately funded judicial body.

Judicial training should include the teaching of the law, judicial skills and the social context including ethnic and gender issues.

---

3   The Guidelines clearly recognise that, in certain jurisdictions, appropriate mechanisms for judicial appointments not involving a judicial service commission are in place. However, such commissions exist in many jurisdictions, though their composition differs. There are arguments for and against a majority of senior judges and in favour of strong representation of other branches of the legal profession, members of parliament and of civil society in general.

4   The making of non-permanent judicial appointments by the executive without security of tenure remains controversial in a number of jurisdictions.

5   The provision of adequate funding for the judiciary must be a very high priority in order to uphold the rule of law, to ensure that good governance and democracy are sustained and to provide for the effective and efficient administration of justice. However, it is acknowledged that a shortfall in anticipated national income might lead to budgetary constraints.

    Finance ministries are urged to engage in appropriate consultations in order to set realistic and sustainable budgets which parliaments should approve to ensure adequate funds are available.

6   This is an area where the sponsoring associations can play a cost-effective role in co-operation with the Commonwealth Secretariat. Resources need to be provided in order to support the judiciary in the promotion of the rule of law and good governance.

The curriculum should be controlled by judicial officers who should have the assistance of lay specialists.

For jurisdictions without adequate training facilities, access to facilities in other jurisdictions should be provided.

Courses in judicial education should be offered to practising lawyers as part of their ongoing professional development training.[7]

Preserving the independence of parliamentarians[8]

1   Article 9 of the Bill of Rights 1688 is reaffirmed. This article provides:

> That the Freedome of Speech and Debates or Proceedings in Parlyement ought not to be impeached or questioned in any court or place out of Parlyement.

2   Security of members during their parliamentary term is fundamental to parliamentary independence and therefore:

   (a) the expulsion of members from parliament as a penalty for leaving their parties (floor-crossing) should be viewed as a possible infringement of members' independence; anti-defection measures may be necessary in some jurisdictions to deal with corrupt practices;[9]

   (b) laws allowing for the recall of members during their elected term should be viewed with caution, as a potential threat to the independence of members;

   (c) the cessation of membership of a political party of itself should not lead to the loss of a member's seat.

3   In the discharge of their functions, members should be free from improper pressures and accordingly:

   (a) the criminal law and the use of defamation proceedings are not appropriate mechanisms for restricting legitimate criticism of the government or the parliament;

   (b) the defence of qualified privilege with respect to reports of parliamentary proceedings should be drawn as broadly as possible to permit full public reporting and discussion of public affairs;

   (c) the offence of contempt of parliament should be drawn as narrowly as possible.

---

7   The drafters of the Guidelines did not wish by this provision to impinge on either the independence of the judiciary or the independence of the legal profession. However, in many jurisdictions throughout the Commonwealth, magistrates and judges are given no formal training on commencement of their duties. It was felt that appointees to the bench would benefit from some training prior to appointment in order to make them more aware of the duties and obligations of judicial officers and would aid their passage to the Bench.

8   It has been observed that the Guidelines are silent about the elected composition of the popular Chamber. In a number of jurisdictions nominated members may have a decisive influence on the outcome of a vote. If properly used, however, the power of nomination may be used to redress, eg, gender imbalance and to ensure representation of ethnic or religious minorities. The role of non-elected senates or upper chambers must also be considered in this context.

9   There remains controversy about the balance to be struck between anti-floor crossing measures as a barrier against corruption and the potential threat to the independence of MPs.

Women in parliament[10]

1 To improve the numbers of women members in Commonwealth parliaments, the role of women within political parties should be enhanced, including the appointment of more women to executive roles within political parties.
2 Pro-active searches for potential candidates should be undertaken by political parties.
3 Political parties in nations with proportional representation should be required to ensure an adequate gender balance on their respective lists of candidates for election. Women, where relevant, should be included in the top part of the candidates' lists of political parties. Parties should be called upon publicly to declare the degree of representation of women on their lists and to defend any failure to maintain adequate representation.
4 Where there is no proportional representation, candidate search and/or selection committees of political parties should be gender balanced, as should representation at political conventions, and this should be facilitated by political parties by way of amendment to party constitutions; women should be put forward for safe seats.
5 Women should be elected to parliament through regular electoral processes. The provision of reservations for women in national constitutions, whilst useful, tends to be insufficient for securing adequate and long term representation by women.
6 Men should work in partnership with women to redress constraints on women entering parliament. True gender balance requires the oppositional element of the inclusion of men in the process of dialogue and remedial action to address the necessary inclusion of both genders in all aspects of public life.

Judicial and parliamentary ethics

1 Judicial ethics
   (a) A Code of Ethics and Conduct should be developed and adopted by each judiciary as a means of ensuring the accountability of judges;
   (b) the Commonwealth Magistrates' and Judges' Association should be encouraged to complete its Model Code of Judicial Conduct now in development;[11]
   (c) the Association should also serve as a repository of codes of judicial conduct developed by Commonwealth judiciaries, which will serve as a resource for other jurisdictions.
2 Parliamentary ethics
   (a) Conflict of interest guidelines and codes of conduct should require full disclosure by ministers and members of their financial and business interests;
   (b) members of parliament should have privileged access to advice from statutorily-established ethics advisors;

---

10 The emphasis on gender balance is not intended to imply that there are not other issues of equity in representation which need to be considered. Parliament should reflect the composition of the community which it represents in terms of ethnicity, social and religious groups and regional balance. Some countries have experimented with regulation of national political parties to ensure, eg, that their support is not confined to one regional or ethnic group, a notion which would be profoundly hostile to the political culture in other jurisdictions.

11 Following discussion of the Guidelines it has been accepted by the Working Group that a 'uniform' Model Code of Judicial Conduct is inappropriate. Judicial officers in each country should develop, adopt and periodically review codes of ethics and conduct appropriate to their jurisdiction. The Commonwealth Magistrates' and Judges' Association will promote that process in its programmes and will serve as a repository for such codes when adopted.

(c) whilst responsive to the needs of society and recognising minority views in society, members of parliament should avoid excessive influence of lobbyists and special interest groups.

Accountability mechanisms

1 Judicial accountability
   (a) Discipline:
       (i) In cases where a judge is at risk of removal, the judge must have the right to be fully informed of the charges, to be represented at a hearing, to make a full defence, and to be judged by an independent and impartial tribunal. Grounds for removal of a judge should be limited to:
           (A) inability to perform judicial duties; and
           (B) serious misconduct.
       (ii) In all other matters, the process should be conducted by the chief judge of the courts.
       (iii) Disciplinary procedures should not include the public admonition of judges. Any admonitions should be delivered in private, by the chief judge.
   (b) Public criticism:[12]
       (i) Legitimate public criticism of judicial performance is a means of ensuring accountability;
       (ii) the criminal law and contempt proceedings are not appropriate mechanisms for restricting legitimate criticism of the courts.

2 Executive accountability
   (a) Accountability of the executive to parliament:
       Parliamentary procedures should provide adequate mechanisms to enforce the accountability of the executive to parliament. These should include:
       (i) a committee structure appropriate to the size of Parliament, adequately resourced and with the power to summon witnesses, including ministers. Governments should be required to announce publicly, within a defined time period, their responses to committee reports;
       (ii) standing orders should provide appropriate opportunities for members to question ministers and full debate on legislative proposals;
       (iii) the public accounts should be independently audited by the Auditor General who is responsible to and must report directly to parliament;
       (iv) the chair of the Public Accounts Committee should normally be an opposition member;
       (v) offices of the Ombudsman, Human Rights Commissions and Access to Information Commissioners should report regularly to parliament.
   (b) Judicial review:
       Commonwealth governments should endorse and implement the principles of judicial review enshrined in the Lusaka Statement on Government under the Law.

---

12 In certain jurisdictions, the corruption of the judiciary is acknowledged as a real problem. The recommendations contained in the Guidelines are entirely consistent with the Framework for Commonwealth Principles in Promoting Good Governance and Combating Corruption approved by CHOGM in Durban in 1999. There is some support for the creation of a judicial ombudsman who may receive complaints from the public regarding the conduct of judges.

The law making process

1   Women should be involved in the work of national law commissions in the law making process. Ongoing assessment of legislation is essential so as to create a more gender balanced society. Gender-neutral language should be used in the drafting and use of legislation.

2   Procedures for the preliminary examination of issues in proposed legislation should be adopted and published so that:
   (a) there is public exposure of issues, papers and consultation on major reforms including, where possible, a draft bill;
   (b) standing orders provide a delay of some days between introduction and debate to enable public comment unless suspended by consent or a significantly high percentage vote of the chamber; and
   (c) major legislation can be referred to a select committee allowing for the detailed examination of such legislation and the taking of evidence from members of the public.

3   Model standing orders protecting members' rights and privileges and permitting the incorporation of variations, to take local circumstances into account, should be drafted and published.

4   Parliament should be serviced by a professional staff independent of the regular public service.

5   Adequate resources to government and non-government back benchers should be provided to improve parliamentary input and should include provision for:
   (a) training of new members;
   (b) secretarial, office, library and research facilities;
   (c) drafting assistance including Private Members' Bills.

6   An all party committee of members of parliament should review and administer parliament's budget which should not be subject to amendment by the executive.

7   Appropriate legislation should incorporate international human rights instruments to assist in interpretation and to ensure that ministers certify compliance with such instruments, on introduction of the legislation.

8   It is recommended that 'sunset' legislation (for the expiry of all subordinate legislation not renewed) should be enacted subject to power to extend the life of such legislation.

The role of non-judicial and non-parliamentary institutions

1   The Commonwealth Statement on Freedom of Expression[13] provides essential guarantees to which all Commonwealth countries should subscribe.

2   The Executive must refrain from all measures directed at inhibiting the freedom of the press, including indirect methods such as the misuse of official advertising.

3   An independent, organised legal profession is an essential component in the protection of the rule of law.

---

13   Since the Guidelines were drafted, the draft Statement on Freedom of Expression has been subject to further consideration and the reference should take account of the new developments. The Commonwealth Heads of Government, in the Coolum Declaration of 5 March 2002, included a commitment to freedom of expression: 'We stand united in our commitment to democracy, the rule of law, good governance, freedom of expression and the protection of human rights ...'

4   Adequate legal aid schemes should be provided for poor and disadvantaged litigants, including public interest advocates.

5   Legal professional organisations should assist in the provision, through *pro bono* schemes, of access to justice for the impecunious.

6   The executive must refrain from obstructing the functioning of an independent legal profession by such means as withholding licensing of professional bodies.

7   Human Rights Commissions, Offices of the Ombudsman and Access to Information Commissioners can play a key role in enhancing public awareness of good governance and rule of law issues, and adequate funding and resources should be made available to enable them to discharge these functions. Parliament should accept responsibility in this regard.

Such institutions should be empowered to provide access to alternative dispute resolution mechanisms.

Measures for implementation and monitoring compliance

These Guidelines should be forwarded to the Commonwealth Secretariat for consideration by law ministers and Heads of Government.[14]

If these Guidelines are adopted, an effective monitoring procedure, which might include a Standing Committee, should be devised under which all Commonwealth jurisdictions accept an obligation to report on their compliance with these Guidelines.

Consideration of these reports should form a regular part of the meetings of law ministers and of Heads of Government.

Human Rights Today Caribbean Symposium

Background

The majority of Commonwealth members are small States. The Human Rights Today Caribbean Symposium, which was co-sponsored by the CLEA, brought together participants from around the Caribbean, including those from some British Overseas

---

14   The Guidelines were considered by Commonwealth law ministers in November 2001. They 'noted that the principles of good governance and judicial independence had been clearly endorsed by Commonwealth Heads of Government and welcomed the general thrust of the declaration of those principles in the Guidelines'. Subject to revisions of the provisions of the Guidelines relating to judicial appointment mechanisms and the control of funds (now incorporated into the text of this document), senior officials agreed that the Guidelines would be laid before law ministers at their meeting in November 2002. The Guidelines were also considered by the Law Ministers and Attorney-Generals of Small Commonwealth jurisdictions Meeting in May 2000, where the Guidelines were welcomed as 'reflecting valuable and fundamental concepts'. The sponsoring organisations have under active consideration the creation of a monitoring procedure outside official Commonwealth processes. This initially may involve an 'annual report' on the implementation of the Guidelines in all Commonwealth jurisdictions, noting 'good' and 'bad' practice.

Territories (OTs), to discuss their particular concerns against the background of the UN Decade for Human Rights Education. The final Symposium Resolution encapsulates the concerns of many small States in the Commonwealth.

Resolution

We, the participants at the Human Rights Today Symposium held in the Cayman Islands from September 11–14, 2001

- Reaffirming the principles of the Universal Declaration of Human Rights and in particular that the recognition of the inherent dignity and of the equal and inalienable rights of all members of the human family is the foundation of freedom, justice and peace in the world;
- Deeply conscious that disregard for human rights as exemplified by the appalling acts of terrorism which have been perpetrated in the United States of America on the very day on which this Symposium commenced have resulted in barbarous acts that have outraged the conscience of all people;
- Recognising that the traditions of freedom and justice in the Caribbean Region which have been created through centuries of struggle against oppression and exploitation, as well as the richness of the Region's cultural and ethnic diversities, provide a unique opportunity to the Region to contribute to the creation of a better world of justice, peace and better standards of life in larger freedom;
- Accepting that human rights are universal and interdependent and should not be denied to any person whether on the grounds of race, gender, age, place of birth or residence, religion, political opinion, status or otherwise;
- Acknowledging that the promotion and protection of human rights are the lifeblood of every democratic society.

BE IT RESOLVED THAT:

1 It is the duty of governments to promote and protect human rights and the rule of law;
2 Governments are called upon expeditiously to draw up national action plans for the promotion and protection of human rights, to include broad-based educational and public information programmes on human rights; it is the duty of governments to conduct programmes of public education in the field of human rights and of governments to introduce in educational institutions at the primary, secondary and tertiary levels (including law schools), schemes for the teaching of human rights;
3 Governments should initiate a process of continual review and reform to ensure that those territories which have no existing constitutional guarantee of human rights incorporate such provisions in their constitutions and that States which already have such guarantees make such revisions as will bring them into conformity with international human rights norms;
4 In conducting the processes of constitutional review and reform, governments should procure the full participation of civil society and widespread public discussion;
5 Governments should conduct a thorough review of existing legislative provisions to ensure they are in harmony with constitutional and conventional human rights norms;

6   In the formation or reformation of Bills of Rights, savings clauses which preserve colonial or other laws which are inconsistent with the fundamental rights provisions must be excluded;

7   In the promotion and protection of human rights, constitutional and legislative provisions must be made to protect family life, and the rights of children, the elderly, and the disabled as members of a family and a community;

8   Governments have a duty to protect the security of the person and property of persons governed by them, and victims who suffer injury or loss should be given appropriate compensation by the State; family members and communities are called upon to lend support to such victims;

9   Cultural and ethnic diversity must be treated as an impetus to respect for the human rights of all and not as an excuse for restricting the full realisation of human rights by some;

10 The right to self-determination implies that decisions affecting the welfare of the people of any country or territory should only be made after full consultation with and approbation of the people of that country or territory;

11 It is the duty of government to provide human rights education to public servants and, in particular, court officials, law enforcement and prison personnel, customs and immigration officers;

12 Regional and national non-governmental organisations and inter-Governmental organisations concerned with men, women, children, labour, development, food, housing, health care, environmental, as well as other social justice groups, human rights advocates, religious organisations and the media shall undertake specific activities of formal and non-formal human rights education;

13 Governments must accept as one of their primary responsibilities the provision of adequate resources and facilities for the administration of justice, including financial and material support for the court system, legal aid and free access to the courts;

14 Lawyers and judges must remain sensitive to the principles of international human rights law and courts must endeavour to apply these principles in adjudicating on questions touching on the human rights of any person;

15 The independence of the judiciary is of cardinal importance to democratic government, the rule of law and the ability of the judiciary to protect and enforce human rights. Governments are therefore encouraged to ensure that the method of appointment of judicial officers and the terms and conditions of judicial service are objective and fair and in keeping with the Latimer House Guidelines adopted in 1998 and aimed at attracting to and keeping in the judiciary, the most able jurists;

16 Members of the legal profession, the judiciary and law enforcement officers must not be subject to political or any other intimidation or interference in the discharge of their responsibilities to protect the human rights of all citizens;

17 Civil servants and others must not be subject to political or any other intimidation or interference in the discharge of their responsibilities to protect the human rights of all citizens;

18 The democratic process must be strengthened by increased openness, transparency and accountability in public administration and the freedoms of information, expression and communication must be maintained and the independence of journalists protected;

19 The governments of independent States should expeditiously take appropriate steps to ratify and accede to the international and regional human rights instruments without reservations and to incorporate them into their domestic law; they should permit where available the rights of their citizens to submit petitions to the appropriate international bodies;

20 It is the duty of governments responsible for dependent territories to take appropriate steps expeditiously to extend, ratify and accede to, on behalf of the said territories, international and regional human rights instruments without reservations and commit to the right of their citizens to submit petitions to the appropriate international bodies;

21 In the process of reform of the criminal law, governments shall ensure that no legislation is passed that would infringe the rights of accused persons as established by international conventions or Bills of Rights;

22 Governments should be encouraged to establish effective human rights commissions and/or offices of the ombudsman;

23 The important role of teachers as the persons who are primarily entrusted with the education and sensitisation of our children for the appreciation of their human rights should be recognised by governments and teachers should be provided with the necessary means and appropriate terms and conditions to allow them to discharge all their duties and to ensure that suitably qualified persons are attracted to and kept within the profession.

Cayman Islands, 11–14 September 2001

CLEA and the Commonwealth Human Rights Initiative (CHRI)

The CLEA is one of the supporting bodies of CHRI. The CHRI is now the largest dedicated body working for human rights in the Commonwealth. It began in 1987 as a voluntary network, but by 2002 had a staff of more than 25 spread around three offices – in New Delhi (currently the main office, though the Initiative is required to rotate its international headquarters), in London and in Accra.

It is an independent NGO that has been constituted by Commonwealth associations with overlapping concerns for human rights. The first three to support it were the Commonwealth Journalists Association, the Commonwealth Lawyers Association and the Commonwealth Trade Union Council. These three lobbied the Commonwealth summit in Vancouver in 1987, calling for a new and wider push for human rights by an organisation which at that time was concerned largely with anti-racism and the need for development. Many member countries were one-party States or governed by the military, and the Cold War was still being fought.

These three were soon joined by the CLEA and the Commonwealth Medical Association. In the 1990s, three more became its sponsors – the Commonwealth Parliamentary Association, the Commonwealth Press Union and the Commonwealth Broadcasting Association. The Harare Commonwealth Declaration 1991, with a commitment to fundamental human rights for which the CHRI had pressed, opened the door to significant progress – including the suspension of military or abusive governments from Commonwealth membership (after 1995) and the spread of national human rights institutions.

Mission and activities

The CHRI was set up both as a lobbying and a project organisation. Its first major lobbying exercise was in the run-up to the Commonwealth Heads of Government Meeting (CHOGM) in Harare, in 1991, when it published the first comprehensive description of human rights issues in the association entitled *Put our World to Rights*. It supported three African bodies in a conference of Commonwealth African human rights NGOs which took place just prior to the meeting of the Commonwealth leaders. This demonstrated the widespread desire for stronger protection for human rights on the continent.

Since then the Initiative has published substantial documents every two years, prior to each CHOGM, on topics varying from freedom of expression and the impact of religious and communal conflict to the proliferation of light weapons (*Over a Barrel*, 1999) and the role of a rights-based approach in reducing poverty (*Human rights and Poverty Eradication*, 2001). It has sought to cover topics involving substantial numbers of people, and many Commonwealth countries.

At the same time it has lobbied on more specialised topics and carried out fact-finding missions (for instance, to Nigeria in 1995 and to the Fiji Islands in 2000). Since the Commonwealth Ministerial Action Group was established in 1995 by governments, to ensure compliance with the basic political values of the association – including adherence to fundamental human rights – the CHRI has been the only NGO to make regular submissions on situations of concern. It has taken a particular interest in this instrument because, following its report on Nigeria in 1995 (*Nigeria – Stolen by Generals*), it had called for inter-governmental machinery to be set up to realise the guarantees of the Harare Declaration.

The theoretical remit of the Action Group was wide but, from 1995 to 2001, it was restricted in practice to countries where a military coup had taken place (at different times Nigeria, The Gambia, Sierra Leone, Pakistan and the Fiji Islands). The CHRI never accepted this limitation and referred to several other countries in its submissions. In 2001, it campaigned for the inclusion of Zimbabwe on the CMAG remit, where it had evidence that the civilian government was abusing the human rights of political opponents and others. The Commonwealth summit in Coolum in March 2002 agreed a formula under which situations not the result of a military coup could lead to the attention of CMAG, and the following month the civilian regime of President Mugabe was suspended from the Councils of the Commonwealth. [Editor's note: for further details of CMAG, see Section 2 below.]

The CHRI is an independent organisation. It has sometimes criticised Commonwealth governments and the Commonwealth Secretariat, which works on their behalf. In particular it published a critique of the modest status and reduced funding of the Secretariat's small Human Rights Unit in 1999 (*Rights Must Come First*). At the same time it has collaborated where appropriate with the Secretariat (the related Commonwealth Fund for Technical Co-operation helped fund a CHRI workshop on refugee rights in Kenya in 1993) and with the Commonwealth Foundation. The CHRI will respond to the appeal in the 2002 Coolum Declaration for more co-operation among members of the 'Commonwealth family', recognising that its resources are considerably larger than those devoted to human rights by the inter-governmental bodies.

The Initiative, with its main office in New Delhi (it had moved from London in 1993), has developed a variety of programmes. These include work on prisons and police reform (originally in South Asia, but now also in East Africa); a right to information campaign, which particularly addresses the needs of poorer and sometimes illiterate communities (started in India, this campaign is now also being run in Ghana); work on constitutional revision, which stresses the participation of citizens and NGOs and the need for gender equality (this has involved several workshops in Africa, and inputs to the constitutional revision process in India, and to the creation of a Northern Ireland Human Rights Commission); and an active interest in the development of national human rights institutions in the Commonwealth.

These programmes have involved training workshops and publications (information is available from the website: www.humanrightsinitiative.org). They have been supported by a variety of agencies, including the Ford Foundation, the UK Government's Human Rights Fund, the Canadian International Development Agency, German foundations, and funds generated inside India. Although some of this work is long term in nature, the Initiative seeks to evaluate each programme on a regular basis. All CHRI offices can be contacted by email. The Delhi office is at: chriall@nda.vsnl.net.in. The Accra office is at: chri@britishcouncil.org.gh. The London office is at: chri@sas.ac.uk.

Governance and accountability

The CHRI is an organisation of organisations, not built on a direct paying membership. The Memorandum of Understanding which gave it a constitution in 1992, provides for three levels of participation by the organisations which support CHRI. Firstly, an international Advisory Commission; secondly, an Executive Committee in the country which hosts the Head Office; thirdly a Trustee Committee based in the UK. An Advisory Committee for the new African office, based in Accra, will be formed.

The function of each body is different. The Advisory Commission, which meets annually, is concerned with the overall policy of the Initiative. Its Secretary is the Director of CHRI. All supporting bodies are entitled to representation and a regional and gender balance is maintained. Co-option is possible. A principal concern of the commission is a biennial report to the Commonwealth, and to Commonwealth governments in particular, on human rights issues of current and overriding concern. Such reports are issued in the name of the commission.

The Executive Committee is the day to day accountability and reference body for the Director and staff in the capital which hosts the main office of the CHRI. It meets quarterly and, like the Advisory Commission, aims to represent national affiliates of the eight supporting Commonwealth NGOs. It too has a capacity to co-opt members. It is responsible for finance, and for the Director's contract (which is also subject to approval of the Trustee Committee). In each country where there is a CHRI office there is separate financial reporting, and the equivalent of charitable status.

The Trustee Committee in London, where the head offices of the supporting bodies are located, was originally designed as a 'long-stop' committee, concerned to ensure that the overall purposes of the CHRI were maintained, and that the head office was rotated in a rational manner. It meets quarterly, with representation from the eight supporting bodies, and with some co-options. It has evolved slightly enlarged functions because the key Commonwealth inter-governmental bodies are based in London, and for reasons of financial convenience.

In principle, these tiers of responsibility provide for two-way communication between the CHRI and its member organisations. In practice, this can be more difficult than it seems because many of the supporting organisations are small and over-stretched, and links between head offices and national affiliates around the Commonwealth can be tenuous. However, the object of the CHRI is to strengthen the human rights work of its supporting bodies where possible, to benefit from their expertise, and to operate jointly wherever it can. The Right to Information campaign, which has been a strong feature of the CHRI in recent years, is obviously of particular interest to the Commonwealth Journalists Association, to the Commonwealth Press Union and to the Commonwealth Broadcasting Association.

Commonwealth Judicial Colloquia on the Domestic Application of International Human Rights Norms

In February 1988, a judicial colloquium was held in Bangalore, India. The central issue discussed in this was the relevance of international human rights standards to the task of national courts in interpreting and applying their national constitutions and legislation and in developing the common law. Further colloquia have since been held in Harare, Zimbabwe; Banjul, The Gambia; Abuja, Nigeria; Bloemfontein, South Africa; Oxford, UK; Georgetown, Guyana; and a 10th anniversary meeting, again in Bangalore.

The Bangalore Principles were developed at the 1988 meeting. These have had an enormous influence on encouraging judges in many Commonwealth jurisdictions to make use of the rich body of international and comparative Commonwealth human rights law.

Whilst not directly involved in the process, CLEA members attended several of the colloquia. The Association fully supports the principles enshrined in the various state-ments emanating from the colloquia, several of which link directly into the Latimer House Guidelines and which emphasise the significance of the development of human rights jurisprudence by Commonwealth judges. The challenge for Commonwealth law teachers to contribute to the development of human rights jurisprudence is also clearly recognised. As para 14 of the Georgetown Conclusions states:

> There is a need for courses in law schools and other institutions of learning to educate the next generation of judges, administrators and lawyers in human rights jurisprudence. The urgent necessity remains to bring the principles of human rights into the daily activities of government and public officials alike, and for ordinary men and women. In this way a global culture of respect for human rights can be fostered.

The main sets of principles and declarations are set out below.

Bangalore Principles (1988)

1   Fundamental human rights and freedoms are inherent in all humankind and find expression in constitutions and legal systems throughout the world and in the international human rights instruments.
2   These international human rights instruments provide important guidance in cases concerning fundamental human rights and freedoms.

3   There is an impressive body of jurisprudence, both international and national, concerning the interpretation of particular human rights and freedoms and their application. This body of jurisprudence is of practical relevance and value to judges and lawyers generally.

4   In most countries whose legal systems are based upon the common law, international conventions are not directly enforceable in national courts unless their provisions have been incorporated by legislation into domestic law. However, there is a growing tendency for national courts to have regard to these international norms for the purpose of deciding cases where the domestic law – whether constitutional, statute or common law – is uncertain or incomplete.

5   This tendency is entirely welcome because it respects the universality of fundamental human rights and freedoms and the vital role of an independent judiciary in reconciling the competing claims of individuals and groups of persons with the general interests of the community.

6   While it is desirable for the norms contained in the international human rights instruments to be still more widely recognised and applied by national courts, this process must take fully into account local laws, traditions, circumstances and needs.

7   It is within the proper nature of the judicial process and well-established judicial functions for national courts to have regard to international obligations which a country undertakes – whether or not they have been incorporated into domestic law – for the purpose of removing ambiguity or uncertainty from national constitutions, legislation or common law.

8   However, where national law is clear and inconsistent with the international obligations of the state concerned, in common law countries the national court is obliged to give effect to national law. In such cases the court should draw such inconsistency to the attention of the appropriate authorities since the supremacy of national law in no way mitigates a breach of an international legal obligation which is undertaken by a country.

9   It is essential to redress a situation where, by reason of traditional legal training which has tended to ignore the international dimension, judges and practising lawyers are often unaware of the remarkable and comprehensive developments of statements of international human rights norms. For the practical implementation of these views it is desirable to make provision for appropriate courses in universities and colleges, and for lawyers and law enforcement officials; provision in libraries of relevant materials; promotion of expert advisory bodies knowledgeable about developments in this field; better dissemination of information to judges, lawyers and law enforcement officials; and meetings for exchanges of relevant information and experience.

10 These views are expressed in recognition of the fact that judges and lawyers have a special contribution to make in administration of justice in fostering universal respect for fundamental human rights and freedoms.

Bangalore, 30 December 1988

Harare Declaration of Human Rights (1989)

1　Fundamental human rights and freedoms are inherent in humankind. In some cases, they are expressed in the constitutions, legislation and principles of common law and customary law of each country. They are also expressed in customary international law, international instruments on human rights and in the developing international jurisprudence on human rights.

2　The coming into force of the African Charter on Human and Peoples' Rights is a step in the ever widening effort of humanity to promote and protect fundamental human rights declared both in universal and regional instruments. The gross violations of human rights and fundamental freedoms which have occurred around the world in living memory (and which still occur) provide the impetus in a world of diminishing distances and growing interdependence, for such effort to provide effectively for their promotion and protection.

3　But fine statements in domestic laws or international and regional instruments are not enough. Rather it is essential to develop a culture of respect for internationally stated human rights norms which sees these norms applied in the domestic laws of all nations and given full effect. They must not be seen as alien to domestic law in national courts. It is in this context that the Principles on the Domestic Application of International Human Rights Norms stated in Bangalore in February 1988 are warmly endorsed by the participants. In particular, they reaffirmed that, subject always to any clearly applicable domestic law to the contrary, it is within the proper nature of the judicial process for national courts to have regard to international human rights norms – whether or not incorporated into domestic law and whether or not a country is party to a particular convention where it is declaratory of customary international law – for the purpose of resolving ambiguity or uncertainty in national constitutions and legislation or filling gaps in the common law. The participants noted many recent examples in countries of the Commonwealth where this had been done by courts of the highest authority – including in Australia, India, Mauritius, the United Kingdom and Zimbabwe.

4　There is a particular need to ensure that judges, lawyers, litigants and others are made aware of applicable human rights norms – stated in international instruments and otherwise. In this respect the participants endorsed the spirit of Article 25 of the African Charter. Under that Article, States Parties to the Charter have the duty to promote and ensure through teaching, education and publication, respect for the rights and freedoms (and corresponding duties) expressed in the Charter. The participants looked forward to the Commission established by the African Charter developing its work of promoting an awareness of human rights. The work being done in this regard by the publication of the Commonwealth Law Bulletin, the Law Reports of the Commonwealth and the Bulletin of Interights (the International Centre for the Legal Protection of Human Rights) was especially welcomed. But to facilitate the domestic application of international human rights norms more is needed to be done. So much was recognised in the Principles stated after the Bangalore Colloquium which called for new initiatives in legal education, provision of material to libraries and better dissemination of information about developments in this field to judges, lawyers and law enforcement officers in particular. There is also a role for non-government organisations in these as in other regards, including the development of public interest litigation.

5 As a practical measure to carrying forward the objectives of the Principles stated at Bangalore, the participants requested that the Legal Division of the Commonwealth Secretariat arrange for a handbook for judges and lawyers in all parts of the Commonwealth to be produced, containing at least the following:
   - the basic texts of the most relevant international and regional human rights instruments;
   - a table for ease of reference to and comparison of applicable provisions in each instrument; and
   - up to date references to the jurisprudence of international and national courts relevant to the meaning of the provisions in such instruments.

6 If the judges and lawyers in Africa, and indeed of the Commonwealth and of the wider world, have ready access to reference material of this kind, opportunities will be enhanced for the principles of international human rights norms to be utilised in proper ways by judges and lawyers performing their daily work. In this way, the long journey to universal respect of basic human rights will be advanced. Judges and lawyers have a duty to familiarise themselves with the growing international jurisprudence of human rights. So far as they may lawfully do so, they have a duty to reflect the basic norms of human rights in the performance of their duties.

In this way the noble words of international instruments will be translated into legal reality for the benefit of the people we serve but also ultimately for that of people in every land.

Harare, 22 April 1989

Georgetown Conclusions (1996)

1–3 ...

4 The international human rights instruments and their developing jurisprudence enshrine values and principles of equality, freedom, rationality and fairness, now recognised by the common law. They should be seen as complementary to domestic law in national courts ...

5 Commonwealth Caribbean judges in the discharge of their functions should give increasing effect to relevant international human rights norms (including those of the Inter-American international human rights instruments) when interpreting and applying their national constitutions and laws. The constitutional guarantees should be interpreted with the generosity appropriate to charters of freedom, avoiding the austerity of tabulated legalism.

6 It is the vital duty of an independent, impartial, well qualified judiciary, assisted by an independent well trained legal profession, to interpret and apply national constitutions and ordinary legislation, and to develop the common law in the light of these values and principles ... 'The protections enjoyed by judges, including financial independence and security of tenure, are an important defence against improper interference and free the judiciary to discharge the particular responsibilities given to it within national constitutional frameworks.'

7 Both civil and political rights and economic, social and cultural rights are integral, indivisible and complementary parts of one coherent system of global human

rights. The implementation of economic, social and cultural rights is a primary duty for the legislative and executive branches of government. However, even those economic, social and cultural rights which are not justiciable can serve as vital points of reference for judges as they interpret their constitutions and develop the common law, making choices which it is their responsibility to make in a free, equal and democratic society. Respect for human rights under the rule of law provides the best environment for the economic, social and cultural development of everyone in all parts of the world.

8   Fundamental human rights are more than mere pious aspirations. They form part of the public law of every nation, protecting individuals and minorities against the misuse of power by public authorities of all kinds. It is the special province of judges to see to it that the law's undertakings are realised in the daily life of the people. In a society ruled by law, all public institutions and authorities – legislative, executive and judicial – must act in accordance with the constitution and the law.

9   The legislative and executive branches of government have a duty to provide the necessary means to secure the equal protection of the law, speedy and effective access to justice, and effective legal remedies. To achieve this, there is a need for adequate funds for the proper functioning of the courts, and adequate legal aid, advice and assistance for people who cannot otherwise obtain legal services. It is also essential for each branch of government to introduce and maintain appropriate rules and procedures to promote compliance, in discharging their functions, with the international human rights instruments by which they are bound.

10   The provision of equal justice requires a competent and independent judiciary and legal profession trained in the discipline of the law and sensitive to the needs and aspirations of all the people. It is fundamental for a country's judiciary and legal profession to enjoy the broad confidence of the people they serve.

11   Judicial review and effective access to the courts are indispensable, not only in normal times, but also during periods of public emergency. It is at such times that basic human rights are most at risk and when courts must be especially vigilant in their protection.

12   Freedom of expression must be jealously protected as essential to the safeguarding of democracy and human rights. The courts must be zealous to protect free speech and expression in their widest sense, and at all times.

13   In relation to the death penalty, the participants recommended:
   (i)   that it should not be extended to any new offences to which it is not now applied in the particular state;
   (ii) that states whose independence constitutions preclude the determination by the courts as to whether the sentence is inhuman and degrading, if the punishment was lawful prior to the achievement of national status, should amend their constitutions to remove this fetter on judicial determination;
   (iii) that the death penalty should not be carried out until the exhaustion of all domestic and international legal remedies available to the applicant.

14   There is a need for courses in law schools and other institutions of learning to educate the next generation of judges, administrators and lawyers in human rights jurisprudence. The urgent necessity remains to bring the principles of human rights into the daily activities of government and public officials alike, and

of ordinary men and women. In this way a global culture of respect for human rights can be fostered.

15   The participants recognised the need to adopt a generous approach to the matter of legal standing in public law cases, while ensuring that the courts are not overwhelmed with frivolous cases. The courts should allow themselves to be assisted by well focused *amicus curiae* submissions from independent non-governmental organisations (NGOs), such as Interights, in novel and important cases where international and comparative law and practice may be relevant. National laws should enable NGOs and expert advocates (whether local or otherwise) to provide specialist legal advice, assistance and representation in important cases of public interest. Bar Associations and Law Societies should ensure that public interest cases are able to be effectively presented *pro bono publico*.

16   The participants expressed concern that the legislatures of some countries pass amendments to their constitutions or laws designed to erode or diminish fundamental rights and freedoms as interpreted and applied by national courts and international human rights fora. They recommended that this practice of diluting the internationally and nationally guaranteed human rights of the individual should not be resorted to, and that no amendment should be made which would destroy or impair the essential features of democratic societies governed by the rule of law.

17   The participants urged closer links and co-operation across national frontiers ... on the interpretation and application of human rights law. They attached the highest importance to disseminating to the judiciary and other lawyers knowledge about the human rights norms of international law, the jurisprudence of international and regional human rights bodies and the decisions of courts throughout the Commonwealth.

The Challenge of Bangalore: Making Human Rights a Practical Reality (1998)

The participants reaffirmed the general principles stated at the conclusion of the Commonwealth Judicial Colloquium in Bangalore in 1988 and developed by subsequent colloquia in Harare, Zimbabwe in 1989; in Banjul, The Gambia in 1990; in Abuja, Nigeria in 1991; in Balliol College, Oxford, UK in 1992; in Bloemfontein, South Africa in 1993; and in Georgetown, Guyana in 1996. What follows is both a restatement and further development of those principles.

1   Fundamental human rights and freedoms are universal. They find expression in constitutional and legal systems throughout the world; they are anchored in the international human rights codes to which all genuinely democratic states adhere; their meaning is illuminated by a rich body of case law, both international and national.

2   The universality of human rights derives from the moral principle of each individual's personal and equal autonomy and human dignity. That principle transcends national political systems and is in the keeping of the judiciary.

3   It is the vital duty of an independent, impartial and well qualified judiciary, assisted by an independent, well trained legal profession, to interpret and apply national

constitutions and ordinary legislation in harmony with international human rights codes and customary international law, and to develop the common law in the light of the values and principles enshrined in international human rights law.

4 Fundamental human rights form part of the public law of every nation, protecting individuals and minorities against the misuse of power by every public authority and any person discharging public functions. It is the special province of judges to see to it that the law's undertakings are realised in the daily life of the people.

5 Both civil and political rights and economic, social and cultural rights are integral, indivisible and complementary parts of one coherent system of global human rights. The implementation of economic, social and cultural rights is a primary duty for the legislative and executive branches of government. However, even those economic, social and cultural rights which are not justiciable can serve as vital points of reference for judges as they interpret their constitutions and ordinary legislation and develop the common law. Likewise, even where human rights treaties have not been ratified or incorporated into domestic law, they provide important guidance to law-makers, public officials and the courts.

6 The legislative and executive branches of government have a duty to secure the equal protection of the law, speedy and effective access to justice and effective legal remedies. This requires adequate funds for the proper functioning of the courts and adequate legal aid and advice for people who cannot otherwise obtain legal services. It is also essential for each branch of government to introduce and maintain appropriate rules and procedures to promote compliance, in discharging their functions, with the international human rights instruments by which they are bound. Where States have accepted the jurisdiction of supra-national human rights courts and Commissions to provide redress to victims of breaches of human rights, national courts should strive to ensure effective recourse to such redress.

7 Independent human rights commissions are needed with powers to assist victims to seek redress; to bring cases on issues of public interest and importance; and, by means of investigation, monitoring, research and public education, to foster a climate of respect for human rights.

8 The provision of equal justice requires a competent and independent judiciary and legal profession trained in the discipline of the law and sensitive to the needs and aspirations of all the people. It is fundamental for a country's judiciary and legal profession to enjoy the broad confidence of the people they serve. Public confidence in the judiciary depends not only on the institutional arrangements for protecting its independence from political pressures but also on the transparency and legitimacy of the manner in which judges are selected. Any mechanism, including judicial service commissions, should ensure that persons are selected because of their proven integrity, ability and independence and that the views of the existing judiciary are given appropriate weight.

9 Judicial review and effective access to the courts are indispensable not only in normal times but also during periods of public emergency. It is at such times that basic human rights are most at risk and when courts must be especially vigilant in their protection.

10 Freedom of expression is essential to safeguard democracy and human rights. The protection of freedom of expression in its widest sense is a chief responsibility of the judiciary.

11 All persons are equal. Equality means full and unfettered membership in every aspect of the democratic social order. Equality not only signifies equal protection of the law, but also equality of opportunity and treatment, together with equal sharing in the dignity which is the individual birthright of all. Equality does not imply homogeneity or diminution of personal liberty. Equality celebrates the priceless individuality and the right to fulfilment of every human being.

12 The principle of equal treatment forbids not only intentional or direct discrimination but also forbids practices and procedures which have a disparate adverse impact upon vulnerable groups and which have no objective justification. It is essential to secure the elimination not only of overt discrimination but also of indirect discrimination of this kind.

13 The principle of equality may require public authorities to take affirmative action to diminish and eliminate conditions which cause or perpetuate discrimination and to ensure equal access to and enjoyment of basic human rights and freedoms. Such affirmative action must be no more than is appropriate and necessary as a means to achieve equality.

14 Equality and justice both require a sensitive understanding of the needs, realities and perspective of women so that they may be free from violence and from infringement of their personal dignity and privacy. Violence against women is an affront to human dignity, a violation of human rights, and a barrier to the achievement of real equality. It is the duty of the judiciary to understand the nature, extent and impact of violence against women in the conduct of proceedings in their courts and in their judgments. Training is needed for judges, lawyers, law enforcement agencies, prosecutors, the prison service and other public authorities.

15 Lessons should be drawn from such advances as have been made in the protection of the rights of women for others suffering unfair discrimination, for example, because of gender, sex or because they are living with HIV/AIDS or because they are mentally or physically disabled.

16 The fundamental human rights of everyone must be protected by the public authorities of the state with effective remedies for breaches of human rights by those acting or purporting to act in an official capacity. Claims based on national security, State and individual immunity and political expediency ought not to deprive victims of such breaches of access to justice, or shield from criminal liability those individuals who commit genocide, war crimes, crimes against humanity or other gross breaches of human rights.

17 It is a matter of public concern that some legislatures pass amendments to their constitutions or laws designed to erode or diminish fundamental rights and freedoms as interpreted and applied by national courts and by international human rights fora. This practice should not be resorted to and no amendment should be made which would destroy or impair the essential features of democratic societies governed by the rule of law.

18 The criminal justice system should function in a manner that is impartial and independent, ensuring justice to the accused but at the same time protecting the victims and society at large. The proper working of the criminal justice system requires free legal assistance to an indigent accused to ensure a fair investigation and trial.

19 The death penalty should not be extended to any offences to which it is not now applied in the particular country. States whose constitutions preclude the determination by the courts as to whether the sentence is inhuman and degrading

should amend their constitutions to remove this fetter on judicial determination. The death penalty should be carried out, if at all, only after the exhaustion of all domestic and international legal remedies.

20 Public interest litigation has a special role to play in protecting the human rights of disadvantaged sections of the population. Judgments in such cases should be based on clear constitutional and legal criteria; they should be enforceable and effective, keeping in mind the rights and interests of those not party to the litigation; and they should be subject to appeal or judicial review.

21 Courts should adopt a generous approach to the matter of legal standing in public law cases. They should also welcome *amicus curiae* submissions in significant cases.

22 The principles of human rights should be brought into the daily activities of government and public officials alike, as well as of ordinary men and women. Furthermore the jurisprudence of international and regional human rights bodies and the decisions of courts throughout the Commonwealth should be disseminated to judges, lawyers and public officials. In these ways a global culture of respect for human rights can be fostered.

23 A South Asian charter of human rights, similar to regional human rights conventions elsewhere, would make a significant contribution to the protection of human rights throughout South Asia. The making of such a charter should be given a high priority. [Editor's note: An Asian Human Rights Charter was prepared under the auspices of the non-governmental Asian Human Rights Commission. This is available at www.ahrck.net.net/charter/index.html. Law Asia and the Association of Asian Parliamentarians for Peace, amongst others, have also drafted their own versions of such a charter.]

Bangalore, 30 December 1998

SECTION 2
THE COMMONWEALTH

THE COMMONWEALTH

INTRODUCTION

The modern Commonwealth dates from a 1949 meeting in London, at which Prime Ministers of the then eight countries of the British Commonwealth – Australia, Britain, Canada, Ceylon (as Sri Lanka was then known), India, New Zealand, Pakistan and South Africa – agreed the *London Declaration*. This was a watershed document in that before its adoption, constitutional allegiance to the British Crown was a condition of membership of the Commonwealth. After its adoption this was no longer the case. Under what was called the 'Nehru formula', it was decided that the then British monarch would become the symbol of their association as free and independent States and as such the Head of the Commonwealth. However, members would no longer need to recognise the monarch as their Head of State and no longer swear an oath of allegiance. In fact the duties of the Head of the Commonwealth would be entirely distinct from those of the British monarch. This in turn meant that countries with republican constitutions could be admitted and that India, which was about to become a republic, could therefore remain in the Commonwealth.

The 1949 London Declaration transformed the whole character of the Commonwealth from a relic of Empire into a co-operative association based on the voluntary membership of free and sovereign States working to promote their mutual interest. The association thus formally became the 'Commonwealth' and ceased to be the 'British Commonwealth'. Eight years later Ghana and Malaya (as it was then known) joined. Then from 1960 the Commonwealth expanded rapidly as the process of decolonisation gathered pace, with virtually all the newly independent States opting to join the association.

The first Commonwealth Secretary-General, Mr Arnold Smith, described such decisions as at once pragmatic and forward looking:

> When statesmen who have led their nations to independence have decided to seek membership in the Commonwealth, they have not appeared to be motivated by sentimentality about the past, but by a constructive vision of the future and by realistic assessments about their country's national interest. For many of them the past included memories of racial discrimination, political struggle and jail. The decision was taken because these leaders saw practical value for their countries and for humanity, in retaining and building on the positive aspects of an association that linked races and continents, and in surmounting past inequities, rather than in using unpleasant memories and resentments for nation building based on the perpetuation of suspicions and divisions, as lesser politicians have so often done. (*Annual Report of the Commonwealth Secretary-General*, 1966, London: Commonwealth Secretariat.)

Today, the Commonwealth is the largest association of independent States after the United Nations (UN). Its 54 independent member countries, with a total population estimated at over 1.7 billion, span all major political groupings, regions and economic zones and comprise some of the largest (eg, India) and smallest (eg, Nauru) countries in the world as well as some of the poorest and some of the richest. It embraces major parts of Africa and Asia, almost all of the Caribbean and much of the Pacific and Australasia, as well as having members in Europe and America. It also contains a high proportion of small States, whose interests the Commonwealth is particularly anxious to protect. It embraces a variety of different political systems, but all Member States acknowledge the British Queen as Head of the Commonwealth. A list of Member States is provided at the end of this section. That States still value membership is shown by the fact the three countries that left the Commonwealth have since returned to membership: South Africa (withdrew in 1961 but returned in 1994); Pakistan (left in 1972 but returned 1989 – although it is currently (2002) suspended from the Councils of the Commonwealth); and the Fiji Islands (membership lapsed in 1987 but returned in 1997 – although it too was later suspended from the Councils of the Commonwealth).

All Member States, with the exception of Mozambique, have experienced direct or indirect British rule or have been linked administratively to another Commonwealth country. In 1997, Commonwealth Heads of Government at their meeting in Edinburgh agreed that in order to become a member, a State must comply with three criteria:

- It should have had a constitutional association with an existing Commonwealth Member State.
- It should comply with Commonwealth values, principles and priorities as set out in the Harare Commonwealth Declaration of 1991.
- It should accept Commonwealth norms and conventions.

The Commonwealth is remarkable in that it has neither a charter nor any formal constitutional structure. Its members voluntarily co-operate with each other in furtherance of their common interests and seek to reach decisions by consensus. As a result, it has gone through a gradual evolution over time as its membership has expanded and issues of joint concern have changed. This is one of the things that distinguishes it from the UN. The principles and aims of the organisation are set out in the form of declarations or statements which have been issued at the biennial meetings of Commonwealth Heads of Government (CHOGM). The major ones are set out below. *The Report by the Commonwealth High Level Review Group to Commonwealth Heads of Government* (set out below) also contains useful background material on the Commonwealth.

The Commonwealth is administered by the Commonwealth Secretariat, which was established in 1965. Up to that year, the association's affairs, including the meetings of its Prime Ministers, were administered by the British Government through the Commonwealth Relations Office. This was clearly unsatisfactory to newly independent States and it was agreed to establish an independent Secretariat and thus turn the Commonwealth into a fully fledged international organisation. Since then the Commonwealth Secretariat has been housed in Marlborough House in London. It is here that the Commonwealth Legal Education Association (CLEA) also has its headquarters. The Commonwealth Secretary-General (S-G) heads the Secretariat. He (there has never been a woman S-G) plays a key role in the association's work on preventive diplomacy and conflict resolution. His 'good offices' role in particular has been used to help resolve actual or potential internal crises in several Commonwealth countries. For example, in March 2002, the S-G was mandated to 'engage with the Government of Zimbabwe to ensure that the specific recommendations from the Commonwealth Observer Group Report, notably on the management of future elections, in Zimbabwe are implemented'. His 'good offices' role also now forms a key part of the work of the Commonwealth Ministerial Action Group (CMAG) (see below).

Commonwealth Law Ministers' Meetings (LMM) are also held regularly. One of its major achievements has been the agreement to implement the Commonwealth schemes on mutual assistance, extradition (rendition of fugitive offenders), cultural heritage and transfer of prisoners. The LMM also sets the agenda for the work of the Legal and Constitutional Affairs Division (LCAD) at the Secretariat.

Unlike most other international organisations, the Commonwealth is not only an association of governments, but also of peoples. There are numerous sophisticated Commonwealth connections at the non-governmental level, involving a wide range of human endeavour. The three major 'legal-professional' associations: the CLEA, Commonwealth Lawyers' Association and Commonwealth Magistrates' and Judges' Association work closely *inter se* and with the LCAD on a variety of projects, with perhaps the most notable being the *Latimer House Guidelines*, details of which appear in Section 1 above. Representatives of the three associations are also invited to attend and participate in both LMM and Meetings of Senior Officials of Law Ministries.

THE LEGAL LEGACY

In the constitutional and legal field, Commonwealth countries have much in common:

- Common language: whilst the people of the Commonwealth speak many languages, they communicate with each other through the shared language of English. As a result, their written laws and decisions of their superior courts are almost invariably available in English.
- Common legal heritage: the laws and legal system of the vast majority of Commonwealth States are based on the English common law. Countries with an Islamic law or Roman-Dutch law tradition also make extensive use of common law principles in some areas.
- Common constitutional principles: the Westminster model constitution was used as the basis for the independence constitutions of many Commonwealth Member States. This commonality has encouraged courts to share jurisprudence on constitutional matters and to develop common principles of constitutional interpretation.
- Common legal problems: there is an enormous amount of co-operation between Commonwealth countries, for example, through the use of the various Commonwealth schemes that were noted earlier.

The result is that for law teachers, legal practitioners and judges, there is a wealth of comparative Commonwealth jurisprudence that is not only readily available but of enormous value for teaching and research purposes. This has also encouraged the CLEA to establish its curriculum development programme based, to a large extent, on comparative Commonwealth materials. It is also no coincidence that in recent years it has become commonplace for judges to make extensive use of jurisprudence from around the Commonwealth. The obtaining of such information has become considerably easier thanks to the internet, and details of access to legal materials in specific Commonwealth countries (much of it is available free of charge) appear in the appropriate country entries in this directory.

MAJOR COMMONWEALTH DECLARATIONS AND STATEMENTS

This section includes the major Commonwealth declarations and principles as agreed to by Commonwealth Heads of Government. The first major declaration – which remains the statement of core beliefs – is the Declaration of Commonwealth Principles, issued by Commonwealth Heads of Government at their meeting in Singapore in 1971.

Declaration of Commonwealth Principles 1971

The Commonwealth of Nations is a voluntary association of independent sovereign States, each responsible for its own policies, consulting and co-operating in the common interests of their peoples and in the promotion of international understanding and world peace.

Members of the Commonwealth come from territories in the six continents and five oceans, include people of different races, languages and religions, and display every stage of economic development, from poor developing nations to wealthy industrialised nations. They encompass a rich variety of cultures, traditions and institutions.

Membership of the Commonwealth is compatible with the freedom of member governments to be non-aligned or to belong to any other grouping, association or alliance.

Within this diversity all members of the Commonwealth hold certain principles in common. It is by pursuing these principles that the Commonwealth can continue to influence international society for the benefit of mankind.

We believe that international peace and order are essential to the security and prosperity of mankind; we therefore support the United Nations and seek to strengthen its influence for peace in the world, and its efforts to remove the causes of tension between nations.

We believe in the liberty of the individual, in equal rights for all citizens regardless of race, colour, creed or political belief, and in their inalienable right to participate by means of free and democratic political processes in framing the society in which they live. We therefore strive to promote in each of our countries those representative institutions and guarantees for personal freedom under the law that are our common heritage.

We recognise racial prejudice as a dangerous sickness threatening the healthy development of the human race and racial discrimination as an unmitigated evil of society. Each of us will vigorously combat this evil within our own nation. No country will subscribe to regimes which practise racial discrimination assistance, which in its own judgement directly contributes to the pursuit or consolidation of this evil policy.

We oppose all forms of colonial domination and racial oppression and are committed to the principles of human dignity and equality. We will therefore use all our efforts to foster human equality and dignity everywhere, and to further the principles of self-determination and non-racialism.

We believe that the wide disparities in wealth now existing between different sections of mankind are too great to be tolerated; they also create world tensions; our aim is their progressive removal. We therefore seek to use our efforts to overcome poverty, ignorance and disease, in raising standards of life and achieving a more equitable international society. To this end our aim is to achieve the freest possible flow of international trade on terms fair and equitable to all, taking into account the special requirements of the developing countries. Moreover, to encourage the flow of adequate resources, including governmental and private resources, to the developing countries, bearing in mind the importance of doing this in a true spirit of partnership, and of establishing for this purpose, in the developing countries, conditions which are conducive to sustained investment and growth.

We believe that international co-operation is essential in removing the causes of war, promoting tolerance, combating injustice, and securing development among the peoples of the world; we are convinced that the Commonwealth is one of the most fruitful associations for these purposes.

In pursuing these principles, the members of the Commonwealth believe that they can provide a constructive example of the multinational approach which is vital to peace and progress in the modern world. The association is based on consultation, discussion and co-operation. In rejecting coercion as an instrument of policy they recognise that the security of each Member State from external aggression is a matter of concern to all members. It provides many channels for continuing exchanges of knowledge and views on professional, cultural, economic, legal and political issues among Member States.

We intend these relationships to foster and extend, for we believe that our multinational association can expand human understanding and understanding among nations, assist in the elimination of discrimination based on differences of race, colour or creed, maintain and strengthen personal liberty, contribute to the enrichment of life for all, and provide a powerful influence for peace among nations.

Singapore, 22 January 1971

Much of the work of the Commonwealth has been dominated by the struggle against racism. This is well illustrated by the efforts over many years to address the problems of minority rule in Rhodesia and South Africa. The following declaration made in 1979 at the CHOGM in Lusaka, Zambia remains a fundamental pillar of the Association.

Lusaka Declaration of the Commonwealth on Racism and Racial Prejudice

We, the Commonwealth Heads of Government, recalling the Declaration of Commonwealth Principles made at Singapore on 22 January 1971 and the statement on Apartheid in Sport, issued in London on 15 June 1977, have decided to proclaim our desire to work jointly as well as severally for the eradication of all forms of racism and racial prejudice.

The Commonwealth is an institution devoted to the promotion of international understanding and world peace, and to the achievement of equal rights for all citizens regardless of race, colour, sex, creed or political belief, and is committed to the eradication of the dangerous evils of racism and racial prejudice.

We now, therefore, proclaim this Lusaka Declaration of the Commonwealth on Racism and Racial Prejudice.

United in our desire to rid the world of the evils of racism and racial prejudice, we proclaim our faith in the inherent dignity and worth of the human person and declare that:

- the peoples of the Commonwealth have the right to live freely in dignity and equality, without any distinction or exclusion based on race, colour, sex, descent, or national or ethnic origin;
- while everyone is free to retain diversity in his or her culture and lifestyle, this diversity does not justify the perpetuation of racial prejudice or racially discriminatory practices;
- everyone has the right to equality before the law and equal justice under the law;
- everyone has the right to effective remedies and protection against any form of discrimination based on the grounds of race, colour, sex, descent, or national or ethnic origin.

We reject as inhuman and intolerable all policies designed to perpetuate apartheid, racial segregation or other policies based on theories that racial groups are or may be inherently superior or inferior.

We reaffirm that it is the duty of all the peoples of the Commonwealth to work together for the total eradication of the infamous policy of apartheid which is internationally recognised as a crime against the conscience and dignity of mankind and the very existence of which is an affront to humanity.

We agree that everyone has the right to protection against acts of incitement to racial hatred and discrimination, whether committed by individuals, groups or other organisations.

We affirm that there should be no discrimination based on race, colour, sex, descent or national or ethnic origin in the acquisition or exercise of the right to vote: in the field of civil rights or access to citizenship; or in the economic, social or cultural fields, particularly education, health, employment, occupation, housing, social security and cultural life.

We attach particular importance to ensuring that children shall be protected from practices which may foster racism or racial prejudice. Children have the right to be brought up and educated in a spirit of tolerance and understanding so as to be able to contribute fully to the building of future societies based on justice and friendship.

We believe that those groups in societies who may be especially disadvantaged because of residual racist attitudes are entitled to the fullest protection of the law.

We recognise that the history of the Commonwealth and its diversity require that special attention should be paid to the problems of indigenous minorities. We recognise that the same special attention should be paid to the problems of immigrants, immigrant workers and refugees.

We agree that special measures may in particular circumstances be required to advance the development of disadvantaged groups in society. We recognise that the effects of colonialism or racism in the past may make desirable special provisions for the social and economic enhancement of indigenous populations.

Inspired by the principles of freedom and equality which characterise our association, we accept the solemn duty of working together to eliminate racism and racial prejudice. This duty involves the acceptance of the principle that positive measures may be required to advance the elimination of racism, including assistance to those struggling to rid themselves and their environment of the practice.

Being aware that legislation alone cannot eliminate racism and racial prejudice, we endorse the need to initiate public information and education policies designed to promote understanding, tolerance, respect and friendship among peoples and racial groups.

We are particularly conscious of the importance of the contribution the media can make to human rights and the eradication of racism and racial prejudice by helping to eliminate ignorance and misunderstanding between people and by drawing attention to the evils which afflict humanity. We affirm the importance of truthful presentation of facts in order to ensure that the public are fully informed of the dangers presented by racism and racial prejudice.

In accordance with established principles of international Law and, in particular, the provisions of the International Convention on the Elimination of All Forms of Racial Discrimination, we affirm that everyone is, at all times and in all places, entitled to be protected in the enjoyment of the right to be free of racism and racial prejudice.

We believe that the existence in the world of apartheid and racial discrimination is a matter of concern to all human beings. We recognise that we share an international responsibility to work together for the total eradication of apartheid and racial discrimination.

We note that racism and racial prejudice, wherever they occur, are significant factors contributing to tension between nations and thus inhibit peaceful progress and development. We believe that the goal of the eradication of racism stands as a critical priority for governments of the Commonwealth, committed as they are to the promotion of the ideals of peaceful and happy lives for their people.

We intend that the Commonwealth, as an international organisation with a fundamental and deep-rooted attachment to principles of freedom and equality, should co-operate with other organisations in the fulfilment of these principles. In particular the Commonwealth should seek to enhance the co-ordination of its activities with those of other organisations similarly committed to the promotion and protection of human rights and fundamental freedoms.

Lusaka, Zambia, 7 August 1979

In 1989, Heads of Government set up a 10 person High Level Appraisal Group with the remit to consider the future of the Commonwealth. The Group's Report led to Heads of Government at their meeting in Harare, Zimbabwe in 1991 adopting the Harare Commonwealth Declaration. This not only reaffirmed their commitment to the 1971 Declaration of Commonwealth Principles but went further by setting out the association's priorities based on two themes: the promotion of the Commonwealth's fundamental political values – democracy, the rule of law and human rights – and sustainable economic development.

Harare Commonwealth Declaration 1991

The Heads of Government of the countries of the Commonwealth, meeting in Harare, reaffirm their confidence in the Commonwealth as a voluntary association of sovereign independent States, each responsible for its own policies, consulting and co-operating in the interests of their peoples and in the promotion of international understanding and world peace.

Members of the Commonwealth include people of many different races and origins, encompass every State of economic development, and comprise a rich variety of cultures, traditions and institutions.

The special strength of the Commonwealth lies in the combination of the diversity of its members with their shared inheritance in language, culture and the rule of law. The Commonwealth way is to seek consensus through consultation and the sharing of experience. It is uniquely placed to serve as a model and as a catalyst for new forms of friendship and co-operation to all in the spirit of the Charter of the United Nations.

Its members also share a commitment to certain fundamental principles. These were set out in a Declaration of Commonwealth Principles agreed by our predecessors at their meeting in Singapore in 1971. Those principles have stood the test of time, and we reaffirm our full and continuing commitment to them today. In particular, no less today than 20 years ago:

- we believe that international peace and order, global economic development and the rule of international law are essential to the security and prosperity of mankind;
- we believe in the liberty of the individual under the law, in equal rights for all citizens regardless of gender, race, colour, creed or political belief, and in the individual's inalienable right to participate by means of free and democratic political processes in framing the society in which he or she lives;
- we recognise racial prejudice and intolerance as a dangerous sickness and a threat to healthy development, and racial discrimination as an unmitigated evil;
- we oppose all forms of racial oppression, and we are committed to the principles of human dignity and equality;
- we recognise the importance and urgency of economic and social development to satisfy the basic needs and aspirations of the vast majority of the peoples of the world, and seek the progressive removal of the wide disparities in living standards amongst our members.

In Harare, our purpose has been to apply those principles in the contemporary situation as the Commonwealth prepares to face the challenges of the 1990s and beyond.

Internationally, the world is no longer locked in the iron grip of the Cold War. Totalitarianism is giving way to democracy and justice in many parts of the world. Decolonisation is largely complete. Significant changes are at last under way in South Africa. These changes, so desirable and heartening in themselves, present the world and the Commonwealth with new tasks and challenges.

In the last 20 years, several Commonwealth countries have made significant progress in economic and social development. There is increasing recognition that commitment to market principles and openness to international trade and investment can promote economic progress and improve living standards. Many Commonwealth countries are poor and face acute problems, including excessive population growth, crushing poverty, debt burdens and environmental degradation. More than half our Member States are particularly vulnerable because of their very small societies.

Only sound and sustainable development can offer these millions the prospect of betterment. Achieving this will require a flow of public and private resources from the developed to the developing world, and domestic and international regimes conducive to the realisation of these goals. Development facilitates the task of tackling a range of problems which affect the whole global community such as environmental degradation, the problems of migration and refugees, the fight against communicable diseases, and drug production and trafficking.

Having reaffirmed the principles to which the Commonwealth is committed, and reviewed the problems and challenges which the world, and the Commonwealth as part of it, face, we pledge the Commonwealth and our countries to work with renewed vigour, concentrating especially in the following areas:

- the protection and promotion of the fundamental political values of the Commonwealth;
- democracy, democratic processes and institutions which reflect national circumstances, the rule of law and independence of the judiciary, just and honest government;
- fundamental human rights, including equal rights and opportunities for all citizens regardless of race, colour, creed or political belief;
- equality for women, so that they may exercise their full and equal rights;
- provision of universal access to education for the population of our countries;
- continuing action to bring about the end of apartheid and the establishment of a free, democratic, non-racial and prosperous South Africa;
- the promotion of sustainable development and the alleviation of poverty in the countries of the Commonwealth through:
  - a stable international economic framework within which growth can be achieved;
  - sound economic management recognising the central role of the market economy;
  - effective population policies and programmes;
  - sound management of technological change;
  - the freest possible flow of multilateral trade on terms fair and equitable to all, taking account of the special requirements of developing countries;
  - an adequate flow of resources from the developed to developing countries, and action to alleviate the debt burdens of developing countries most in need;
  - the development of human resources, in particular through education, training, health, culture, sport and programmes for strengthening family and community support, paying special attention to the needs of women, youth and children;
  - effective and increasing programmes of bilateral and multilateral co-operation aimed at raising living standards;
  - extending the benefits of development within a framework of respect for human rights;
  - the protection of the environment through respect for the principles of sustainable development which we enunciated at Langkawi;
  - action to combat drug trafficking and abuse and communicable diseases;
  - help for small Commonwealth States in tackling their particular economic and security problems;
  - support of the United Nations and other international institutions in the world's search for peace, disarmament and effective arms control; and in the promotion of international consensus on major global political, economic and social issues.

To give weight and effectiveness to our commitments, we intend to focus and improve Commonwealth co-operation in these areas. This would include strengthening the capacity of the Commonwealth to respond to requests from members for assistance in entrenching the practices of democracy, accountable administration and the rule of law.

We call on all inter-governmental institutions of the Commonwealth to seize the opportunities presented by these challenges. We pledge ourselves to assist them to develop programmes which harness our shared historical, professional, cultural and linguistic heritage, and which complement the work of other international and regional organisations.

We invite the Commonwealth Parliamentary Association and non-governmental Commonwealth organisations to play their full part in promoting these objectives, in a spirit of co-operation and mutual support.

In reaffirming the principles of the Commonwealth and in committing ourselves to pursue them in policy and action in response to the challenges of the 1990s, in areas where we believe that the Commonwealth has a distinctive contribution to offer, we the Heads of Government express our determination to renew and enhance the value and importance of the Commonwealth as an institution which can and should strengthen and enrich the lives not only of its own members and their peoples, but also of the wider community of peoples of which they are a part.

Harare, Zimbabwe, 20 October 1991

In 1995, at the CHOGM in Auckland, New Zealand, the Harare Principles were strengthened by the adoption of the Commonwealth Millbrook Action Programme. This provides an operating structure for the two central declarations: the Declaration of Commonwealth Principles and the Harare Commonwealth Declaration. It also defines the Commonwealth's role in global and national affairs.

Amongst other things it set up the CMAG for dealing with serious or persistent violations of the principles contained in the Harare Declaration. The role, mandate and activities of CMAG are noted in later Commonwealth documents, notably the Coolum Declaration (set out below). A note on the work of CMAG also appears separately towards the end of this section.

Millbrook Commonwealth Action Programme on the Harare Declaration

At Harare in 1991, we pledged to work for the protection and promotion of the fundamental political values of the association, namely democracy, democratic processes and institutions which reflect national circumstances, fundamental human rights, the rule of law and independence of the judiciary, and just and honest government. We agreed at the same time to work for the promotion of socio-economic development, recognising its high priority for most Commonwealth countries. During our retreat at Millbrook, we decided to adopt a Commonwealth Action Programme to fulfil more effectively the commitments contained in the Harare Commonwealth Declaration. This Programme is in three parts:

I   Advancing Commonwealth Fundamental Political Values;
II   Promoting Sustainable Development; and
III   Facilitating Consensus-Building.

I Advancing Commonwealth fundamental political values

A Measures in Support of Processes and Institutions for the Practice of the Harare Principles

The Secretariat should enhance its capacity to provide advice, training and other forms of technical assistance to governments in promoting the Commonwealth's fundamental political values, including:

- assistance in creating and building the capacity of requisite institutions;
- assistance in constitutional and legal matters, including selecting models and initiating programmes of democratisation;
- assistance in the electoral field, including the establishment or strengthening of independent electoral machinery, civic and voter education, the preparation of Codes of Conduct, and assistance with voter registration;
- observation of elections, including by-elections or local elections where appropriate, at the request of the member governments concerned;
- strengthening the rule of law and promoting the independence of the judiciary through the promotion of exchanges among, and training of, the judiciary;
- support for good government, particularly in the area of public service reform; and other activities, in collaboration with the Commonwealth Parliamentary Association and other bodies, to strengthen the democratic culture and effective parliamentary practices.

B Measures in Response to Violations of the Harare Principles

Where a member country is perceived to be clearly in violation of the Harare Commonwealth Declaration, and particularly in the event of an unconstitutional overthrow of a democratically elected government, appropriate steps should be taken to express the collective concern of Commonwealth countries and to encourage the restoration of democracy within a reasonable timeframe. These include:

- immediate public expression by the Secretary-General of the Commonwealth's collective disapproval of any such infringement of the Harare Principles;
- early contact by the Secretary-General with the *de facto* government, followed by continued good offices and appropriate technical assistance to facilitate an early restoration of democracy;
- encouraging bilateral démarches by member countries, especially those within the region, both to express disapproval and to support early restoration of democracy;
- appointment of an envoy or a group of eminent Commonwealth representatives where, following the Secretary-General's contacts with the authorities concerned, such a mission is deemed beneficial in reinforcing the Commonwealth's good offices role;
- stipulation of up to two years as the timeframe for the restoration of democracy where the institutions are not in place to permit the holding of elections within, say, a maximum of six months;
- pending restoration of democracy, exclusion of the government concerned from participation at ministerial level meetings of the Commonwealth, including CHOGMs;

- suspension of participation at all Commonwealth meetings and of Commonwealth technical assistance if acceptable progress is not recorded by the government concerned after a period of two years; and
- consideration of appropriate further bilateral and multilateral measures by all Member States (eg, limitation of government to government contacts; people to people measures; trade restrictions; and, in exceptional cases, suspension from the association), to reinforce the need for change in the event that the government concerned chooses to leave the Commonwealth and/or persists in violating the principles of the Harare Commonwealth Declaration even after two years.

C   Mechanism for Implementation of Measures

We have decided to establish a Commonwealth Ministerial Action Group on the Harare Declaration in order to deal with serious or persistent violations of the principles contained in that Declaration. The Group will be convened by the Secretary-General and will comprise the Foreign Ministers of eight countries, supplemented as appropriate by one or two additional ministerial representatives from the region concerned. It will be the Group's task to assess the nature of the infringement and recommend measures for collective Commonwealth action aimed at the speedy restoration of democracy and constitutional rule.

The composition, terms of reference and operation of the Group will be reviewed by us every two years.

II   Promoting sustainable development

We reaffirmed our view that the Commonwealth should continue to be a source of help in promoting development and literacy and in eradicating poverty, particularly as these bear on women and children. With a view to enhancing its capacity in this area, we agreed on the following steps:

- to strengthen the Secretariat's capacity for undertaking developmental work through support for its various Funds and especially by restoring the resources of the CFTC to their 1991/92 level in real terms, and to provide adequate resources to the Commonwealth of Learning and to the Commonwealth Foundation;
- to support a greater flow of investment to developing member countries through such schemes as the Commonwealth Private Investment Initiative;
- to work for continued progress in assisting countries with unsustainable debt burdens and to promote enhanced multilateral concessional financial flows to developing countries, in particular, to support new and innovative mechanisms for relief on multilateral debt, such as the one proposed by the British Chancellor of the Exchequer at the 1994 Commonwealth Finance Ministers Meeting in Malta, and reiterated subsequently;
- to support the Secretariat in facilitating the adoption by more Commonwealth countries of successful self-help schemes, with non-governmental agencies and others acting as catalyst agents, for mobilising the energies of people in alleviating poverty;
- to support the efforts of small island developing States to mitigate the effects on their development of environmental change, natural disasters and the changing international trading system; and

- to combat the spread of HIV/AIDS, which threatens large parts of the younger population of many countries, recognising that the effective exploitation of economic opportunities requires a healthy and educated population; and to provide further resources to renew the core funding of the Southern African Network of AIDS Organisations (SANASO), along with increased funding for UNICEF initiatives in Southern Africa.

III   Facilitating consensus building

We were convinced that the Commonwealth, with its global reach and unique experience of consensus building, was in a position to assist the wider international community in building bridges across traditional international divides of opinion on particular issues. We therefore agreed that there was scope for the association to play a greater role in the search for consensus on global issues, through:

- use of their governments' membership of various regional organisations and attendance at other international gatherings to advance consensual positions agreed within the Commonwealth;
- use, where appropriate, of special missions to advance Commonwealth consensus positions and promote wider consensus on issues of major international concern; and
- use of formal and informal Commonwealth consultations in the wings of meetings of international institutions with a view to achieving consensus on major concerns.

Millbrook, Queenstown, New Zealand, 12 November 1995

The 2001 CHOGM was postponed following the events of 11 September. Commonwealth Heads of Government eventually met in Coolum, Australia, in March 2002. The Coolum Declaration is highly significant for several reasons. Two in particular are worth noting here: first, it commits Commonwealth States 'individually and collectively to take concerted and resolute action to eradicate terrorism'. Secondly, Heads of Government agreed to adopt the High Level Review Group Report which 'sets out concrete steps to build a Commonwealth for the 21st century'. This report appears after the Coolum Communiqué.

Coolum Declaration 2002: The Commonwealth in the 21st Century: Continuity and Renewal

At the outset of this new millennium we, the Heads of Government of the Commonwealth of Nations, meeting at Coolum, Australia, renew our enduring commitment to the values and principles which we share. We stand united in:

- our commitment to democracy, the rule of law, good governance, freedom of expression and the protection of human rights;
- our respect for diversity and human dignity; our celebration of the pluralistic nature of our societies and the tolerance it promotes; and our implacable opposition to all forms of discrimination, whether rooted in gender, race, colour, creed or political belief;

- our determination to work to eliminate poverty, to promote people centred and sustainable development, and thus progressively to remove the wide disparities in living standards among us and overcome the special challenges facing our small State and less developed country members; and
- our collective striving after international peace and security, the rule of international law and the elimination of people smuggling and the scourge of terrorism.

We reiterate in the strongest terms our condemnation of all forms and manifestations of terrorism. In the aftermath of the events of 11 September 2001 and following our statement of 25 October 2001, we solemnly reaffirm our resolve as a diverse community of nations individually and collectively to take concerted and resolute action to eradicate terrorism. We pledge to work together in fulfilling our international obligations to deny any safe haven for terrorists.

We cannot accept that nearly half the world's population should live in poverty, nor that disease, illiteracy and environmental degradation should continue to blight the lives of many of our people, nor the fact that in too many societies women continue to face discrimination. The benefits of globalisation must be shared more widely and its focus channelled for the elimination of poverty and human deprivation. We stress the importance of equality of access to economic opportunities and the need to apply new international standards, such as the OECD Harmful Tax Initiative, evenly, equitably and without exception.

The Fancourt Declaration and the UN Millennium Declaration have laid a firm base for us to push back the frontiers of poverty and under-development. In pursuit of the Millennium Development Goals, we call on governments to seize the opportunities presented by the Financing for Development Conference (Monterrey, Mexico, 18–22 March 2002) and the World Summit on Sustainable Development (Johannesburg, August/September 2002) to chart a more sustainable and equitable growth path for the world. We also welcome the groundbreaking proposal from Africa to tackle poverty through the New Partnership for Africa's Development, and will use our best efforts to support similar partnerships in other regions of the Commonwealth. More broadly, we call on all nations to work to reduce the growing gap between rich and poor, and to enhance international support to democracies fighting poverty.

Recognising the links between democracy and good governance on the one hand, and poverty, development and conflict on the other, we call on the Commonwealth Secretary-General to constitute a high level expert group to recommend ways in which we could carry forward the Fancourt Declaration. This group should focus on how democracies might best be supported in combating poverty, and should report to the next CHOGM.

We are deeply conscious of the threat HIV/AIDS poses to hard-won social and economic progress in much of Africa and elsewhere. As leaders committed to each one of our citizens developing their human potential to the full, we pledge ourselves to combating this pandemic and the spread of other communicable diseases. We urge both the public and private sector, and international organisations, to join with us in a renewed effort to tackle the challenge HIV/AIDS presents to our countries and their people, and to humanity itself.

We recognise the particular vulnerabilities of small States, as well as the need for concerted action by the international community to address their special needs. We further appreciate the importance of systemic changes to respond to these needs, and we commit the Commonwealth to pursue innovative and practical support mechanisms for small States. Many other challenges confront us daily. As leaders guiding our nations into the 21st century, we need a Commonwealth that both builds on our enduring values and adapts to our evolving needs. We seek a Commonwealth in tune with the future: an organisation which draws on its history, plays to its strengths, vigorously pursues its members' common interests and seizes the opportunities open to it to shape a better world for our children.

We envisage a modern and vibrant Commonwealth working to serve its peoples, with a simplified structure and a clear focus on what it does best. We want the Commonwealth to be an effective defender of democratic freedoms and a peacemaker in conflict, and to work tirelessly in promoting people-centred economic development.

We have adopted the attached High Level Review Group (HLRG) Report which charts a clear future course for the Commonwealth in line with this vision. The HLRG Report sets out concrete steps to build a Commonwealth for the 21st century:

- **we determine materially to strengthen the Commonwealth's capacity to support its members' pursuit of democratic values and the rule of law.** We have clarified the conditions under which the Commonwealth Ministerial Action Group will in future address serious or persistent violations of the Harare Principles, which go beyond the unconstitutional overthrow of member governments. A clear set of procedures – in which the Secretary-General and the Chairperson in Office will have an important part to play – will help ensure transparent and effective dealing with any Member State concerned. We are committed to strengthening the Good Offices role of the Commonwealth Secretary-General and have agreed to strengthen the Commonwealth's work in supporting democratic practice, in resolving tensions, in conflict prevention and resolution, and in post-conflict rebuilding, working in consultation with regional organisations as appropriate;

- in pursuit of a more equitable distribution of the benefits of globalisation and in pursuit of the Millennium Development Goals, **we are committed to forging new opportunities for our members in trade, in investment and in private sector development.** We have agreed steps which will help our organisation better identify and promote its members' economic and development needs in an increasingly competitive international environment. We recognise the importance of enhancing market access in the global trading system, particularly for the poorest and smallest countries. To this end, we welcome and give our strong support to the agreement reached in Doha on the World Trade Organisation's new multilateral trade negotiations. Through an enhanced facilitation role, we want our organisation to help Member States get better access to international assistance, and to focus the Commonwealth's own related programmes more effectively on the assistance it is best equipped to provide. We support the HLRG's strategy to bridge the information and communications technology gap between rich and poor;

- recognising that the Commonwealth's future lies in the hands of its youth, **we have agreed to create a pan Commonwealth 'Youth for the Future' initiative** composed of four related components for technology and skills transfer, and for fostering youth enterprise. We seek to engage youth, young professionals and youth volunteers more closely, harnessing their skills and enthusiasm to make a major practical contribution to the work of the Commonwealth;

- **we seek to rationalise and streamline the Commonwealth's governance and organisation to provide a simplified structure** capable of responding more quickly and effectively to members' needs;
- we call on the many inter-governmental, professional and civil society bodies which help to implement our Commonwealth values, **to join with us in building closer Commonwealth 'family' links, and strengthening consultation and collaboration.** We are convinced of the need for stronger links and better two-way communication and co-ordination between the official and non-governmental Commonwealth, and among Commonwealth NGOs. This will give Commonwealth activities greater impact, ensuring that every programme produces lasting benefit. [Original emphasis.]

We cherish our shared history and are proud of what we have achieved together over the years. We are convinced that acting on the recommendations of the HLRG Report will better equip the Commonwealth to meet the challenges of the future. Our common values and unique ways of working together provide a special strength in this, which we treasure. We call on our Secretary-General to work assiduously with the Chairman in Office, the new governing mechanisms and the wider Commonwealth family to translate the outcomes of the review into a practical reality which benefits all our people.

Coolum, Australia, 5 March 2002

Coolum Communiqué

1   Commonwealth Heads of Government met in Coolum from 2–5 March 2002. Of the 51 countries which attended the meeting, 35 were represented by their Heads of State or Government. The meeting was chaired by the Prime Minister of Australia, the Hon John Howard.

2   ...

3   ...

4   Heads of Government welcomed the Prime Minister of Tuvalu which became a full member of the Commonwealth in 2000 and attended the CHOGM for the first time. Heads of Government were also pleased to welcome the Fiji Islands' return to the Councils of the Commonwealth.

5   Heads of Government adopted the Commonwealth Coolum Declaration, and approved the recommendations of the High Level Review Group on the Special Theme 'The Commonwealth in the 21st Century: Continuity and Renewal'.

Terrorism

6   Heads of Government reiterated their absolute condemnation of all acts of terrorism in whatever form or wherever they occur or by whomsoever perpetrated, with the consequent tragic loss of human life and severe damage to political, economic and social stability. They emphasised that terrorism constitutes a threat to all countries and peoples, irrespective of faith, nationality, culture or community. They reaffirmed their commitment to work together as a diverse community of nations, individually, and collectively under the auspices and authority of the United Nations, to take concerted and resolute action to eradicate terrorism. There is no justification for terrorism. While terrorist activities are unconscionable and should be eradicated forthwith, the challenge is to

understand the root causes of those despicable acts and to deal with them appropriately.

7   Heads of Government welcomed the Report of the Commonwealth Committee on Terrorism and the Plan of Action based on their Statement on Terrorism of 25 October 2001. They agreed that the Committee should monitor the implementation of the Plan of Action and to that end meet annually to review progress. They requested the Secretary-General to implement the measures identified by the Committee. They urged all member countries to take the steps outlined in the Plan of Action and to give assistance to small and less developed members of the Commonwealth to enable them to meet their obligations under United Nations Security Council Resolution 1373; and agreed to support efforts to mitigate the economic loss experienced by poor and vulnerable States. Heads of Government requested all member countries to work for a speedy conclusion of the comprehensive United Nations Convention on the Elimination of Terrorism.

Fundamental political values

8   Heads of Government reaffirmed their commitment to the fundamental political values of the Commonwealth as set out in the Harare Commonwealth Declaration and reinforced by the Millbrook Action Programme. They reiterated in particular their commitment to international peace and order, democracy, good governance, human rights, freedom of expression and the rule of law.

9   Heads of Government expressed strong support for the Good Offices role of the Secretary-General in conflict prevention and resolution. They also recorded their support for the Commonwealth's work in reinforcing democratic processes and institutions in member countries.

Commonwealth Ministerial Action Group on the Harare Declaration

10   Heads of Government received a Report from the Commonwealth Ministerial Action Group on the Harare Declaration (CMAG) covering CMAG's deliberations in the period since the Durban Commonwealth Heads of Government Meeting in 1999.

11   Heads of Government took note of the progress made in the restoration of democracy in the Fiji Islands, particularly through the elections of 25 August to 5 September 2001, and endorsed CMAG's decision to lift Fiji Islands' suspension from the Councils of the Commonwealth with effect from 20 December 2001. In recognition of the ongoing legal proceedings over the constitutionality of the Government of the Fiji Islands, they agreed that CMAG should keep the Fiji Islands on its agenda.

12   Heads of Government noted CMAG's decision to remove The Gambia from its agenda following the repeal of Decree 89 in that country.

13   Heads of Government agreed that Pakistan's suspension from the Councils of the Commonwealth should remain unchanged pending the restoration of a democratic government. In that regard, they welcomed the commitment of the Government of Pakistan to hold democratic elections by October 2002, and agreed that the Commonwealth Secretary-General should have an active monitoring role in the period leading up to the restoration of democracy, including the deployment of Commonwealth observers at the Provincial and National Elections and the provision of technical assistance.

14 Heads of Government welcomed the improvement in the security situation and the conclusion of the disarmament process in Sierra Leone. They noted CMAG's decision to remove Sierra Leone from its agenda and the need to provide continued appropriate technical assistance.

15 Heads of Government welcomed the recent national Parliament elections in Solomon Islands, and acknowledged the role of regional governments for their support in assisting with the conduct of those elections. They expressed support for the Government of Solomon Islands, noting that much remains to be done to consolidate peace and stability. Heads of Government commended the role of the International Peace Monitoring Team, led by Australia and New Zealand, in overseeing the peace process and agreed that in recognition of the difficulties in that country, Solomon Islands should continue to be on CMAG's agenda for the purpose of promoting good governance, peace and stability and economic development.

16 Heads of Government adopted a Statement on Zimbabwe on 4 March 2002, which is attached.

17 Heads of Government decided that CMAG would have the following members with immediate effect, until the next CHOGM – Australia, The Bahamas, Bangladesh, Botswana, India, Malta, Nigeria and Samoa.

18 Heads of Government acknowledged that the current limitation of two terms of membership of CMAG could be made more flexible. They decided that in future a member could be retained for a third term if this was deemed desirable to preserve continuity; institutional knowledge; or to provide linkages with relevant international organisations.

Cyprus

19 Recalling and reaffirming previous United Nations Security Council Resolutions and reaffirming their previous communiqués on Cyprus, Heads of Government welcomed the resumption of talks between the two sides under the auspices of the United Nations Secretary-General within the framework of his mandate of good offices mission as described in Security Council Resolution 1250.

20 They noted that progress could only be made at the negotiating table and encouraged all concerned to co-operate fully with the Secretary-General and his Special Adviser to show flexibility and negotiate to the conclusion of a just and lasting settlement consistent with relevant Security Council Resolutions.

21 Heads of Government reiterated their support for a Cyprus settlement that ensures the independence, sovereignty, territorial integrity and unity of a reunited Cyprus.

Belize

22 Heads of Government reaffirmed their firm support for the territorial integrity, security and sovereignty of Belize. They welcomed the progress being made in the dialogue taking place under the auspices of the Organisation of American States and pledged support for this facilitation process. Heads of Government mandated the Secretary-General to convene the Ministerial Committee on Belize whenever necessary. They noted that proposals for a final settlement were expected to contain a provision for the establishment of a development fund to be used for the benefit of border communities and urged member countries to contribute to it generously.

Guyana

23 Heads of Government reaffirmed their solidarity with Guyana in light of the continuing threat to its sovereignty and territorial integrity by Venezuela. In this context they regretted Guyana's inability to fully exploit all its natural resources in the Essequibo region in accordance with the Geneva Agreement.

24 Heads of Government commended the United Nations good offices process in finding a solution to the controversy and urged both countries to continue to avail themselves of this mechanism to resolve their differences in a spirit of good neighbourliness. They further requested the Secretary-General to convene the Commonwealth Ministerial Group on Guyana when occasion required it.

Landmines/International Criminal Court

25 Heads of Government noted the progress made in addressing the global landmines problem in recent years through the comprehensive framework for mine action provided by the Convention on the Prohibition of the Use, Stockpiling, Protection and Transfer of Anti-Personnel Mines and on their Destruction, and urged all countries that are in a position to do so to accede to the Convention. They also encouraged member countries to accede to the Rome Statute establishing the International Criminal Court.

World economic situation

26 Heads of Government noted that the tragic events of 11 September 2001 had worsened the global economic slowdown which could threaten achievement of the Millennium Development Goals. Heads of Government also stressed the need to assist developing and vulnerable countries to cope with the challenges of a more adverse external environment.

Multilateral trade issues

27 Heads of Government emphasised the crucial importance, especially for developing countries, of trade liberalisation and access to markets in overcoming poverty. With particular regard to the development objectives of the Doha Agenda, they urged the removal of barriers to exports and the elimination of trade-distorting subsidies, including agricultural subsidies.

28 Heads of Government reiterated their strong support for a transparent, equitable and rules based multilateral trading system and welcomed the launch of the WTO Work Programme agreed at Doha, Qatar, in November last year. Heads of Government welcomed the development agenda adopted at Doha, including negotiations focused on improving market access for agricultural goods, industrial products and services for the benefit of all members and particularly for developing and least developed countries; the resolution of outstanding implementation issues; and the work programme for small economies. Heads of Government pledged to work together for a successful conclusion of the Doha Work Programme to achieve an overall balance in the outcome, consistent with the mandate and within the timeframe set out in the Doha Development Agenda to ensure the early realisation of these benefits. They noted that a successful conclusion will also support the multilateral trading system's contribution to sustainable development.

29 Heads of Government confirmed the importance of technical assistance to help to build capacity so that all members can fully participate in the WTO.

Debt

30 Heads of Government noted the report of the Heavily Indebted Poor Countries (HIPC) Ministerial Forum, held in Malawi this year, and welcomed the progress made to implement the HIPC Initiative. They stressed that countries, in the process, needed to benefit from the flexibility that the Initiative provided to compensate for exogenous shocks, and, where appropriate, from additional concessional support to achieve a sustainable exit from their debt burden.

International economic co-operation

31 Heads of Government called on the international community to embrace global dialogue and co-operation aimed at enhancing development and good governance. They encouraged participation by governments at the highest level in the UN Conference on Financing for Development and the World Summit on Sustainable Development. They welcomed the initiative aimed at Africa's renewal through fostering closer co-operation and partnership among the industrial countries, Africa and the private sector worldwide, as enunciated in the New Partnership for Africa's Development (NEPAD) and called upon all Commonwealth institutions to assist with the effective implementation of NEPAD. They recognised that all these initiatives provide important opportunities to develop strategies for tackling poverty and building global stability with a focus on the needs of developing countries.

Strengthening financial systems

32 Heads of Government reaffirmed the right of sovereign nations to determine their own tax and fiscal policies and welcomed the proposed adjustments being made to the OECD Harmful Tax Competition Initiative and hoped that the dialogue, promoted by the Commonwealth, would ensure that the process continued to be inclusive. They reiterated that the standards and timelines for non-OECD jurisdictions should be no more onerous than those for OECD members. They requested the Secretariat to support the affected jurisdictions to mobilise assistance to meet international standards, strengthen and deepen their financial sectors and diversify their economies.

33 ...

Good corporate governance

34 Noting that foreign direct investment is crucial for their economies, Heads of Government reiterated the importance of good corporate governance and urged foreign investors to act in accordance with national laws, legal requirements and social obligations.

35 ...

Climate change

36 Heads of Government expressed concern about the consequences of global warming and climate change, especially for vulnerable small island States and other low lying areas. They welcomed progress made by the Iwokrama

International Rain Forest Centre in Guyana in conserving and sustainably utilising tropical rain forest resources.

Small States

37 Heads of Government reaffirmed their view that small States are particularly vulnerable to international developments and natural disasters and confront a range of structural challenges to sustainable development. They stressed the need for further concerted action by the international community to address these challenges. Heads of Government regretted the cancellation of the proposed Summit on Small States due to practical considerations and hoped that it would be convened at an appropriate time. They welcomed the Report of the Ministerial Group on Small States (MGSS) and the actions being taken in the Commonwealth, the World Bank and other international institutions to implement the Recommendations of the Report of the Joint Commonwealth Secretariat/World Bank Task Force on Small States.

38 Heads of Government acknowledged, at the same time, the need for systemic changes in dealing with small States' concerns and the creation of new delivery and support mechanisms. In that context, they endorsed the New Agenda for the Commonwealth's work on small States, which identified key priorities for the short and medium term. These included notably that the Commonwealth should provide appropriate assistance on trade issues, including working with the international community to strengthen small States' representation at the WTO, promote dialogue on the OECD Harmful Tax Initiative and take action to help mitigate the impact on small States of the events of 11 September and their aftermath. They also stressed that the upcoming UN Conference on Financing for Development and the World Summit on Sustainable Development were important platforms for promoting issues particularly relevant to small States. They endorsed the call of their ministers that these meetings produce outcomes beneficial to small economies.

39 Heads of Government mandated the Ministerial Group on Small States to develop a framework of action for consideration at the next CHOGM on how the Commonwealth could work with partner organisations to develop appropriate responses to the challenges facing small States ...

Coolum, 5 March 2002

Report of the Commonwealth High Level Review Group to Commonwealth Heads of Government, Coolum, Australia

[As adopted by Heads of Government at their meeting in Coolum on 3 March 2002.]

1 Commonwealth Heads of Government established our Group at their meeting in South Africa in November 1999, in order to review the role of the Commonwealth and advise on how best it could respond to the challenges of the new century.

2 We met in New York in September 2000, and again in Coolum on 2 March 2002 to conclude our task. We greatly benefited from the participation of the Commonwealth Secretary-General in our discussions. We also benefited from the work of our Officials, who met several times. In the course of our work, we invited all other Commonwealth member governments to share their views with us. We

also invited submissions from, and consulted with, various Commonwealth organisations, including non-governmental organisations, and several eminent Commonwealth citizens.

I   The Commonwealth's values and assets

3   The modern Commonwealth is a family of 54 independent States who share a commitment to certain core values and principles, as enunciated by Heads of Government at Singapore (1971), Harare (1991), Edinburgh (1997) and Fancourt (1999). We reiterate our commitment to the following values, in particular: respect for diversity and human dignity; opposition to all forms of discrimination, be it rooted in race, ethnicity, creed or gender; adherence to democracy, the rule of law, good governance, freedom of expression and the protection of human rights; the elimination of poverty and the promotion of people-centred development; and progressive removal of the wide disparities in living standards among our members; and international peace and security, the rule of international law and opposition to terrorism.

4   The Commonwealth's special strength lies not only in this shared commitment to core values and principles, but also in the combination of the diversity of its members with their shared history, language, traditions and commitment to the rule of law. Its inter-governmental and people to people links, its consensual, informal and flexible ways of working, and its global reach give it a unique place in addressing the problems of a changing world.

5   The Commonwealth is endowed with the following assets, in particular:

- It is a cross-section of the globe representing diverse constituencies from the north, south, rich, poor, large and small. This provides a fertile arena for dialogue and bridge building in a number of areas.
- Its democratic decision making, with all members having an equal voice, creates a high degree of trust and confidence in its official multilateral processes.
- Its common language, shared traditions and similarities in administrative, legal and education systems enable it to share experience and improve standards through functional co-operation in a number of sectors.
- Its inclusiveness helps it to advance the interests of its smaller and weaker members, whose voices are otherwise not heard in international negotiations.
- It is able to draw on the knowledge and resources of a vibrant network of Commonwealth professional and non-governmental organisations.

II   The Commonwealth in the 21st century

6   Today's Commonwealth has played an important supportive role in the process of decolonisation and the dismantling of apartheid. It has come of age as a force for conflict resolution, democratic freedoms, good governance, sustainable economic development, and for meeting the special needs of small States. Our task as Commonwealth leaders now, at the dawn of the 21st century, is to chart a practical vision to meet the challenges of the coming decades.

7   We face many and varied challenges such as absolute poverty, human deprivation, degradation of the environment, the AIDS pandemic and conflicts. Terrorism has emerged as a significant new threat to peace and stability in many

parts of the world, and therefore constitutes a challenge to the Commonwealth's fundamental values and principles, as well as to its efforts to foster development and justice. Democratic freedoms and institutions remain fragile in too many places. While new technologies and freer flow of goods and capital are opening up new opportunities in all walks of life, this is yet to be realised for the majority of our citizens.

8   Against this background, we are convinced of the Commonwealth's enduring relevance and value. We are proud of our heritage and what we have achieved together. And as we look to the future, we need constantly to renew our organisation and recalibrate it to contemporary needs and the aspirations of our peoples. The following action programme thus encompasses a comprehensive series of recommendations for policy and organisational renewal. Our common values and our unique ways of working together provide real strengths in addressing the challenges we face. We envisage a modern and vibrant Commonwealth with a simplified and effective structure. We seek a Commonwealth known, owned and valued by its peoples, responsive to their evolving needs, and invigorated by a more focused and productive partnership between governments and civil society. We believe that our Commonwealth for the 21st century will need to be one which draws on its history, plays to its strengths, and seizes the opportunities open to it to add value in critical areas of international endeavour.

III   The political role of the Commonwealth

9   The modern Commonwealth is an association of democracies committed to the principles of good governance, democratic processes, just and honest government and fundamental human rights, the rule of law and the independence of the judiciary, freedom of expression and the enjoyment of such rights by all individuals regardless of gender, race, colour, creed or political belief. The Commonwealth has committed itself to oppose all forms of racial oppression and to uphold human dignity. By setting out its core values in the Singapore and Harare Declarations of 1971 and 1991, and by having the courage to enforce adherence to these core values, the Commonwealth has set itself apart and established a standard to which others now aspire.

10   At the same time that it set out its fundamental political principles in the Singapore and Harare Declarations, the Commonwealth recognised that these values were inseparable from sustainable development, given that economic and social progress work to enhance the sustainability of democracy. We reaffirm the centrality of mutually reinforcing Commonwealth activities that support its fundamental political values.

11   In the promotion and enhancement of these fundamental political values, the Commonwealth is committed to respecting the well established practice of keeping bilateral issues between Member States out of Commonwealth multilateral discussions.

12   We recognise the parliaments and legislatures of the Commonwealth – national, regional and local – as essential elements in the exercise of democratic government, and welcome the contribution of the Commonwealth Parliamentary Association in advancing the democratic culture of the Commonwealth. We

believe also that not only governments but all political parties, other organs of civil society and the public at large share responsibility for upholding and promoting the democratic ethic.

(i) Conflict Prevention and Resolution

13 The challenge for the Commonwealth in the 21st century is to assist its members to strengthen adherence to the Harare Principles, in order to realise the benefits of just and stable government and freedom from internal conflict. We believe the Commonwealth has built a reputation for working quietly to resolve disputes in its Member States and this tradition of quiet diplomacy is highly effective. The Secretary-General's key role in deploying his Good Offices will remain the most important element of this work. At the same time, Commonwealth measures in support of conflict prevention and resolution will continue to take account of varying traditions and cultures across the Commonwealth.

14 We recommend that:

14.1 The Good Offices Role of the Secretary-General should be strengthened through dedicated and enhanced staff capacity to assist him/her in that work. With such an enhanced capacity, the Commonwealth's focus would shift more towards peace building, including conflict prevention and post-conflict capacity-building. This would increase the Secretariat's ability to provide high quality advice and expertise with regard to situations arising in any part of the Commonwealth. Existing resources from within the Secretariat and expertise from outside would be drawn upon in achieving this.

14.2 The Secretary-General should continue to deploy the services of former Heads of Government/State and other eminent persons from within the Commonwealth in support of his/her Good Offices Role.

14.3 The Secretary-General should consult more closely with regional organisations and key regional players in the exercise of his/her Good Offices Role.

14.4 The Good Offices Role of the Secretary-General should be strengthened through the support of the CHOGM Chairperson-in-Office.

(ii) Promoting and Enhancing the Commonwealth's Fundamental Political Values

15 We believe there is a need to intensify efforts to assist members in strengthening democracy and democratic institutions through the provision of constitutional, electoral and legal assistance. The work of Commonwealth Observer Groups, where invited, will remain a strong element in Commonwealth efforts to ensure the free expression of will by electors, and a key measure of the priority the Commonwealth attaches to this fundamental tenet of democracy.

16 We recommend that:

16.1 The Secretariat's capacity should be strengthened and adequately resourced to support democracy and democratic institutions through enhanced electoral observation, technical assistance to promote sound and sustainable electoral practices and institution building.

16.2 It is important to promote and strengthen national and regional human rights mechanisms and promote gender equality in all areas of national life, including in the political sphere.

16.3 Greater priority should be given to supporting member governments in the review and strengthening of democratic institutions, including constitutions, judiciaries and judicial processes, the training of legislative draftspersons, and public service reform.

(iii) The Future Role of the Commonwealth Ministerial Action Group on the Harare Declaration

17 The Commonwealth Ministerial Action Group (CMAG) remains the most tangible expression of the Commonwealth's commitment to the fundamental political values to which all Commonwealth members subscribe. As the custodian of the Harare Principles, it has been charged by Heads of Government to address all serious or persistent violations of those Principles by member countries.

18 At their meeting in Durban, Heads of Government commended the role played by CMAG as a custodian of the Harare Principles. They agreed that CMAG should continue to address serious or persistent violations of those Principles and that its future mandate should be considered further by the Commonwealth High Level Group.

19 We have accordingly considered the CMAG paper '*Realising Millbrook*' which addresses the issue of the Group's remit.

20 We agreed that CMAG's mandate, as it relates to the unconstitutional overthrow of a democratically elected government, is clearly defined in the Millbrook Commonwealth Action Programme and needs no further elaboration.

21 We felt that the issue requiring attention was the need to clarify procedures to apply in other circumstances where a member country is perceived to be in serious or persistent violation of the Harare Commonwealth Principles. We recommend that:

(i) Where such a perception was formed by the Chairperson-in-Office, the Secretary-General or a member government, particular steps should be instituted to establish the basis on which such a perception was founded, before CMAG engages itself with that situation.

(ii) When a member country raises such a concern in respect to another member, it must in the first instance bring the matter to the attention of the Secretary-General with evidence as to the basis of that concern.

(iii) The member country which is the subject of such concern must also be afforded the opportunity to respond to the points made.

(iv) Should the Secretary-General consider that the case so warrants, he or she should then apply his or her Good Offices Role with a view to encouraging the country concerned to move towards full compliance with the Harare Principles.

(v) The Chairperson-in-Office and the Secretary-General should consult appropriately in the application of the Good Offices Role.

(vi) CMAG would examine a case of perceived violation of the Harare Principles once such Good Offices activities have been exhausted.

22 We further agreed that, in the circumstances referred to in para 21, CMAG might consider applying a similar but differentiated and flexible set of steps as those outlined in the Millbrook Commonwealth Action Programme.

IV   Enhancing the Commonwealth's economic and developmental role

23   At Harare, leaders recognised the importance of economic and social development to satisfy the basic needs and aspirations of the Commonwealth's members as an enduring and fundamental Commonwealth principle. They pledged to this principle in facing the challenges of the 1990s and beyond. There have been promising successes, for example, in debt relief, and partnership with the World Bank in dealing with the particular problems confronting small States.

24   The challenges remain, and it is time to renew this commitment in the 21st century, identify ways of being even more effective and strengthen the Commonwealth's commitment to the achievement of the Millennium Development Goals. As leaders noted at Fancourt, globalisation is a reality, but its benefits must be shared more widely and its forces channelled for the elimination of poverty and human deprivation. It demands higher levels of international co-operation than have been seen hitherto, and a concerted effort to enable developing countries to take advantage of new opportunities in areas like trade and information and communications technology. The Fancourt Declaration, which was followed up by specific targets agreed upon in the Millennium Declaration of the UN in terms of globalisation, indicates that strong export growth remains a key element in the ability of developing countries to improve their living standards. The Fancourt Declaration stresses that developing countries need to be assisted to improve their capacities to achieve this. The Commonwealth can and needs to give a lead in this, in a strategic manner that accords with the interests of its members and makes good use of the human and financial resources made available to the Commonwealth by its members. This is a task which demands the focussed attention and co-ordinated effort of the entire Commonwealth family – Commonwealth member governments, the Commonwealth Secretariat, other multilateral Commonwealth agencies, the private sector, the non-official Commonwealth and civil society working together.

25   Gender equality is a fundamental value of the Commonwealth. It contributes not only to the advancement of political rights and empowerment of women, but also to peace building, poverty reduction and economic and social progress. Taking account of its Plan of Action on Gender and Development, the Commonwealth should continue to support gender mainstreaming and advocacy of gender equality.

26   While the Commonwealth does play a good advocacy role there is scope for enhancement. Debt relief, HIV/AIDS and the vulnerability of small States are examples of areas where the Commonwealth has in the past used its representative nature and internal strengths to contribute to international debate and outcomes which meet the interests of its members.

27   The Commonwealth is well placed to play a constructive role on, and be an effective advocate for, international co-operation in areas such as sustainable development. Through capacity building to enable member countries to engage more effectively in international bodies and negotiations, and by promoting open dialogue on key sustainable development issues at major international meetings, the Commonwealth has the potential to promote a stronger commitment to poverty reduction and sustainable development in other international fora.

28   The pace and complexity of developments in international trading and financial arrangements is ever increasing. Many of the Commonwealth's smaller members do not have sufficient capacity to influence all these developments or to update their own systems in line with evolving international standards. The Commonwealth should help to safeguard the interests of smaller members and address this need, including through facilitating dialogue between its members and the relevant international agencies and through support for members in developing the necessary capacity. More specifically, attention should be given to building capacity within Member States in order to improve their access to markets and investment.

29   We recommend that:

29.1   The Commonwealth's strategic advocacy and political influence should be focussed more effectively in areas of shared concern. This is particularly important for those global issues where high level Commonwealth political engagement can be deployed in support of members' economic and development interests. These include giving greater attention to the Commonwealth's role in promoting dialogue and co-operation to develop a global response to major environmental challenges such as climate change and sea level rise. The Commonwealth should also influence the broader global debate and the possible emerging consensus on sustainable development.

29.2   The Secretariat's capacity for strategic policy development should be strengthened through enhanced staff capacity, including through short term contracts, so that it may help to identify, develop and support such Commonwealth interventions on global issues, as in the ground breaking Commonwealth/World Bank work on small States' issues and on debt relief.

29.3   Issues warranting such engagement would be determined and reviewed by Heads of Government at successive CHOGMs, but might be adjusted inter-sessionally by the Secretary-General in consultation with the CHOGM Chairperson-in-Office.

29.4   In pursuing this important work, the Commonwealth should prioritise its efforts and take fully into account sensitive technical debates taking place in other international fora.

29.5   Without duplicating the work of other organisations, the Commonwealth should work to facilitate capacity building in its Member States to enhance their participation in the multilateral trade system and their access to investment, and to seek opportunities to use its network of member countries to promote dialogue and bridge building on major international issues, notably:

- by pressing for improved access to key international institutions and processes for Commonwealth members, especially small States and developing countries, and improved support from those international institutions for such members;
- by helping to develop members' human resources capacities in national advocacy in trade negotiation; and
- by strengthening the private sector and working in partnership with it to promote good economic management, trade, investment and technological innovation.

Commonwealth Statement on Terrorism

On 25 October 2001, Commonwealth Heads of Government issued the following statement that calls for concerted and resolute action against terrorism. Senior officials of law ministries, at a meeting in November 2001, recognised that the Commonwealth is well placed to assist member countries with the development of technical legal measures to combat terrorism. As a result, a group of experts met in London in January 2002 to prepare drafting instructions for model legislation, as well as guidelines for administrative and other measures which countries can use as a basis for developing a domestic strategy to implement fully Security Council Resolution 1373 of 28 September 2001. Details of the recommendations of the group as well as specimen legislation is set out in the Report of Expert Working Group on Legislative and Administrative Measures to Combat Terrorism which is available from the Criminal Law Unit, Commonwealth Secretariat.

1   We, the leaders of the Commonwealth, have consistently condemned in the strongest terms all forms and manifestations of terrorism and in particular the heinous acts of terrorism that took place in the United States on 11 September 2001. The Commonwealth affirms its resolve as a diverse community of nations to, individually and collectively, take concerted and resolute action against terrorism.

2   We will not be divided by race, nationality, religion or geography. We reject any attempt to link terrorism with any faith. Our diversity is our strength and binds us together. The perpetrators of these atrocious acts, and those who harboured or assisted them, have attacked the values and freedoms enshrined in the open, democratic, plural and multicultural societies that the Commonwealth represents. Terrorism threatens the peace, development, security and stability of the entire world, and all nations, races and religions and is aimed at the destruction of human rights, fundamental freedoms and democracy.

3   Recalling that many members of the Commonwealth have suffered casualties in the terrorist attacks in the United States and that Commonwealth member countries have themselves suffered from terrorism over many years, the importance of our renewed commitment to combating terrorism worldwide has never been greater.

4   We welcome UN Security Council Resolution 1373 of 28 September 2001, which provides an important framework for international action against terrorism. We are committed to fully implementing this resolution. We pledge to assist each other in so doing. Our actions will reflect the fundamental values upon which the Commonwealth is based including democracy, human rights, the rule of law, freedom of belief, freedom of political opinion, justice and equality.

5   We condemn any nation which harbours, supports or provides assistance to terrorist activity. Any member country that aids, supports, instigates, finances or harbours terrorists, or permits such activities within its jurisdiction, violates the fundamental values of our association and should have no place in it.

6   As Heads of Government of the largest association of democracies in the world, we call for firm deterrent measures by the international community. We will work towards the universal implementation of the numerous international conventions already in place to address terrorism. The Commonwealth urges all countries that have not already done so to take steps to sign, ratify, and, most importantly, implement these instruments. The importance of bringing to a successful conclusion the ongoing negotiations on a Comprehensive Convention against Terrorism cannot be overstated.

7   The Commonwealth adds its distinctive voice to calls for greater international co-operation and the strengthening of national, regional and international legal frameworks to combat terrorism in a comprehensive manner. We underscore the important role which can be played by the association due to our similar legal systems, and in particular through Commonwealth schemes for mutual assistance to counter crime. We undertake, as part of our contribution to the endeavours of the international community against terrorism, to redouble our efforts to prevent the use and abuse of our financial services sectors by fully co-operating with the international community in the tracing, freezing and confiscation of the assets of terrorists, their agents, sponsors and supporters.

8   We are deeply conscious that terrorist attacks hurt economic growth worldwide and the impact will be most acutely felt by poor and vulnerable States. We support the efforts of the international and regional financial institutions to develop strategies and programmes to mitigate the economic loss experienced by such countries.

9   There is no justification for terrorism. The Commonwealth is determined to fight this scourge and fully commits itself to a strengthened international campaign against it. The impact of terrorism has encouraged the Commonwealth to redouble its commitment to the cause of peace and stability and the elimination of poverty, injustice and discrimination. The Commonwealth calls on all nations of the world to stand resolute in rooting out hatred, intolerance and extremism. This is a struggle against terrorism, not against any community or faith.

25 October 2001

The Commonwealth Ministerial Action Group (CMAG)

At the Commonwealth Heads of Government Meeting in Auckland, New Zealand, in 1995, leaders accepted an initiative by Canada's Prime Minister and South Africa's President to put the Harare Principles into practical action by giving the Commonwealth an expanded mandate on democracy, including mechanisms for responding to problems when they arise in member countries. The result was the Millbrook Action Programme, authorising increased Commonwealth action to promote democracy, development, and consensus building.

The Millbrook Programme also established the CMAG which would comprise a pan-Commonwealth selection of ministers of foreign affairs. The Group is tasked with investigating serious and persistent violations of the Harare Declaration by Commonwealth members and recommends collective Commonwealth action. The composition, terms of reference and operation of the Group are reviewed by the Heads of Government at each CHOGM. In 2002, the members were Australia, Bangladesh, Botswana, India, Malta, Nigeria, and The Bahamas.

CMAG holds regular meetings at the ministerial level, and has sent ministerial missions to the Fiji Islands, Nigeria, Pakistan, Sierra Leone, Solomon Islands and The Gambia.

Fiji Islands: The CMAG held an emergency meeting in June 2000 following a crisis in the Fiji Islands that saw the transfer of power from a democratic government to a government appointed by the military. The Group suspended the Fiji Islands from the Councils of the Commonwealth and sent a ministerial delegation to visit there to encourage the interim government to commit itself to a timetable for restoring democracy. In December 2000, the Commonwealth Secretary-General named a special envoy to help resolve the situation.

Commonwealth and UN observers found Fiji Island's national elections in early September 2001 to be free and fair. At a meeting held in London on 20 December 2001, the CMAG decided that, given its progress in restoring democracy, Fiji Island's suspension from the Councils of the Commonwealth should be lifted. However, the Group decided to retain the Fiji Islands on the agenda and to continue to monitor the situation.

Nigeria: In 1995, Nigeria, which was then under a military regime, was suspended from the Commonwealth as a result of serious violations of the Harare Principles, including the execution of Ken Saro-Wiwa and other human rights activists. CMAG ministers met with representatives of the regime, as well as NGOs and civil society, in efforts to support the peaceful transition to democratic government. The CMAG also instituted a series of military, trade and visa sanctions aimed at encouraging change. Following peaceful democratic elections in early 1999, CMAG ministers recommended that Commonwealth Heads of Government lift Nigeria's suspension. Nigeria was formally welcomed back into the Commonwealth with the peaceful handover of power and the inauguration of President Obasanjo in May 1999.

Pakistan: A CMAG mission went to Pakistan in 1999 following a military coup. Pending its return to democratic government, Pakistan has been suspended from the Councils of the Commonwealth.

Sierra Leone: The CMAG, which had worked to provide political support to Sierra Leone's fragile democracy, removed Sierra Leone from the agenda in October 2001 in recognition of the improved political situation, but requested the Secretary-General to continue to monitor events in that country.

Solomon Islands: In June 2000, a CMAG delegation held talks with officials of the Solomon Islands and principal combatants in an effort to avoid having the democratically elected government overthrown. In October 2000, a peace agreement was signed under the auspices of the Australian government. Although elections held on 5 December 2001 were judged free and fair by a Commonwealth Observer Group, the CMAG has retained the Solomon Islands on their agenda to further help it promote good governance, peace and stability, and economic development.

The Gambia: Commonwealth concerns over The Gambia's Decree 89, which restricted political activity by certain political parties and specific individuals, prompted the CMAG in March 2001 to ask the Secretary-General to help that country create an environment in which all political parties and individuals can freely take part in the political process. The Gambia was removed from the Group's agenda in December 2001 following the repeal of Decree 89.

Zimbabwe: Since May 2000, the CMAG has expressed concern about reports of politically motivated violence and intimidation of the judiciary and the media in

Zimbabwe. In March 2001, ministers decided to send a mission to consult with the government, convey its concerns, and offer assistance, but Zimbabwe refused to receive the mission.

At a meeting held in Nigeria on 6 September 2001, the Committee of Commonwealth Foreign Ministers on Zimbabwe won commitments from the government of Zimbabwe to stop further occupation of farmland, to restore the rule of law to land reform, to protect constitutionally guaranteed freedom of speech, and to act firmly against violence and intimidation. However, during a follow up meeting in Zimbabwe in October 2001 the group concluded that Zimbabwe had not lived up to its commitments.

On 30 January 2002, the CMAG condemned recently enacted and proposed legislation in Zimbabwe that, in its view, further curbed freedom of speech of the press and of association. The group called on Zimbabwe to ensure that there is an immediate end to violence and intimidation, that the police and army refrain from party political statements and activities, that all parties in the election of 9–10 March 2002, have the opportunity to campaign without fear of recrimination, and that the people of Zimbabwe can make an unfettered and informed choice in the elections. The group also called for the deployment of Commonwealth observers to Zimbabwe's presidential elections, and for the full co-operation by the government with all international and domestic observers during the election period.

As noted above, Commonwealth Heads of Government at their Meeting in Coolum, Australia, then mandated the Commonwealth Chairpersons' Committee on Zimbabwe to determine the appropriate action in the event of an adverse report from the Commonwealth Observer Group to the March 2002 presidential election. On 19 March the Committee made the following statement.

Marlborough House Statement on Zimbabwe

1   The Commonwealth Chairpersons' Committee on Zimbabwe, consisting of the Prime Minister of Australia, Rt Hon John Howard, the President of Nigeria, HE Chief Olusegun Obasanjo, and the President of South Africa, HE Mr Thabo Mbeki, met at Marlborough House, London, on 19 March 2002, to discuss the situation in Zimbabwe. The Commonwealth Secretary-General, Rt Hon Don McKinnon, also attended the discussions.

2   The Committee recalled the mandate given to them by Commonwealth Heads of Government at their recent meeting in Coolum, Australia, to determine appropriate Commonwealth action on Zimbabwe, in the event of an adverse report from the Commonwealth Observer Group to the Zimbabwe Presidential Election, in accordance with the Harare Commonwealth Declaration and the Millbrook Commonwealth Action Programme.

3   The Committee noted that the Commonwealth Observer Group, led by General Abdulsalami Abubakar of Nigeria, had concluded that the Presidential Election was marred by a high level of politically motivated violence and that 'the conditions in Zimbabwe did not adequately allow for a free expression of will by the electors'. They deemed these conclusions, together with other aspects of the Report of the Observer Group, to be an adverse reflection on the electoral process, requiring an appropriate Commonwealth response.

4   The Committee took note of the various recommendations contained in the Commonwealth Observer Group Report. It also received a report from the Commonwealth Secretary-General on his consultations with other Commonwealth leaders.

5   The Committee expressed its determination to promote reconciliation in Zimbabwe between the main political parties. To this end, the Committee strongly supported the initiatives of the President of Nigeria and the President of South Africa in encouraging a climate of reconciliation between the main political parties in Zimbabwe which they considered essential to address the issues of food shortages, economic recovery, the restoration of political stability, the rule of law and the conduct of future elections.

6   The Committee called upon the international community to respond to the desperate situation currently in Zimbabwe, especially the shortages of food.

7   The Committee noted the reference in the Commonwealth Observer Group Report to national reconciliation being a priority and that the Commonwealth should assist in this process, and requested the President of Nigeria and the President of South Africa to continue to actively promote the process of reconciliation in Zimbabwe between the main political parties and to appoint special representatives to remain engaged with all the parties concerned towards this end.

8   The Committee decided to suspend Zimbabwe from the Councils of the Commonwealth for one year with immediate effect. This issue will be revisited in 12 months' time, having regard to progress in Zimbabwe based on the Commonwealth Harare Principles and reports from the Commonwealth Secretary-General.

9   The Committee mandated the Commonwealth Secretary-General to engage with the Government of Zimbabwe to ensure that the specific recommendations from the Commonwealth Observer Group Report, notably on the management of future elections in Zimbabwe, are implemented.

10   In line with the Abuja Agreement and the Coolum Statement, the Committee stated that land is at the core of the crisis in Zimbabwe and cannot be separated from other issues of concern, and the Commonwealth will be ready to assist Zimbabwe to address the land issue and to help in its economic recovery in co-operation with other international agencies. The Committee requested the Commonwealth Secretary-General to remain actively involved with the UN Development Programme in promoting transparent, equitable and sustainable measures for land reform in Zimbabwe.

11   The Committee will actively promote the implementation of all the goals contained in this Statement in consultation with the Commonwealth Secretary-General and will meet at the request of the Commonwealth Chairperson-in-Office.

Marlborough House, London, 19 March 2002

COMMONWEALTH MEMBER STATES

As at June 2002, the Commonwealth has 54 member countries.

Member country	Joined Commonwealth
Antigua and Barbuda	1981
Australia	1931 (Statute of Westminster*)
The Bahamas	1973
Bangladesh	1972
Barbados	1966
Belize	1981
Botswana	1966
Brunei Darussala	1984
Cameroon	1995
Canada	1931 (Statute of Westminster*)
Cyprus	1961 (independent 1960)
Dominica	1978
Fiji Islands	1997
The Gambia	1965
Ghana	1957
Grenada	1974
Guyana	1966
India	1947
Jamaica	1962
Kenya	1963
Kiribati	1979
Lesotho	1966
Malawi	1964
Malaysia	1957
Maldives	1982 (independent 1965)
Malta	1964
Mauritius	1968
Mozambique	1995 (independent 1975)
Namibia	1990
Nauru	1968 (full member from 1999)
New Zealand	1931 (Statute of Westminster*)
Nigeria	1960 (suspended 1995–99)
Pakistan	1989 (rejoined, having left in 1972**)
Papua New Guinea	1975
St Kitts and Nevis	1983
St Lucia	1979
St Vincent and the Grenadines	1979
Samoa	1970
Seychelles	1976

Member country	Joined Commonwealth
Sierra Leone	1961
Singapore	1965
Solomon Islands	1978
South Africa	1994 (rejoined, having left in 1961)
Sri Lanka	1948
Swaziland	1968
Tonga	1970
Trinidad and Tobago	1962
Tuvalu	1978 (full member from September 2000)
Uganda	1962
United Kingdom	
United Republic of Tanzania	1961
Vanuatu	1980
Zambia	1964
Zimbabwe	1980***

*The Statute of Westminster of 1931 gave effective independence to the Dominions of Australia, Canada, New Zealand and South Africa.

**Following the displacement of the democratically elected government in May 2000, and pending restoration of democracy, the Fiji Islands was suspended from the Councils of the Commonwealth. Following the overthrow of the democratically elected government in October 1999, Pakistan was suspended from the Councils of the Commonwealth pending the restoration of democracy in the country.

***In March 2002, Zimbabwe was suspended from the Councils of the Commonwealth.

SECTION 3
DIRECTORY OF COMMONWEALTH
LAW SCHOOLS

AUSTRALIA

There are 28 law schools in Australia, the number having doubled over the past decade. All are situated within universities located in the six States and two Territories within Australia. Virtually all law schools offer a combined degree programme in which the degree in Law (LLB) is undertaken together with another degree over five years (eg, in arts, economics or science). About half also offer a straight LLB degree which is undertaken in four years. Many law schools also offer a coursework Masters in Law (LLM), often in an area of specialisation. Access to the websites of all Australian universities is available through http://jurist.law.mq.edu.au/lawschl.htm.

Admission to legal practice is dependent upon the completion of practical legal training requirements following graduation with an LLB degree. A period of conditional admission is also required in most States for new practitioners, during which they are required to work under the supervision of an experienced practitioner. Admission is regulated on a State by State basis, but considerable effort is being made to achieve uniformity of requirements across the various jurisdictions. Usually, the relevant admitting authority is the Supreme Court in each State.

The CLEA country contact is Ros Macdonald of the Queensland University of Technology (address below) (email: r.macdonald@qut.edu.au).

The Australasian Law Teachers Association (ALTA) is the professional body that represents the interests of teachers of law in Australia, New Zealand, Papua New Guinea and the Pacific Islands. ALTA seeks to advance legal education (and the interests of law teachers) throughout Australasia, and especially focuses on the encouragement of legal research and the dissemination of its results. Membership is open to teachers of law and law librarians in tertiary institutions in these countries. Associate membership is open to former teachers of law and other persons engaged in or associated with the teaching of, or research into, law in these countries and to teachers of law in other countries in the Asian and Pacific regions. Contact details: email: alta@usyd.edu.au.

The Corporate Law Teachers Association (CLTA) is a body whose aim is to advance corporate law teaching, research and scholarship; promote co-operation and exchange of ideas between corporate law scholars in Australia, New Zealand and elsewhere in the Asia Pacific region; encourage corporate law research and the publication of contributions to legal knowledge; promote active co-operation of corporate law teachers with university and other learned bodies in the region; co-operate with professional legal associations, law reform agencies and other bodies in the work of law reform; collect and publish information about the roles and needs of corporate law teachers and of developments in teaching and scholarship; organise an annual conference and other conferences, workshops and seminars. For further details, contact CLTA website administrator, c/o Faculty of Law, Australian National University, Canberra ACT 0200, Australia (email: ccl.law@anu.edu.au).

The Australian legal system is based on the common law. Each State has its own court system ranging from local and magistrates' courts to a Supreme Court. In addition to this, there is a Federal Court and the High Court of Australia, which is the highest appellate court in the legal system.

Practitioners from other common law systems may apply for admission but will be required to undertake study in relation to various aspects of Australian law, including constitutional law, property law and procedure. Any professional queries should be directed to the Supreme Court of the State in which admission is being sought. The Australian Bar Association can be contacted at info@austbar.asn.au.

LAW REPORTS

There are several series of law reports including:
- *Australian Law Reports* (ALR) (1973–date)
- *Federal Law Reports* (1956–date)
- *Commonwealth Law Reports* (CLR) (1903–date)
- Full text decisions of Federal and State Courts are available free of charge on www.austlii.edu.au

LAW SCHOOLS

ADELAIDE UNIVERSITY

Law School, Ligertwood Building, Adelaide, SA 5005, Australia
Tel: +61 8 83035063; Fax: +61 8 83034344
email: kathleen.mcevoy@adelaide.edu.au
website: www.law.adelaide.edu.au

Courses offered

LLB
LLM
Master of Comparative Laws
PhD

After graduation, students complete the six month Graduate Certificate in Legal Practice course and such a course or programme of post-admission practical legal training as may be approved for that purpose by the Board of Examiners of the Supreme Court of South Australia

Journals

1 *Adelaide Law Review* (biannually) (focuses on general legal topics of particular relevance to both academics and practitioners)
2 *Australian Journal of Legal History* (biannually)
3 *Corporate and Business Law Journal* (1988–2000). Journal publication has now been transferred to the Centre for Commercial Law, Australian National University)

AUSTRALIAN NATIONAL UNIVERSITY

Faculty of Law, Canberra, ACT 0200, Australia
Tel: +61 2 61253483; Fax: +61 2 62490103/62493971
email: enquiries.law@anu.edu.au
website: http://law.anu.edu.au

Courses offered

LLB
Master of Laws
Master of Legal Studies
Doctor of Juridical Science (SJD)
MPhil
PhD

The LLB degree (in any combination) is recognised for admission to practice in all Australian jurisdictions

Centres

1   Centre for Law and Economics
2   Australian Centre for Environmental Law (ACEL) (aims to meet the growing demand for environmental law expertise – in practice, in teaching, in research and in public policy development)
3   Australian Centre for Intellectual Property in Agriculture (ACIPA) (is a national facility for education and training, and research and policy development in intellectual property issues as they apply to agricultural biotechnology)
4   Centre for Commercial Laws
5   Centre for International and Public Law
6   Centre for Law and Economics

Journals

1   *Australian Yearbook of International Law*
2   *Federal Law Review* (biannually) (website: http://uniserve.anu.edu.au/law) (examines legal and policy questions relating to the nature of federalism, Commonwealth constitutional and administrative law and international law in so far as it affects the Commonwealth)

BOND UNIVERSITY

School of Law, University Drive, Robina, Queensland 4229, Australia
Tel: +61 7 55951111; Fax: +61 7 55952246
email: eric_calvin@bond.edu.au
website: www.bond.edu.au

Courses offered

Bachelor of Business Law
Bachelor of Jurisprudence
LLB
Juris Doctor (Professional Qualification)
LLM
Doctor of Legal Science (SJD)
PhD
Doctor of Laws (LLD)

Graduates gain admission to practise in all Australian States

Journals

1   *Bond Law Review* (biannually)
2   *Bond Dispute Resolution News*
3   *Revenue Law Journal* (annual) (provides an international focus on all aspects of taxation)

Centres

1   Centre for Transnational Business Law
2   Commercial Law Centre
3   Dispute Resolution Centre

UNIVERSITY OF CANBERRA

School of Law, Division of Management and Technology, ACT 2601, Australia
Tel: +61 2 62015762; Fax: +61 2 62015764
email: dmtlaw@management.canberra.edu.au
website: www.dmt.canberra.edu.au/law

Courses offered

LLB
LLM
Masters in Corporate Law
PhD in Corporate Law
Professional Doctorate in Law (SJD)

Journals

1   *Australian Journal of Corporate Law*
2   *Canberra Law Review*
3   *Corporate and Business Law Journal*

Centre

National Centre for Corporate Law and Policy Research (focuses on corporate and business law and policy in Australia and the Asia Pacific region)

DEAKIN UNIVERSITY

School of Law, 221 Burwood Highway, Burwood, Victoria 3125, Australia
Tel: +61 3 92446062; Fax: +61 3 92446063
email: law@deakin.edu.au
website: www.law.deakin.edu.au

Courses offered

LLB
LLB (joint degree programmes)
LLM
Master of International Trade and Investment Law
Master of Commercial Law

Doctor of Juridical Science (SJD)
PhD

Journal

Deakin Law Review (contains articles, case notes and book reviews on a broad range of law topics) (email: deakinlawreview@hotmail.com; website: www.austlii.edu.au/au/journals/DLR)

FLINDERS UNIVERSITY OF SOUTH AUSTRALIA

School of Law, GPO Box 2100, Adelaide 5001, Australia
Tel: +61 8 82013539; Fax: +61 8 82013630
email: law@flinders.edu.au
website: wwwehlt.flinders.edu.au/law

Courses offered

Bachelor of Laws and Legal Practice (LLB/LP)
LLM
PhD

Journal

Flinders Journal of Law Reform (biannually) (email: fjlr@flinders.edu.au)

Centre

National Aboriginal Youth Law Centre (jointly with Northern Territory University)

GRIFFITH UNIVERSITY

Faculty of Law, Nathan Campus, GU Nathan, Brisbane, Queensland 4111, Australia
Tel: +61 7 38755339 ; Fax: +61 7 38755599
email: s.collins@mailbox.gu.edu.au
website: www.gu.edu.au/school/law

Courses offered

LLB
LLB (joint degree programmes)
LLM
MA (law)
MPhil
PhD

Centres

1   Social-Legal Research Centre
2   Family Law Research Unit
3   Centre for Intellectual Property Research

Journal

Griffith Law Review (biannually) (publishes work in any area of law and legal studies, particularly inter-disciplinary or socio-legal work)

JAMES COOK UNIVERSITY OF NORTH QUEENSLAND

Faculty of Law, Townsville, Queensland 4811, Australia
Tel: +61 7 47814111; Fax: +61 7 47796371
email: thomas.middleton@jcu.edu.au
website: www.jcu.edu.au/school/law

Courses offered

LLB
LLB (joint degree programmes)
LLM
PhD
LLB (accredited for purposes of admission as a barrister or solicitor in Queensland)

LA TROBE UNIVERSITY

School of Law and Legal Studies, Bundoora, Victoria 3086, Australia
Tel: +61 3 94792284; Fax: +61 3 94791607
email: law&legal@latrobe.edu.au
website: www.latrobe.edu.au/law

Courses offered

Bachelor of Legal Studies (BLS)
LLB
LLB (joint degree programmes)
LLM
MA
PhD

MACQUARIE UNIVERSITY

Division of Law, North Ryde, Sydney, NSW 2109, Australia
Tel: +61 2 98507097; Fax: +61 2 98507686
email: Info@law.mq.edu.au
website: www.law.mq.edu.au

Courses offered

LLB
LLB (joint degree programmes)
LLM Environmental Law
Master of Commercial Law (MComLaw)
PhD

The combined LLB and external LLB programmes are accepted as fulfilling the academic requirements for admission to practice

Journal

Australian Journal of Law and Society (annually)

Centre

Centre for Environmental Law

UNIVERSITY OF MELBOURNE

Melbourne Law School, 185 Pelham Street, Victoria 3010, Australia
Tel: +61 3 83446164; Fax: +61 3 83444546
email: dean@law.unimelb.edu.au
website: www.law.unimelb.edu.au

Courses offered

LLB
LLB (+ joint degree programmes)
LLM
PhD
Doctor of Juridical Science (SJD)

Centres

1   Asian Law Centre (Room 0726, Level 7, Melbourne Law School; Tel: +61 3 83446847; Fax: +61 3 83444546; email: alc@law.unimelb.edu.au; website: www.law.unimelb.edu.au/alc/welcome)
    Objectives
    •   To promote the teaching of Asian law in Australia at both graduate and undergraduate levels, and the teaching of Australian law in Asia.
    •   To promote the development of Asian studies and Asian languages in other disciplines and to encourage a linkage with law studies.
    •   To improve Australia's knowledge of the laws of the region and to research the legal framework for trade and investment.
    •   To develop specialised legal training programmes for Australians and Asians.
    •   To promote exchanges of staff and students between the law school and Asian universities and institutions.
    •   To support the rule of law in Asia.

2   Centre for Comparative Constitutional Studies

Journals

1   *Melbourne University Law Review* (three issues annually) (email: mulr@law.unimelb.edu.au; website; www.law.unimelb.edu.au/mult) (encourages debate on contemporary legal issues)
2   *Australian Journal of Asian Law* (biannually) (provides a forum for debate on the laws and legal cultures of Asia. It publishes multi-disciplinary, historical and fieldwork contributions). (Contact: The Editors, *The Australian Journal of Asian Law*, PO Box 4318, University of Melbourne, Victoria 3052, Australia; Tel: +61 03 83446847; Fax: +61 03 83444546; email: asianlawj@law.unimelb.edu.au.)
3   *Melbourne Journal of International Law* (website: www.law.unimelb.edu.au/mjil)

MONASH UNIVERSITY

Faculty of Law, PO Box 12, Victoria 1800, Australia
Tel: +61 3 99053356; Fax: +61 3 99053300
email: enquiries@law.monash.edu.au
website: www.law.monash.edu.au

Courses offered

LLB
LLB (+ joint degree programmes)
Master of Laws
Master of Laws (Internet and Electronic Law)
Master of Laws (International and Comparative Law)
Master of Laws (Banking and Finance Law)
Master of Laws (Intellectual Property Law)
Master of Laws (Commercial Law)
Master of Laws (Tribunal Processes)
LLD
PhD

Journals

1   *Alternative Law Journal* (bimonthly) (goals of the journal include promotion of social justice issues; community legal education) (website: www.altlj.org)
2   *Monash University Law Review* (biannually)

Centres

1   Castan Centre for Human Rights Law
2   Centre for Law in the Digital Economy (CLIDE)
3   International Institute of Forensic Studies
4   National Australia Bank's Banking Law Centre
5   Privatisation and Public Accountability Centre

MURDOCH UNIVERSITY

School of Law, GPO 51400, Murdoch, Perth, WA 6849, Australia
Tel: +61 9 3602979; Fax: +61 9 3106671
email: inquiries@law.murdoch.edu.au
website: wwwlaw.murdoch.edu.au

Courses offered

LLB
Bachelor of Legal Studies (BLS)
LLB (+ joint degree programmes)
MPhil
PhD

Centres

1   Asia Pacific Intellectual Property Law Institute
2   Asia Pacific Centre for Human Rights and the Prevention of Ethnic Conflict
3   Southern Communities Legal Advisory and Education Service (email: scales@murdoch.edu.au)
4   International Commission of Jurists (WA Branch)

Journals

1   *Digital Technology Law Journal* (a wholly online periodical – website: www.law.murdoch.edu.au/dtlj) (publishes papers on issues of law relevant to digital technology)
2   *Murdoch University Electronic Journal of Law* (website: www.murdoch.edu.au/elaw)
3   *Sister in Law* (a feminist legal journal that deals with all aspects of women and the law)
4   *Asia Pacific Journal on Human Rights and the Law*

UNIVERSITY OF NEWCASTLE

Faculty of Business and Law, University Drive, Callagham, Newcastle, NSW 2308, Australia
Tel: +61 2 49215022; Fax: +61 2 49216931
email: law-enquiries@law.newcastle.edu.au
website: www.law.newcastle.edu.au

Courses offered

LLB
LLB (+ joint degree programmes)
LLM
PhD

Centres

1   Centre for Health Law Ethics and Policy
2   Centre for Legal Education
3   The Justice Policy Research Centre

UNIVERSITY OF NEW ENGLAND

School of Law, Armidale, NSW 2351, Australia
Tel: +61 2 67733598; Fax: +61 2 67733602
email: hgeddes@metz.une.edu.au
website: www.une.edu.au

Courses offered

LLB
LLB (+ joint degree programmes)
LLM

THE COLLEGE OF LAW, NEW SOUTH WALES

PO Box 2, St Leonard's, NSW 2065, Australia
Tel: +61 2 99650333; Fax: +61 2 92315809
email: fogrady@fl.asn.au
website: www.lawsocnsw.asn.au

The College of Law Professional Programme is approved by the Legal Practitioners Admission Board as a requirement for admission to practise in New South Wales. It is offered in two stages:

(i)   15 weeks of full time instruction conducted at the college premises in St Leonard's; and
(ii)   75 hours of continuing practical training to be undertaken during a period of practical experience in the workplace, equivalent to 15 weeks of full time work.

UNIVERSITY OF NEW SOUTH WALES

Faculty of Law, Sydney NSW 2052, Australia
Tel: +61 2 9385 2227; Fax: +61 2 9385 1175
email: law@unsw.edu.au
website: www.law.unsw.edu.au

Courses offered

LLB
BJuris
LLB (+ joint degree programmes)
LLM
Graduate Diploma in Law (Grad Dip Law)
Master of Legal Studies (MLS)
Graduate Diploma in Legal Studies (Grad Dip LS)
PhD
Doctor of Juridical Science (SJD)

To be admitted as a solicitor, the holder of an LLB degree must undertake a six month full time practical skills course at the College of Law

Centres

1   Australian Human Rights Centre (AHRC) (encourages multidisciplinary teaching and research in the area of human rights at the national, regional and international levels)
2   Australian Human Rights Centre (AHRC)
3   Australasian Legal Information Institute (AustLII)
4   Baker and McKenzie Cyberspace Law and Policy Centre
5   Centre for Continuing Legal Education
6   Communications Law Centre
7   Diplomacy Training Program
8   European Law Centre
9   Financial Services Consumer Policy Centre (FSCPC)
10   Gilbert and Tobin Centre of Public Law
11   Indigenous Law Centre

12   Kingsford Legal Centre
13   National Children's and Youth Law Centre Social Justice Project

Journals

1   *University of New South Wales Law Review* (three times a year) (email: law.journal@unsw.edu.au) (publishes articles which are relevant to academics legal and business professionals)
2   *Australian Journal of Human Rights* (focuses on human rights developments in Australia and the Asia-Pacific region. It deals not only with the legal aspects of human rights but also with philosophical, historical, sociological, economic and political issues as they relate to human rights in Australia and the Asia-Pacific Region)
3   *Human Rights Defender* (email: dtp@unsw.edu.au) (quarterly human rights bulletin, published jointly by the Diplomacy Training Program and the Human Rights Centre at the University of New South Wales)
4   *Indigenous Law Bulletin* (undertakes research and reporting on the relationship between Indigenous people and the law) (email: ilc@unsw.edu.ac)
5   *Australian Indigenous Law Reporter* (email: ailr@unsw.edu.au; website: www.worldlii.org.ac/journals/AILR)
6   *Privacy Law and Policy Reporter* (PLPR) (a monthly review and analysis of privacy laws, policies and intrusions, focusing on Australia, New Zealand, and the Asia-Pacific region)

UNIVERSITY OF NOTRE DAME AUSTRALIA

College of Law, PO Box 1225, Fremantle, WA 6160, Australia
Tel: +61 8 92395720; Fax: +61 8 92395722
email: sderrett@nd.edu.au
website: www.nd.edu.au/law

Course offered

LLB

NORTHERN TERRITORY UNIVERSITY

Faculty of Law, Darwin, NT 0909, Australia
Tel: +61 8 89466833; Fax: +61 8 89466852
email: law@darwin.ntu.edu.au
website: www.ntu.edu.au/faculties/law

Courses offered

LLB
BJuris
LLB (+ joint degree programmes)
LLM in Comparative Law
PhD

Core units of the LLB degree plus two elective skill units, Legal Ethics and Trust Accounts, are the academic requirements to practice as a barrister and solicitor of the Supreme Court of the Northern Territory

Centre

Centre for South-East Asian Law

UNIVERSITY OF QUEENSLAND

TC Beirne School of Law, Queensland 4072, Australia
Tel: +61 7 33653498; Fax: +61 7 33651454
email: a.bigg@law.uq.edu.au
website: www.law.uq.edu.au

Courses offered

LLB
LLB (+ joint degree programmes)
Master of Legal Science
LLM
Master of Applied Law (MappLaw)
Master of Comparative Law
PhD
LLD

Journals

1   *University of Queensland Law Journal* (annually)
2   *International Trade and Business Law Annual*
3   *Bulletin of the Australian Society of Legal Philosophy*

Centres

1   Australian Institute of Foreign and Comparative Law (promotes research and teaching in foreign and comparative law with a special emphasis on areas of the law relating to international trade and commerce)
2   Centre for Legal and Economic Study of Institutions (promotes cross-disciplinary research into legal and economic institutions and their interface)
3   Corrs Chambers Westgarth Dispute Management Centre (promotes dispute management skills by offering a range of courses dealing with the various forms of dispute management, or: alternative dispute resolution, negotiation, mediation, case appraisal and arbitration)
4   Centre for Technology Law (promotes teaching and research in industrial and intellectual property law with particular emphasis on continuing education for lawyers, patent attorneys and others involved with legal aspects of the administration of intellectual property rights)
5   Centre for Maritime Law

QUEENSLAND UNIVERSITY OF TECHNOLOGY

Faculty of Law, 2 George Street, GPO Box 2434, Brisbane, Queensland 4001, Australia
Tel: +61 7 38642707; Fax: +61 7 38642222; 38641152
email: law_enquiries@qut.edu.au
website: www.qut.edu.au/law

Courses offered

LLB
LLB (+ joint degree programmes)
Master of Laws
Doctor of Juridical Science (SJD)
PhD
Bar Practice Course (a prerequisite for admission as a barrister in Queensland)
Legal Practice Course (completion of the course allows conditional admission as a solicitor in Queensland)

The QUT LLB is an approved degree for the purpose of practising as a solicitor and/or barrister throughout Australia and also in West and East Malaysia, Fiji Islands and Papua New Guinea

Centres

1   Centre for Commercial and Property Law (Fax: +61 7 3864 1161)
2   Centre for Law and Social Justice

Journal

Queensland University of Technology Law and Justice Journal (email: c.ktschkin@qut.edu.au; website: www.law.qut.edu.au/about/ljjl)

SOUTHERN CROSS UNIVERSITY

School of Law and Justice, PO Box 157, Lismore, NSW 2480, Australia
Tel: +61 66 203109; Fax: +61 66 224167
email: law@scu.au.edu.au
website: www.scu.edu.au/schools/lawj

Courses offered

Associate Degree in Law (Paralegal Studies)
Bachelor of Legal and Justice Studies
Double Degree including Law
LLM
PhD

Journal

Southern Cross University Law Review

UNIVERSITY OF SYDNEY

Faculty of Law, 173 Phillip Street, Sydney 2000, Australia
Tel: +61 2 93510351; Fax: +61 2 93510200
email: info@law.usyd.edu.au
website: www.law.usyd.edu.au

Courses offered

LLB
LLB (+ joint degree programmes)
PhD
Doctor of Juridical Science (SJD)

Centres

1   Australian Centre for Environmental Law
2   Centre for Plain Legal Language
3   National Children's and Youth Law Centre
4   Institute of Criminology
5   Centre of Asian and Pacific Law

Journals

1   *Sydney Law Review* (website: www.law.usyd.edu.au/slr)
2   *Current Issues in Criminal Justice*
3   *Sydney Law Reports*

UNIVERSITY OF TASMANIA

Law School, GPO Box 252-89, Hobart 7001, Australia
Tel: +61 3 62262066; Fax: +61 3 62267623
email: Don.Chalmers@utas.edu.au
website: www.law.utas.edu.au

Courses offered

LLB
LLB (+ joint degree programmes)
LLM
PhD

The LLB degree qualifies the holder for admission subject to passing the examination of the Legal Practice Programme and undertaking a 12 months' apprenticeship

Journals

1   *Journal of Law and Information Science* (biannually)
2   *University of Tasmania Law Review* (biannually)
3   *Antarctic and Southern Ocean Law and Policy Papers* (annually)
4   *University of Tasmania Law School Occasional Papers* (biannually)

Centre

The Tasmania Law Reform Institute (established on the 23 July 2001 by agreement between the Government of the State of Tasmania, the University of Tasmania and the Law Society of Tasmania). The Institute undertakes law reform work and research on topics proposed by the Government, the community, the University and the Institute itself

UNIVERSITY OF TECHNOLOGY, SYDNEY

Faculty of Law, GPO Box 123, Broadway, NSW 2007, Australia
Tel: +61 2 95143444; Fax: +61 2 95153400
email: davidb@law.uts.edu.au
website: http://lexsun.law.uts.edu.au

Courses offered

LLB
LLB (+ joint degree programme)
Bachelor of Indigenous Law
LLM
Master of Dispute Resolution (MDR)
Master of Taxation (MTax)
PhD
Doctor of Juridical Sciences (SJD)

Journal

UTS Law Review (email: utslawreview@law.uts.edu.au)

Centres

1   Unit for Dispute Resolution
2   Community Law and Research Centre
3   Australasian Legal Information Institute

VICTORIA UNIVERSITY

School of Law, PO Box 14428, Melbourne City MC, Victoria 8001,
Australia
Tel: + 61 3 96885083
email: neil.andrews@vu.edu.au
website: www.business.vu.edu.au

Courses offered

LLB
LLB (+ joint degree programmes)
Master of Comparative Commercial law
Master of Business
PhD

UNIVERSITY OF WESTERN AUSTRALIA

Faculty of Law, Law Building, Nedlands, Perth, WA 6907, Australia
Tel: +61 9 3802945; Fax: +61 9 3801045
email: rbartlet@ecel.uwa.edu.au
website: www.law.ecel.uwa.edu.au/law

Courses offered

LLB
LLB (+ joint degree programme)
LLM
Master of Banking and Finance Law
Master of Criminal Justice
Master of Taxation Studies
PhD
Doctor of Juridical Science (SJD)

The LLB degree qualifies the holder for admission as a barrister and solicitor after the completion of one year as articled clerk

Journal

University of Western Australia Law Review

Centre

Crime Research Centre

UNIVERSITY OF WESTERN SYDNEY

School of Law, Locked Bag 1797, Penrith 1797, NSW, Australia
Tel: +61 2 46203653; Fax: +61 2 46203887
email: c.sappideen@uws.edu.au
website: www.uws.edu.au/law

Courses offered

LLB
LLB (+ joint degree programmes)
Masters of Dispute Resolution
Master of Law (international business)
LLM
Doctor of Juridical Science (SJD)
PhD

Journals

1   *Australian International Law Journal*
2   *Elder Law Review*
3   *University of Western Sydney Law Review*

Centre

Centre for Elder Law (www.uws.edu.au/law/elderlaw)

UNIVERSITY OF WOLLONGONG

Faculty of Law, Northfields Avenue, Wollongong, NSW 2522, Australia
Tel: +61 2 42213555; Fax: +61 2 42213188
email: law@uow.edu.au
website: www.uow.edu.au

Courses offered

LLB
LLB (+ joint degree programme)
LLM (international and comparative law)
PhD

Journals

1   *The Australasian Journal of Natural Resources Law and Policy*
2   *Law Text Culture*

Centres

1   Centre for Court Policy and Administration
2   Centre for Natural Resources Law and Policy
3   Centre for Maritime Policy

BANGLADESH

Legal education in Bangladesh is conducted in the law faculties of the University of Chittagong, University of Dhaka and Rajshahi University. Holders of the LLB degree who wish to practise as advocates must pass the qualifying examination conducted by the Bangladesh Bar Council and undertake a period of articleship.

There is no formal association of law teachers in Bangladesh.

The CLEA country contact is M Habibur Rahman of Rajshahi University (address below) (Fax: +880 721 750064; email: habiburlaw@yahoo.com.).

The laws of Bangladesh are based on English common law, albeit extensively modified. Many pre-August 1947 Indian statutes and Pakistani statutes enacted before December 1971 are part of Bangladesh law. Islamic and Hindu law is applicable in the area of family law.

The superior court system consists of a Supreme Court of Bangladesh which comprises an appellate division and the High Court Division (whose permanent seat is in Dhaka) and which hears cases throughout the country.

The legal profession is fused. Practitioners from other common law systems may apply for the right of audience on an *ad hoc* basis in the Bangladeshi courts. Those from foreign jurisdictions who wish to practise in Bangladesh should contact the Bangladesh Bar Council, Bangladesh Bar Council Building, Ramna Dhaka 1000, Bangladesh (Tel: +880 257759; Fax: +880 863409). The National Bar Association of Bangladesh can be contacted as follows: 35/A Purana Paltan Line, VIP Road, Dhaka 1000, Bangladesh (Tel: +880 293 37695; Fax: +880 283 9427).

LAW REPORTS

- *Dhaka Law Reports* (DLR)
- *Bangladesh Legal Decisions* (BLD)

LAW SCHOOLS

UNIVERSITY OF CHITTAGONG

Faculty of Law, University Post Office, Chittagong, Bangladesh
Tel: +880 31 682031 to 39; Fax: +880 31 726310
email: cu@ctgu.edu
website: www.ctgu.edu

Courses offered

LLB (Hons)
LLM

DHAKA UNIVERSITY

Faculty of Law, Ramna, Dhaka-1000, Bangladesh
Tel: +880 2 861 3724; 966 1900 to 59; Fax: +880 2 861 5583
email: lawfac@bangla.net; duregstr@bangla.net
websites: www.du.bangla.net; www.univdhaka.edu

Courses offered

LLB (Hons)
LLM
MPhil
PhD
Clinical Legal Education Programme

Centre

The Law School is part of the South Asia Legal Education Consortium (SALEC) which encourages greater political and economic integration, religious tolerance and legal development in the region though the development and exchange of ideas, practical training and scholarship (for further details see: www.gwu.edu/salec/default.asp)

Journal

Dhaka University Studies

RAJSHAHI UNIVERSITY

Department of Law, Rajshahi 6205, Bangladesh
Tel: +880 721 750041 to 49; Fax: +880 721 750064
email: ru@ugc.org; ru.phy@drik.bgd.toolnet.org

Courses offered

LLB
LLM
MPhil
PhD

Centre

Part of the South Asia Legal Education Consortium (see entry above)

BOTSWANA

The department of law at the University of Botswana was set up in August 1981 and is the sole provider of legal education in the country. The original course structure followed the pattern evolved from the old joint Universities of Botswana, Lesotho and Swaziland (UBLS), and, later, University of Botswana and Swaziland (UBS).

From August 2002 the department of law will offer two programmes: a Diploma in Law and a Bachelor of Laws (LLB) degree. Graduate programmes leading to the awards of the LLM and MPhil will commence soon.

The Diploma in Law is a four semester (two-year) programme, primarily designed for public and private sector employees requiring specialised training in areas of Botswana law relevant to their work experiences. The object of the programme is to improve the ability of the public and private sector employees to work with, or implement, Botswana legislation relevant to their spheres of work.

The LLB is a 10 semester (five-year) full time programme combining theoretical and practical skills training in law and related courses. The degree awarded is recognised as the basic or founding qualification for admission as a legal practitioner in Botswana. However, holders of the degree are required to fulfil pupillage and other requirements under the Legal Practitioners Act 1996.

The CLEA country contact is Clement Ngongola of the University of Botswana (address below) (email: ngongola@mopipi.ub.bw).

Botswana has a hybrid system of law, which draws from Roman-Dutch law. English common law and customary law. Roman-Dutch law generally applies to civil matters, while criminal law is heavily influenced by the common law.

The superior court system comprises the Court of Appeal for Botswana and the High Court. The principal seat for both courts is in Lobatse, but the High Court has a division in Francistown and goes on circuit in other main centres of the country.

The Legal Practitioners Act 1996 regulates the right of audience on an *ad hoc* basis for practitioners from other common law systems, and the rights of admission for persons admitted to practice in specified countries. Details can be obtained from the Executive Secretary, Law Society of Botswana, PO Box 50889, Gaborone, Botswana (Tel: +267 300777; Fax: +267 300660; email: lawsociety@mega.bw).

LAW REPORTS

- *Botswana Law Reports* (BLR) (1964–date)
- Copies of unpublished decisions may be obtained by writing to The Registrar, High Court of Botswana, Private Bag 1, Lobatse, Botswana

LAW SCHOOL

UNIVERSITY OF BOTSWANA

Department of Law, Faculty of Social Sciences, Private Bag 00705, Gaborone, Botswana
Tel: +267 3552344; Fax +267 585099
email: law@mopipi.ub.bw
website: www.ub.bw

Courses offered

LLB
Diploma in Law

Centre

Legal Aid Clinic

CAMEROON

Legal education in Cameroon is conducted at the University of Buea, Université de Douala, Université de Dschang, Universite de N'gaoundere, Universite de Yaounde I a Ngoa-Ekelle and University of Yaounde II at Soa.

The CLEA country contact is Samgena Galega of the University of Buea (address below) (email: dr_sdgalega@yahoo.com).

To qualify as a legal practitioner an individual must undertake a three-year degree programme, leading to the award of an LLB or *Licence en droit*. A fourth year of study leads to qualification as a *maîtrise*. Following the successful completion of a competitive examination, a candidate qualifies as a pupil lawyer and then spends two years with a law firm before taking a final competitive examination. The successful completion of this qualifies the individual to be sworn in as a legal practitioner.

Due to its colonial links with both France and the United Kingdom, there is a dual legal system in Cameroon based on civil law and common law.

The superior courts system consists of the Supreme Court, Courts of Appeal and High Courts.

Practitioners from foreign jurisdictions seeking a right of audience on an *ad hoc* basis, or who wish to practise in Cameroon, should contact the Cameroon Bar Association, BP 120, Bamenda, Cameroon (Tel: +237 363036).

LAW REPORTS

- *West Cameroon Law Reports* (1962–68)
- *University of Yaounde Law Reports* (1968–73)
- *Cameroon Common Law Reports* (1996–date): for details contact Liberty Publications, PO Box 278, Tiko, Cameroon (Tel/Fax: +237 351138)

LAW SCHOOLS

UNIVERSITY OF BUEA

Department of Law, Faculty of Social and Management Sciences, PO Box 63, Buea, Cameroon
Tel: +237 322134; Fax +237 322272
email: dr_sdgalega@yahoo.com

Course offered

LLB

Centre

Commonwealth Legal Education Resource Centre

UNIVERSITÉ DE DOUALA

Faculté de Sciences Juridiques et Politiques, BP 2701, Douala, Cameroon

UNIVERSITÉ DE DSCHANG

Department of Law, BP 96, Dschar   Cameroon
Tel: +237 451381; Fax: +237 451381
email: mtchuent@sdncmr.undp.org

UNIVERSITÉ DE N'GAOUNDERE

Faculte de Droit et de Sciences Politiques, BP 454, N'gaoundere, Cameroon
Tel: +237 252230 or 252420; Fax:: +237 252573

UNIVERSITY OF YAOUNDE II AT SOA

Faculty of Law and Political Science, BP 1365, Yaounde, Cameroon
website: www.uninet.cm

CANADA

There are 20 law schools in Canada, 14 offering common law programmes and six offering either civil law, or combined civil and common law programmes. All are situated in universities distributed across the Provinces, with the highest concentrations being in Ontario and Quebec. In all Provinces, excluding Quebec, entry into law school is highly competitive and is normally only available to those candidates who have completed a minimum of two years undergraduate study in any discipline. The vast majority of applicants will have obtained an undergraduate degree. Applicants are also required to complete the Law School Aptitude Test that is administrated throughout the year in various locations. In Quebec, entry to law school follows from successful completion of a programme of study at one of the Provinces CEGEPs (*les colleges d'enseignement général et professionel*).

All law degree programmes are three years long and result in the awarding of either the LLB or BCL (Bachelor of Civil Law). Many law schools offer combined law degrees, with either arts or business, and postgraduate studies at both the masters and doctorate levels. All common law Canadian law school programmes are recognised by the respective law societies within the common law Provinces, as are all the civil law school programmes recognised by the Barreau du Quebec and La Chambre des Notaires du Quebec.

After completing a law degree, a person wishing to be admitted as a barrister and solicitor (in common law Provinces, the Bar is fused), or as a notary or advocate in Quebec, must meet the requirements of the respective provincial law societies who control all admission requirements. The exact requirements differ between Provinces but normally entail a combination of the successful completion of a Bar Admission Programme organised by the respective provincial law society; consisting of one or two short periods of instruction, examination of core legal areas, and practical lawyering skills, and a period of articling in which the candidate is employed and mentored by an experienced lawyer. Following successful completion of articles and the Bar Admission Programme, a person is admitted to the unrestricted practice of law in the Province in which his or her call is made. A lawyer may transfer between Provinces usually after completing an examination and having practised for a minimum of three years after being called to the Bar.

The CLEA country contact is Jeff Berryman of the University of Windsor (address below) (email: jberrym@uwindsor.ca).

The Canadian Association of Law Teachers/Association canadienne des professeurs de droit (CALT/ACPD) is the umbrella organisation of law teachers in Canada. The CALT/ACPD is recognised as one of the Canadian learned societies and meets with other such societies drawn from the social sciences and humanities at their annual colloquium. The current President of the Association is Louise Langevin who can be contacted at the Faculté de droit, Université Laval, Pavillon Charles De Koninck, Ste-Foy, Québec G1K 7P4, Canada. The website of the CALT is www2.lexum.umontral.ca/acpd/index.

The Association publishes an annual directory of all members. Copies can be ordered from Debra Smith, Canadian Bar Association, 50 O'Connor Street, Suite 902, Ottawa, Ontario K1P 6L2, Canada (Tel: +1 613 2372925; Fax: +1 613 2370185; email: info@cba.org; website: www.cba.ca). There is also a Canadian Law Student

Association and other national associations of black law students, aboriginal law students and women law students.

At some law schools course materials are available on open-access websites. These can be viewed on: http://jurist.law.utoronto.ca/cour_pgs.htm.

Canada enjoys two distinct legal systems. In all Provinces and territories, excluding Quebec, the system is based on the common law. In Quebec there is a civil law legal system. Throughout the country, criminal law based upon the Criminal Code, constitutional law and much of administrative law follows the common law. Each Province has its own court system although most judges are appointed by the federal government. Each Province has its own appellate court with second tier appeals going to the Supreme Court of Canada, Canada's highest appellate court. There are also federal trial and appellate courts with final appeals to the Supreme Court of Canada.

Practitioners from other common law systems may apply for admission to a provincial Bar (for addresses, see below) but will be required to undertake study at a law school and/or successfully pass a number of challenge examinations on various aspects of Canadian law. All Provinces have agreed to allow the National Committee on Accreditation to evaluate the credentials and prescribe a course of study for practitioners of other countries, or graduates of law programmes other than those provided by Canadian law schools. Any inquiry should be addressed to the National Committee on Accreditation, University of Ottawa, Faculty of Law, Common Law Section, PO Box 450, Station A, Ottawa, Ontario K1N 6N5, Canada. The Committee requires payment of a filing fee before assessing an applicant's credentials.

LAW REPORTS

Law reporting in Canada is organised by private legal publishers, of which there are a number of competing and overlapping services. Each Province has its own report series.

- Nationally, there are the *Dominion Law Reports* (DLR)
- For the Western Provinces there are the *Western Weekly Reports* (WWR)
- There are also numerous topical reports and computerised databases and free internet pages of law reports and statutes. A good starting point is Jurist Canada (http://jurist.lawutoronto.ca), the Canadian Legal Information Institute (www.canlii.org) which contains full text decisions (free of charge) of all the major courts in Canada and legal portal at www.gahtan.com/links

LAW SCHOOLS

UNIVERSITY OF ALBERTA

Faculty of Law, Law Centre, Alberta T6G 2H5, Canada
Tel: +1 780 4923115; Fax: +1 780 4924924
email: kjwilson@law.ualberta.ca
website: www.law.ualberta.ca

Courses offered

LLB
LLB/MBA
LLB/MPM
LLM

Journal

Alberta Law Review (quarterly) (seeks to promote legal research and scholarship and to provide a forum for the discussion of contemporary legal issues) (website: www.albertalawreview.com)

Centres

1   Centre for Constitutional Studies
2   Health Law Institute
3   International Ombudsman Institute
4   Alberta Civil Liberties Research Center

UNIVERSITY OF BRITISH COLUMBIA

Faculty of Law, 1822 East Mall, Vancouver, BC V6T 1Z1, Canada
Tel: +1 604 8223151; Fax: +1 604 8228108
email: wiggs@law.ubc.ca
website: www.law.ubc.ca

Courses offered

LLB
MBA/LLB
LLM
PhD

Centres

1   Centre for Asian Legal Studies
2   International Centre for Criminal Law Reform and Criminal Justice Policy
3   Centre for Feminist Legal Studies
4   Dr Andrew R Thompson Natural Resources Program
5   Nametz International Centre for Conflict Resolution
6   Centre for International Indigenous Legal Studies

Journals

1   *UBC Law Review* (biannually)
2   *Canadian Journal of Family Law* (biannually)

UNIVERSITY OF CALGARY

Faculty of Law, 2500 University Drive, NW, Calgary, Alberta T2N 1N4, Canada
Tel: +1 403 2205447; Fax: +1 403 2828325
email: law@calgary.ca
website: www.law.ucalgary.ca

Courses offered

LLB
LLM

Centres

1   Canadian Institute of Resources Law
2   Canadian Research Institute for Law and the Family

CARLETON UNIVERSITY

Department of Law, C473 Loeb, 1125 Colonel By Drive, Ottawa, Ont K1S 5B6, Canada
Tel: +1 613 5203690; Fax +1 613 5204467
email: law@carleton.ca
website: www.carleton.ca

Course offered

BA Law
MA in Legal Studies

Journal

Jus in Re

DALHOUSIE UNIVERSITY

Dalhousie Law School, 6061 University Avenue, Halifax, Nova Scotia B3H 4H9,
Canada
Tel: +1 902 4942114; Fax: +1 902 4941316
email: lawinfo@dal.ca
website: www.dal.ca/law

Courses offered

LLB
LLM
JSD
Indigenous Black and Mi'kmaq Programme
Maritime and Environmental Law Programme
Marine Affairs Programme
Master of Marine Management
Master of Electronic Commerce

Centres

1   Health Law Institute
2   Law and Technology Institute
3   Marine and Environmental Law Programme

Journals

1   *Dalhousie Law Journal*
2   *Ocean Yearbook*
3   *Canadian Journal of Law and Technology*

UNIVERSITÉ LAVAL

Faculty of Law, Pavillon Charles-de-Koninck, Bureau 2407, Quebec G1K 7P4, Canada
Tel: +1 418 6563036; Fax: +1 418 6567230
email: fd@fd.ulaval.ca
website: www.ulaval.ca/fd

Courses offered

LLB
LLM
LLD
Dip DN

In order to practice law, graduate students must register for a one year programme at Quebec's Bar School followed by six months training in a law firm or government agency. After completing these requirements, students are sworn in, then membership dues are paid annually to Quebec's Bar. Students have to pass the examinations of Quebec's Notary Board. A yearly fee is also payable to the Board by every graduate who wishes to practise

Journal

Les Cahiers de Droit

MCGILL UNIVERSITY

Faculty of Law, Chancellor Day Hall, 3644 Peel Street, Montreal, Quebec H3A 1W9, Canada
Tel: +1 514 3986604; Fax: +1 514 3984659
email: peter.leuprecht@mcgill.ca
website: www.law.mcgill.ca

Courses offered

BCL
LLB
MCL (thesis)
LLM (thesis)
DCL (thesis)

Centres

1   Institute of Comparative Law
2   Institute of Air and Space Law
3   Centre for the Study of Regulated Industries

Journals

1   *Annuals of Air and Space Law* (annually)
2   *McGill Law Journal* (quarterly)

UNIVERSITY OF MANITOBA

Faculty of Law, Room 301, Robson Hall, Winnipeg, Manitoba R3T 2N2, Canada
Tel: +1 204 4749282; Fax: +1 204 2755540
email: faculty-law@umanitoba.ca
website: www.umanitoba.ca/faculties/law

Courses offered

LLB
LLM

Centre

Legal Research Institute

Journal

Manitoba Law Journal

UNIVERSITÉ DE MONCTON

École de Droit, Moncton New Brunswick E1A 3E9, Canada
Tel: +1 506 8584560; Fax: +1 506 8584534
email: edr@umoncton.ca
website: www.umoncton.ca

Courses offered

LLB
LLB/MBA
Diploma ECL

Centres

1   Centre internationale de la common law en français
2   Centre de traduction et de terminologie juridiques

UNIVERSITÉ DE MONTRÉAL

Faculté de Droit, CP 6128, Succursale Centre-ville, Montréal, Quebec H3C 3J7, Canada
Tel: +1 514 3436098; Fax: +1 514 3432199
email: infodroit@droit.umontreal.ca
website: www.droit.umontreal.ca

Courses offered

LLB
LLM

Centres

1   Centre de droit des affaires et du commerce international
2   Institute for European Studies
3   Centre de recherche en droit publique

UNIVERSITY OF NEW BRUNSWICK

Faculty of Law, Ludlow Hall, Box 4400, Fredericton, New Brunswick E3B 5A3, Canada
Tel: +1 506 4534627; Fax: +1 506 4534604
email: lawadmit@unb.ca
website: www.law.unb.ca

Courses offered

LLB
LLB/MBA

Journal

UNB Law Journal (annually)

Centre

Centre for Property Studies

UNIVERSITY OF OTTAWA

Faculty of Common Law, 57 Louis Pasteur Street, PO Box 450, Stn A, Ottawa, Ontario K1N 6N5, Canada
Tel: +1 613 5625927; Fax: +1 613 5625124
Faculty of Civil Law
Tel: +1 613 5625902; Fax: +1 613 5625121
email: comlaw@uottawa.ca
website: www.uottawa.ca/academic/commonlaw

Courses offered

LLB
LLL/LLB
MBA/LLB
MA/LLB
LLM
LLD
Legislative Drafting Programs

Centres

1   Canadian Centre for Linguistic Rights
2   Human Rights Research and Education Centre
3   Center for Trade Policy and Law
4   National Judicial Institute

Journals

1   *Revue Generale De Droit*
2   *Ottawa Law Review*
3   *Canadian Yearbook of International Law* (annually)
4   *Canadian Journal of Women and the Law*

QUEEN'S UNIVERSITY

Faculty of Law, Macdonald Hall, Kingston, Ontario K7L 3N6, Canada
Tel: +1 613 5336000; Fax: +1 613 5336509
email: law@qsilver.queensu.ca
website: http://qsilver.queensu.ca/law

Courses offered

LLB
LLM

Journal

Queen's Law Journal (biannually)

UNIVERSITY OF SASKATCHEWAN

College of Law, 15 Campus Drive, Saskatoon, Saskatchewan S7N 5A6, Canada
Tel: +1 306 9665910; Fax: +1 306 9665874
website: http://law.usask.ca

Courses offered

LLB
LLM

Centres

1   Native Law Centre of Canada
2   Centre for Studies in Agriculture, Law and the Environment
3   Estey Centre for Law and Economics in International Trade

Journals

1   *Saskatchewan Law Review* (biannually)
2   *Native Law Reporter*

UNIVERSITÉ DE SHERBROOKE

Faculté de droit, 2500 boul Université, Sherbrooke, Quebec J1K 2R1, Canada
Tel: +1 819 8217511; Fax: +1 819 8217578
email: cabinet.doyen.droit@USherbrooke.ca
website: www.usherbooke.ca/droit

Courses offered

Baccalauréat en droit régulier (LLB)
Baccalauréat en droit avec cheminement en biotechnologie
Baccalauréat en droit (LLB) avec maîtrise en administration des affaires (MBA)
Diplôme de deuxième cycle en droit notarial (DDN)
Diplôme de deuxième cycle en droit transnational
Diplôme de deuxième cycle en gestion juridique de l'entreprise
Maîtrise et diplôme de deuxième cycle en droit et politiques de la santé (LLM)
Maîtrise en prévention et règlement des différends (LLM)
Maîtrise en environnement (MEnv)
Doctorat en droit (LLD)

Journal

Revue de droit de l'Université de Sherbrooke

UNIVERSITY OF TORONTO

Faculty of Law, 78 Queen's Park, Toronto M5S 2C5, Ont, Canada
Tel: +1 416 9783718; Fax: +1 416 9713026
email: ron.daniels@utoronto.ca
website: www.law.utoronto.ca

Courses offered

LLB
LLM
SJD

Centres

1   University of Toronto Joint Centre for Bioethics
2   Centre for the Study of State and Market
3   Centre for Innovation Law and Policy
4   Health Law Group

Journals

1   *The Advocate*
2   *University of Toronto Law Journal* (quarterly)
3   *University of Toronto Faculty of Law Review*

UNIVERSITY OF VICTORIA

Faculty of Law, PO Box 2400, Victoria, BC V8W 3H7, Canada
Tel: +1 250 7218147; Fax: +1 250 4724299; 7216390
email: apetter@uvic.ca
website: www.law.uvic.ca

Courses offered

LLB
LLB (a programme of the University of Victoria, Faculty of Law in partnership with Nunavut Arctic College and The Akitsiraq Law School Society offered in Iqaluit, Nunavut)

Centre

Institute for Dispute Resolution

UNIVERSITY OF WESTERN ONTARIO

Faculty of Law, Josephine Spencer Niblett Building, London, Ontario N6A 3K7, Canada
Tel: +1 519 6613346; Fax: +1 519 6613790
email: beckyb@uwo.ca
web site: www.law.uwo.ca

Courses offered

Joint Programmes:
LLB/MBA
HBA/LLB
BA(KIN)/LLB
BSc/LLB (computer science)
BESc/LLB
LLB/MA (philosophy)
UWO/Laval Law Joint Programme

Journal

Canadian Journal of Law and Jurisprudence (biannually)

Centres

1   National Tax Centre
2   Canada-US Law Institute
3   Dispute Resolution Centre
4   The Sports Solution
5   Community Legal Services

UNIVERSITY OF WINDSOR

Faculty of Law, 401 Sunset Avenue, Windsor, Ontario N9B 3P4, Canada
Tel: +1 519 2534232 ext 2930; Fax: +1 519 9737064
email: jberrym@uwindsor.ca
website: http://athena.uwindsor.ca/law

Courses offered

LLB
MBA/LLB
JD/LLB (in association with the University of Detroit Mercy)

Centres

1 Canadian-American Research Centre
2 Intellectual Property Law Institute

Journals

1 *Windsor Yearbook of Access to Justice*
2 *Windsor Review of Legal and Social Issues*

YORK UNIVERSITY

Osgoode Hall Law School, 4700 Keele Street, North York, Ontario M3J 1P3, Canada
Tel: +1 416 7365199; Fax: +1 416 7365251
email: lawdean@osgoode.yorku.ca
website: www.osgoode.yorku.ca

Courses offered

LLB
LLM
DJur

Centre

1 Nathanson Centre for the Study of Organised Crime and Corruption
2 Institute for Feminist Legal Studies
3 York University Centre for Public Law and Public Policy

Journal

Osgoode Hall Law Journal

BAR COUNCILS AND LAW SOCIETIES

FEDERATION OF LAW SOCIETIES OF CANADA

Suite 480, 445 Boulevard Saint-Laurent, Montreal, Quebec, Canada
Tel: +1 514 8756350; Fax: +1 514 8756115
email: info@flsc.ca
website: www.flsc.ca

BARREAU DE QUÉBEC

email: battonier@barreau.qc.ca
website: www.barreau.qc.ca

LAW SOCIETY OF ALBERTA

Suite 600, 919-11th Avenue SW, Calgary T2R 1P3, Alberta, Canada
Tel: +1 403 2294700; Fax: +1 403 2281728
email: comdir@lawsocietyalberta.com

LAW SOCIETY OF BRITISH COLUMBIA

8th floor, 845 Cambie Street, Vancouver V6B 4Z9, British Columbia, Canada
Tel: +1 604 6692533; Fax: +1 604 6695232
email: memberinfo@lsbc.org

LAW SOCIETY OF MANITOBA

219 Kennedy Street, Winnipeg R3C 1S8, Manitoba, Canada
Tel: +1 204 9425571; Fax: +1 204 9560624
email: admin@lawsociety.mb.ca

LAW SOCIETY OF NEW BRUNSWICK

Suite 206, 1133 Regent Street, Fredericton E3B 3Z2, New Brunswick, Canada
Tel: +1 506 4588540; Fax: +1 506 4511421
email: general@lawsociety.nb.ca

LAW SOCIETY OF NEWFOUNDLAND

Baird's Cove, 215 Water Street, PO Box 1028, St John's A1C 5M3, Newfoundland,
Canada
Tel: +1 709 7224740; Fax: +1 709 7228902
email: peter.ringrose@lawsociety.nf.ca

LAW SOCIETY OF THE NORTHWEST TERRITORIES

Lower Level, Laurentian Building, 4918-50th Street, PO Box 1298, Yellowknife NT
XIA, Canada
Tel: +1 867 8733828; Fax: +1 867 8736344
email: whitford-lsnt@TheEdge.ca

NOVA SCOTIA BARRISTER'S SOCIETY

Centennial Building, 1101–1645 Granville Street, Halifax B3J 1X3, Nova Scotia, Canada
Tel: +1 902 4221491; Fax: +1 902 4294869
email: infomail@nsbs.ns.ca

LAW SOCIETY OF NUNAVUT

PO Box 149, Iqaluit XOA OHO, NU, Canada
Tel: +1 867 9792330; Fax: +1 867 9792333
email: lawsoc@nunanet.com

LAW SOCIETY OF SASKATCHEWAN

Suite 1100, 2500 Victoria Avenue, Regina S4P 3X2, Saskatchewan, Canada
Tel: +1 306 5698242; Fax: +1 306 3522989
email: reception@lawsociety.sk.ca

LAW SOCIETY OF UPPER CANADA

130 Queen Street West, Toronto M5H 2N6, Ontario, Canada
Tel: +1 416 9473308; Fax: +1 416 9473448
email: mdoyle@lsuc.on.ca

LAW SOCIETY OF YUKON

Suite 201, 302 Steele Street, Whitehorse Y1A 2C5, Yukon, Canada
Tel: +1 867 6684231; Fax: +1 867 6677556
email: lsy@yknet.yk.ca

THE CARIBBEAN

The scheme of legal education in the Caribbean involves a collaboration between the University of the West Indies (UWI) and the University of Guyana. To practise law in any of the Caribbean countries, a student must first obtain an LLB degree from UWI or the University of Guyana.

The faculty of law was established at UWI in 1970, with its headquarters at the Cave Hill Campus in Barbados. The faculty offers both an undergraduate and a postgraduate programme. The LLB course is divided into three parts: Part I is offered at the UWI Cave Hill (Barbados), Mona (Jamaica) and St Augustine (Trinidad) campuses. Parts II and III are offered at the Cave Hill campus only. The University of Guyana also offers a three-year LLB course.

A challenge programme is offered in the non-campus territories to allow persons who are not registered on the undergraduate programme to take examinations in Part I of the LLB. A certificate course is then open to persons who have completed the Part I LLB programme on the challenge programme. These candidates are required to pass two additional courses in order to qualify for the award of the Certificate in Introductory Legal Studies.

The CLEA Executive Committee member for the region is Keith Sobion of the Norman Manley Law School, Jamaica (address below) (email: nmls1@hotmail.com).

Entry into the legal profession of all the Caribbean territories is regulated by the law of the particular territory, but, as a result of a regional agreement, the basic requirements tend to follow a common pattern. Since 1975, a Legal Education Certificate is normally required by a prospective lawyer. This is granted by the Council of Legal Education of the West Indies which was established by treaty in 1971 by several Caribbean countries from The Bahamas in the north to Guyana in the south. The certificate is granted to a student who successfully completes a two-year course of full time training at one of the Council's three law schools: the Norman Manley Law School in Jamaica, the Hugh Wooding Law School in Trinidad and the Eugene Dupuch Law School in The Bahamas. Entry into a law school will normally be granted to any applicant holding an LLB degree from UWI or the University of Guyana. Students who hold law degrees from other universities may be admitted if places are available but the Council has the power to lay down additional entry requirements. The schools also conduct a transitional six-month programme for persons who hold equivalent law degrees and have been admitted to practice in another common law jurisdiction.

Holders of a Legal Education Certificate will be regarded by all governments in the West Indies as having satisfied institutional and educational requirements for practice, although local legislation may add further requirements, such as that of nationality, which must be satisfied before the right to practise is granted in a particular territory. Full details can be obtained from the various professional bodies whose names and addresses are set out below. In those States which have not yet acceded to the Treaty, including The Bahamas, St Lucia, St Vincent, Cayman Islands and the Turks and Caicos Islands, persons qualified in the United Kingdom can be admitted to practice. Trinidad and Tobago also permits a limited right of admission with the fiat of the Attorney-General for persons of 10 years standing who are qualified in the United Kingdom.

Cayman Islands Law School offers a Bachelor of Laws degree in conjunction with the University of Liverpool. It also runs a one-year local professional legal training programme.

There are some variations regarding the court structure between the various jurisdictions. Essentially, however, the structure involves magistrates' courts at the lowest level, together with a Supreme Court which comprises a High Court and a Court of Appeal. The Organisation of Eastern Caribbean States (OECS) which comprises Antigua and Barbuda; Dominica; Grenada, Montserrat, St Kitts and Nevis; Saint Lucia and St Vincent and the Grenadines (with the British Virgin Islands and Anguilla as associate members) share a single Supreme Court. The Eastern Caribbean Supreme Court with its two divisions, the High Court of Justice and the Court of Appeal, administers the laws of each OECS Member State. The Supreme Court is headed by the Chief Justice. High Court judges are based in each Member State, but the judges of the Court of Appeal are resident in St Lucia and travel to each territory to hear appeals from the High Court.

It is likely that a Caribbean Court of Appeal will replace recourse to the Judicial Committee of the Privy Council, which is currently the final court of appeal for the other Caribbean countries.

LAW REPORTS

- *West Indies Law Reports* (a compilation of cases from several Caribbean jurisdictions)
- Some decisions of the Supreme Court of Jamaica are available free of charge from www.sc.gov.jm
- The law library at the Faculty of Law, UWI, Cave Hill, Barbados (address below), has a good collection of unreported decisions from several jurisdictions
- *Cayman Islands Law Reports*
- *Law Reports of The Bahamas* (1965–date)
- Selected decisions from the Supreme Court in The Bahamas are available free of charge from www.lexbahamas.com
- Many decisions of the Judicial Committee of the Privy Council are available free of charge on www.bailii.org.uk/cases

LAW SCHOOLS

CAYMAN ISLANDS LAW SCHOOL

The Tower Building, George Town, Grand Cayman, Cayman Islands, BVI
Tel: +345 2443544; Fax: +345 9461845
email: vaughan.carter@gov.ky

Courses offered

LLB (in conjunction with the University of Liverpool)
Diploma in Legal Studies

Journal

Cayman Islands Law Bulletin (contains local unreported decisions and articles of local interest)

EUGENE DUPUCH LAW SCHOOL

Old National Insurance Building, Farrington Road, Nassau NP, The Bahamas
Tel: +242 3268507/8; Fax: +242 3268504
email: admin@edls.edu.bs

Course offered

Legal Education Certificate

Centre

Legal Aid Clinic

UNIVERSITY OF GUYANA

Faculty of Social Sciences, Department of Law, Turkeyan Campus, Greater
Georgetown, PO Box 101110, Guyana
Tel: +592 2224946; Fax: +592 2224940
email: deptlawuni@solutions2000.net; r_w_james@hotmail.com

Course offered

LLB

Journal

Guyana Law Review (biannually) (contains articles on legal issues of local and regional
interest. Contact the General Editor, Guyana Law Review, Department of Law,
University of Guyana, as above)

NORMAN MANLEY LAW SCHOOL

Council of Legal Education, PO Box 231, Mona, Kingston 7, Jamaica
Tel: +1876 9271235; 9271899; Fax: +1876 9273533
email: nmls1@hotmail.com

Courses offered

LLB (Year 1 only)
Legal Education Certificate

HUGH WOODING LAW SCHOOL

Council of Legal Education, PO Bag 323, Tunapuna, Trinidad
Tel: +1868 6625835; Fax: +1868 6620927
email: clehwls@carib-link.net

Courses offered

LLB (Year 1 only)
Legal Education Certificate

UNIVERSITY OF THE WEST INDIES

Faculty of Law, Cave Hill Campus, St Michael, PO Box 64, Bridgetown, Barbados
Tel: +1246 4174215; 4174216; Fax: +1246 2421788
email: aburgess@uwichill.edu.bb
website: www.uwichill.edu.bb

Courses offered

LLB
LLM (includes a legislative drafting option but this is only open to members of the legal profession who are specifically nominated by their governments)
PhD
Advanced Diploma in Law

Centre

Caribbean Law Institute (jointly with Florida State University)

Journals

1   *Caribbean Law and Business*
2   *The Caribbean Law Review*

BAR ASSOCIATIONS AND LAW SOCIETIES

ORGANISATION OF COMMONWEALTH CARIBBEAN BAR ASSOCIATIONS

email: occba@hotmail.com

ORGANISATION OF EASTERN CARIBBEAN STATES (OECS) BAR ASSOCIATION

website: www.oecsbar.org

ANGUILLA BAR ASSOCIATION

email: mitchellm@candw.com.ai

ANTIGUA AND BARBUDA BAR ASSOCIATION

Roberts & Co, Chambers, Nevis Street, St John's, Antigua
Tel: +1268 4620076; Fax: +1268 4623077

BAHAMAS BAR ASSOCIATION

PO Box N-4632, Nassau, The Bahamas
Tel: +1242 3263276; Fax: +1242 3284615
email: bba@batelnet.bs

BARBADOS BAR ASSOCIATION
Reece Chambers, Motley House, Coleridge Street, Bridgetown, Barbados
Tel: +1246 4377316; Fax: +1246 2281739

BRITISH VIRGIN ISLANDS BAR ASSOCIATION
PO Box 71, Road Town, Tortola, BVI
Tel: +809 4942233; Fax: +809 4943547

CAYMAN ISLANDS LAW SOCIETY
PO Box 10390, APO, George Town, Grand Cayman
Tel: +1345 9498066; Fax: +1345 9498080
email: csj@mapples.candw.ky

DOMINICA BAR ASSOCIATION
PO Box 2000, Roseau, Dominica
Tel: +767 4480200; Fax: +767 4480202
email: bruneym@cwdom.dm

GRENADA BAR ASSOCIATION
c/o R Ferguson, President
email: ciboneychambers@caribsurf.com

GUYANA BAR ASSOCIATION
39 Brickdam, Stabroek, Georgetown, Guyana
Tel: +592 264871; 262671

JAMAICAN BAR ASSOCIATION
78–80 Harbour Street, Kingston, Jamaica
Tel: +1876 9671528; Fax: +1876 9673783

MONTSERRAT BAR ASSOCIATION
PO Box 1, Marine Drive, Plymouth, Montserrat
Tel: +491 2498; Fax: +491 2943

ST KITTS AND NEVIS BAR ASSOCIATION
PO Box 180, Basseterre, St Kitts-Nevis

ST LUCIA BAR ASSOCIATION/ST LUCIA LAW SOCIETY
c/o Mrs L Williams, President
email: williamsl@candw.lc

ST VINCENT AND THE GRENADINES BAR ASSOCIATION
PO Box 951, Marcole Plaza, Halifax Street, Kingstown, St Vincent
Tel: +1784 4561523; Fax: +1784 4562622
email: lawyer@caribsurf.com

LAW ASSOCIATION OF TRINIDAD AND TOBAGO

c/o Marie de Vere Chambers, 90 Maraval Road, Port of Spain, Trinidad and Tobago
Tel: +628 2324; Fax: +628 6271

TURKS AND CAICOS ISLANDS BAR ASSOCIATION

PO Box 97, Wigglesworth Building, Leeward Highway, Providenciales, Turks and
Caicos
Tel: +1809 1 9464344; Fax: +1809 1 9464955

GHANA

The General Legal Council, the statutory body established by the Ghana Legal Profession Act 1960, has responsibility for the organisation of legal education in Ghana. The Council has made arrangements for legal education through a school of law established by the Council itself, that is, the Ghana School of Law; and another independent institution, that is, the faculty of law of the University of Ghana.

The faculty of law offers a three-year LLB/BA law degree that covers the teaching of the core subjects and other law subjects and some selected subjects in humanities. After obtaining the LLB/BA law degree, the student who wishes to be trained as a professional lawyer must proceed to the Ghana School of Law for a further two-year Professional Law Course (PLC). In addition to the PLC, the Ghana School of Law runs two other courses: (a) a two-year Preliminary Law Course for non-graduates who study the seven core subjects. Successful candidates proceed to do the two-year PLC; and (b) a three-month post-call course in two subjects: Ghana constitutional law and customary law for persons already qualified as lawyers outside Ghana, in a country exercising a common law system analogous to Ghana. Candidates who successfully complete the two-year Professional Law Course or the post-call course at the Ghana School of Law, are qualified for enrolment by the General Legal Council as barristers and solicitors after doing six months' pupillage in the chambers of another lawyer of not less than seven years' standing as a lawyer in Ghana. Approximately 70 law students graduate each year for enrolment as barristers and solicitors.

There is no association of law teachers in Ghana. However, all law teachers at the Ghana School of Law and the Faculty of Law Legon – being professional lawyers – are members of the Ghana Bar Association.

The CLEA West Africa Chapter is situated at the Ghana School of Law. The CLEA regional representative is Seth Bimpong-Buta (email: sethbb@hotmail.com).

All matters pertaining to the Ghana Bar Association should be directed to the National Secretary, Ghana Bar Association, PO Box 4150, Accra, Ghana (Tel: +233 21 226748; Fax: +233 21 068115; email: okudzeto@ncs.com.gh).

The system of law is based on the common law which has been defined by Art 11(2) of the 1992 Constitution of Ghana as comprising 'the rules of law generally known as the common law, the rules generally known as the doctrines of equity and the rules of customary law including those determined by the Superior Court of Judicature'.

The legal profession is fused and a person can, after enrolment, practise as a barrister or solicitor or both. Practitioners from other common law systems may apply to the General Legal Council for the right of audience in the Ghana courts on an *ad hoc* basis under s 3(2) of the Legal Profession Act 1960. Persons from foreign jurisdictions who wish to practise permanently in Ghana must satisfy the General Legal Council that they are of good character and possess the qualifying certificate issued by the General Legal Council after passing the Professional Part I and II Examinations conducted by the Board of Legal Education through the Ghana School of Law.

LAW REPORTS

- *Ghana Law Reports* (1938–80)
- *Supreme Court of Ghana Law Reports* (1996–date). For further details contact The Editor in Chief, Advanced Legal Publications, PO Box JT222, James Town, Accra, Ghana (Fax: +233 21 778185)

LAW SCHOOLS

UNIVERSITY OF GHANA

Faculty of Law, PO Box 70, Legon, Ghana
Tel: +233 21 500304; Fax: +233 21 502385
email: Lawfac@ug.gn.ape.org

Courses offered

LLB/BA with Law
LLM

Centre

Human Rights Study Centre

Journal

University of Ghana Law Journal

GHANA SCHOOL OF LAW

PO Box 179, Accra, Ghana
Tel: +233 21 666582; Fax: +233 21 664822
email: gslawlib@Ghana.com

Courses offered

Professional Law Course (candidates must have obtained the LLB/BA with Law with passes in the seven core subjects, that is, law of contracts, law of torts, constitutional law, criminal law, property law, equity and succession and the Ghana legal system)

Preliminary Law Course (this is for non-law graduates and is followed by the two-year Professional Law Course)

Post-Call Course (this consists of courses in Ghanaian constitutional law and customary law for lawyers qualified in another common law jurisdiction)

Journal

Ghana School of Law Journal

HONG KONG

[Note: Since 1 July 1997, Hong Kong has been a special administrative region of the People's Republic of China. In view of the continuing close links between the universities in Hong Kong and the Commonwealth legal fraternity, it was felt appropriate to include this entry in the directory.]

The University of Hong Kong and City University of Hong Kong both offer a three-year LLB programme, and a one-year professional course, the Postgraduate Certificate in Laws, which law graduates must complete before they can proceed to pupillage (one year) or traineeship (two years). Both universities also offer taught LLM programmes as well as postgraduate research degree programmes.

The CLEA country contact is Anton Cooray of the City University of Hong Kong (address below) (email: l.w.cooray@cityu.edu.hk).

Whilst Hong Kong is a special administrative region of the People's Republic of China, its Basic Law provides for the continuation of its common law system, legal profession and system of courts. The only significant change effected by the Basic Law in the courts system is the creation of the Hong Kong Court of Final Appeal to take the place of the Judicial Committee of the Privy Council.

The legal profession consists of barristers and solicitors. There are 720 barristers and 4,700 solicitors in Hong Kong. The addresses of the governing bodies of the two professions are as follows: Hong Kong Bar Association, LG3 Supreme Court Building, 38 Queensway, Hong Kong; Tel: +852 28690210; Fax: +852 28690189; email: info@hkba.org; website: www.hkba.org; Law Society of Hong Kong, 3/F Wing On House, 71 Des Voeux Road, Central District, Hong Kong; Tel: +852 28460500; Fax: +852 28450387; email: sg@hklawsoc.org.hk; website: www.hklawsoc.org.hk.

Foreign lawyers may be admitted to the legal profession provided they pass the Overseas Lawyers Qualification Examination and meet certain other requirements, such as sufficient experience in practice. A legal practitioner from a foreign jurisdiction (so far only from Britain) with the permission of the Court of Appeal, may appear in a Hong Kong court in a specific matter.

LAW REPORTS

- *Hong Kong Law Reports*
- *Hong Kong Cases*
- *Hong Kong Law Reports* and *Digest*

LAW SCHOOLS

UNIVERSITY OF HONG KONG

Faculty of Law, 4/F KK Leung Building, Pokfulam Road, Hong Kong
Tel: +852 28592951; Fax: +852 25593543
email: lawfac@hkusua.hku.hk
website: www.hku.hk

Courses offered

LLB
PCLL (Postgraduate Certificate in Laws)
LLM
MCL (Master of Common Law)
Postgraduate Diploma in Commercial Law
Postgraduate Diploma in the Law Of The People's Republic of China
Postgraduate Diploma in Public Law
Postgraduate Diploma in Information Technology Law
Postgraduate Diploma in International Arbitration and Dispute Resolution
Doctor of Legal Science (SJD)

Centre

Centre for Comparative and Public Law

Journal

Hong Kong Law Journal

CITY UNIVERSITY OF HONG KONG

School of Law, 83 Tat Chee Avenue, Kowloon, Hong Kong
Tel: +852 27888008; Fax: +852 27887530
email: l.w.cooray@cityu.edu.hk
website: www.cityu.edu.hk

Courses offered

LLB
PCLL (Postgraduate Certificate in Laws)
MA in Arbitration and Dispute Resolution
LLM in Chinese and Comparative Law
LLM (joint programme with Renmin University of China)
MA in Language and Law (joint programme with the Department of Chinese, Translation and Linguistics)
Associate of Legal Studies

Centre

Centre for Chinese and Comparative Law

Journals

1 *Asia Pacific Law Review*
2 *Journal of Chinese and Comparative Law*

INDIA

There are 95 recognised universities in India providing legal education. However, there are many more law teaching institutions, most of which are colleges of law run by the State Government or are under private management. The medium of instruction is either English, Hindi, or both. Given their number, the list of law schools does not contain an entry for every law college in the country.

There are now five universities exclusively for legal education: National Law School of India, University at Bangalore; NALSAR University of Law (National Academy of Legal Studies and Research University) at Hyderabad; the National Law University at Jodhpur; National Law Institute University, Bhopal; and the National University of Juridical Science in Kolkata. The establishment of the Dr Ambedkar Law University in Tamil Nadu is another significant development as this brings all the affiliated law colleges in the State under the purview of this university. This is the first ever attempt at bringing all law colleges in a State under a single university.

The CLEA country contacts for India are S Sivakumar of the Kerala Law Academy (email: sivku98@hotmail.com) and A Raghunadha Reddy at the Sri Krishnadevaraya University (address below) (email: raghu_sku@yahoo.com).

The Bar Council of India has statutory powers to prescribe standards of legal education and to recognise degrees for professional qualification purposes. For enrolment as an Advocate, ie, a lawyer qualified to practise law in all courts and tribunals, a candidate must have an LLB (or equivalent) degree under a three-year programme after a first degree in arts, science or commerce, or under a five-year programme after the Higher Secondary School examination. As regards the latter, the Bar Council rules provide that a degree in law shall not be recognised for purposes of enrolment as an advocate unless the following conditions are fulfilled:

(a) That at the time of joining the course of instruction for the degree in law the person concerned has passed an examination in 10 + 2 courses of schooling recognised by the educational authority of the Central or the State Governments or possesses such academic qualifications which are considered equivalent to such 10 + 2 courses by the Bar Council of India.

(b) The law degree has been obtained after undergoing a regular course of study in a duly recognised law college for a minimum period of five years, out of which the first two years shall be devoted to the study of pre-law courses as a prerequisite for admission to a three-year course of study in law to be commenced thereafter. The last six months of the three years of the law course shall include a regular course of practical training.

(c) That during the course of study in law there has been regular attendance for the requisite number of lectures, tutorials, moot courts, and practical training given by a college affiliated to a University recognised by the Bar Council of India.

Practitioners from foreign jurisdictions seeking a right of audience on an *ad hoc* basis or wishing to practise in India should contact the Bar Council of India, 21 Rouse Avenue, International Area, Nr Bal Bhawan, New Delhi 110002, India (Tel: +91 11 3231647; Fax: +91 11 3231767). The Bar Association of India can be contacted at 93 Supreme Court Chambers, Supreme Court Building, New Delhi 110001, India (Tel: +91 11 3322601; Fax: +91 11 3329273).

LAW REPORTS

Law reporting is well developed with the main set of reports being:
- *All India Law Reports* (AIR)
- *Supreme Court Cases* (SCC)
- *Indian Law Reporter* (ILR)
- Decisions of the superior courts are available free of charge on www.judis.nic.in and www.indiancourts.nic.in
- Decisions of the Supreme Court are also available free of charge on www.supremecourtonline.com

LAW SCHOOLS

AGRA UNIVERSITY

Faculty of Law, Agra-282004, India
Tel: + 91 352946

Courses offered

LLB
LLM
PhD

AJMER UNIVERSITY

Law Department, Ajmer, Rajasthan, India

Course offered

LLB

ALIGARH MUSLIM UNIVERSITY

Department of Law, Aligarh, Uttar Pradesh-202 002, India
Tel: +91 400994; 400528
website: www.amu.ac.in

Courses offered

LLB
LLM
PhD
LLD
Diploma in Labour Law and Labour Relations

Journal

Aligarh Law Journal

ALLAHABAD UNIVERSITY

Department of Law, Allahabad, Uttar Pradesh-211002, India
website: www.allduniv.edu

Courses offered

LLB
LLM
LLD

AMRAVATHI UNIVERSITY

Faculty of Law, Amravati 444602, Maharashtra, India
Tel: +91 62173; 62358

Courses offered

Bachelor of General Law (BGL)
PhD

The following law colleges all offer a three-year LLB degree: Dr Panjabrao Deshmukh
College of Law; Sitabal Arts College, Akola; Amolakchand Mahavidyalaya, Yavatmal.
The degree awarded by the University is recognised by the Bar Council of India

ANDHRA UNIVERSITY

Department of Law, Waltair, Visakhapatnam, Andhra Pradesh-530003, India
Tel: +91 891 554871; Fax: +91 891 555547

Courses offered

LLB
BL
Bachelor of General Law
LLM
PhD

Affiliated colleges: All Saints Christian Educational Society College, Visakhapatnam;
CSKM College of Law; Dr BR Ambedkar College of Law, Visakhapatnam

ANNAMALAI UNIVERSITY

Department of Law (Distance Education), Annamalai Nagar, Tamil Nadu 608002,
India

Course offered

LLM

AWADHESH PRATAP SINGH UNIVERSITY

Faculty of Law, Rewa, Madhya Pradesh-486003, India
Tel: +91 22277; 22335

Courses offered

LLB
LLM
PhD

The following law colleges all offer an LLB degree: DCB Law College, Panna; Law College, Satna; Law College, Shadol; ML Nehru, Law College, Chatapur

BANARAS HINDU UNIVERSITY

Law School, Varanasi, Uttar Pradesh 221005, India
website: www.bhu.ac.in

Courses offered

LLB
LLM
PhD

BANGALORE UNIVERSITY

University Law College, Bangalore, Palace Road, Bangalore 560009, India
Tel: +91 80 3303023
website: www.bangaloreuniversity.net

Courses offered

LLB
LLM
PhD

The following affiliated colleges all offer an LLB degree: BMS College of Law, Bangalore Basavagundi, Bangalore; KLE Society's Law College, Bangalore; VV Puram Law College, Visweswara-Puram, Bangalore; Sri Jagadguru Renukachrya Law College, Ananda Rao Circle, Bangalore; Vidyodaya Law College, Tamkur, Bangalore; Dayanand Law College, Bangalore; GV Law College, KGF; Socio-Legal Services and Research Centre Law College, Bangalore

BARKATULLAH VISHWAVIDYALAYA, INSTITUTE OF OPEN AND DISTANCE EDUCATION

Department of Law, Hoshangabad Road, Bhopal 462026, Madhya Pradesh, India
Tel: +91 755 587151; 587236

Course offered

LLB

BERHAMPUR UNIVERSITY

Lingaraj Law College, Bhanja Bihar 760007, Ganjam, Berhampur, Orissa, India
Tel: +91 70615

Courses offered

LLB
LLM

Affiliated college: Ganjam Law College, Berhampur

BHAGALPUR UNIVERSITY

Faculty of Law, Bhagalpur, Bihar 812007, India

Course offered

LLB

BHARATHIDASAN UNIVERSITY

Palkalai Perur, Tiruchirapalli, Tamil Nadu 620024, India
Tel: +91 896245

Course offered

BL

BHARATHIAR UNIVERSITY

Faculty of Law, Coimbatore, Tamil Nadu 641046, India
Tel: +91 422222

Course offered

BL

BHAVNAGAR UNIVERSITY

Faculty of Law, Gaurishanker Lake Road, Bhavnagar, Gujarat 364002, India
website: www.bhavnagar.com/bhavuni/bhavuni.htm

Course offered

LLB

BHOPAL UNIVERSITY

Hamidia Government Postgraduate Law College, Bhopal, Madhya Pradesh, India

Course offered

LLB

BIHAR YOGA BHARATI

Faculty of Law, Muzaffarpur, Bihar State 842001, India

Course offered

BL

UNIVERSITY OF MUMBAI (BOMBAY)

Department of Law, Mumbai, Maharashtra State 400032, India
Tel: +91 22 2652819; 2652825; Fax: +91 22 2652832
email: webmaster@glc.edu
website: www.mu.ac.in

Courses offered

LLB
LLM
PhD

The following law colleges all offer both a BCL and LLB degree programme: Government Law College, Mumbai; KC Law College, Mumbai; New Law College, Mumbai; Siddharth Law College, Mumbai; Jitendra Chauhan College of Law, Vile Parle, W Mumbai; Dr Ambedkar College of Law, Tilak Road, Mumbai; GJ Advani Law College, Bandra, Mumbai; Goa University, Goa; VM Salgaoncar College of Law, Miramar, Goa (email: mrkprasad@indiatimes.com; website: www.vmslaaw.edu); Vidya Vardhak Mandal's GRK College of Law, Margao, Goa; Glam Das Jamatmal Advani Law College, Mumbai

BUNDELKHAND UNIVERSITY

Law Department, Kanpur Road, Jhansi, Uttar Pradesh 284128, India

Course offered

LLB

UNIVERSITY OF BURDWAN

Department of Law, PO Rajbati, Distt Burdwan, West Bengal 713104, India

Courses offered

LLB
LLB
LLM

UNIVERSITY OF CALCUTTA

Faculty of Law, 51/1 Hazra Road, Kolkata, West Bengal 700 019, India; College Street, Calcutta, West Bengal 700072, India
Tel: +91 33 4755801; Fax: +91 33 2413222
website: www.netguruindia.com

Courses offered

LLB
LLB (Hons)
LLM
LLD
PhD

The following law colleges all offer an LLB degree programme: University College of Law, Calcutta; Surendranath Law College, Calcutta; Jogeschchandra Chaudhri Law College, Calcutta; South Calcutta College for Girls, Calcutta

UNIVERSITY OF CALICUT
Government Law College, Marikunnu PO, Calicut 12, India; Thrissur, Kerala, India
website: www.calicutnet.com

Courses offered

LLB
LLM

The holder of an LLB degree is competent to practise as an Advocate

COCHIN UNIVERSITY OF SCIENCE AND TECHNOLOGY
School of Legal Studies, Ernakulam, Kerala 682022, India
Tel: +91 484 555465; Fax: +91 484 555463
email: sls@cusat.ac.in
website: www.cusat.ac.in

Courses offered

LLB
LLM
PhD
Diploma in Labour Law

Journal

Cochin University Law Review

UNIVERSITY OF DELHI
Faculty of Law, Delhi 11007, India
Tel: +91 11 7667725
website: www.du.ac.in

Two more departments are:
Campus Law Centre I and Campus Law Centre II, New Delhi

Courses offered

LLB
LLM
Master of Comparative Laws
PhD

Journals

1   *Delhi Law Review*
2   *Capital National Law Journal*

AMITY LAW SCHOOL

E-27, Defence Colony, New Delhi 110024, India
Tel: +91 11 4621960; 4699700
website: www.amity.edu/als

Course offered

LLB

DIBRUGARH UNIVERSITY

Department of Law, Dibrugarh, Assam 786004, India

Course offered

LLB

GURU NANAK DEV UNIVERSITY

Department of Law, Amritsar, Punjab 143005, India

Course offered

LLB

There are law colleges at Golaghat, Sibsagar, Dibrugarh and Tinsukla, and each award an LLB degree

GOA UNIVERSITY

Department of Law, Bombolim, Santa Cruz, Goa, India

Course offered

LLB

GORAKHPUR UNIVERSITY

Department of Law, Gorakhpur, Uttar Pradesh 273009, India

Courses offered

LLB
LLM
PhD
Diploma in Labour Law

GULBARGA UNIVERSITY

Faculty of Law, Jnana Ganga, Gulbarga, Karnataka-585106, India
Tel: +91 8472 45446
e-mail: gu@vsnl.com
website: www.gulbargauniversity.kar.nic.in

Course offered

LLM

GUWAHATI UNIVERSITY

Department of Law, Gopinath Bardoloi Nagar, Guwahati 781014, Assam, India

Postgraduate Department of Law
LLM
PhD

Journal

Guwahati University Journal of Law

University Law College
LLB
LLM
PhD

The following law colleges also award an LLB degree: JB Law College, Guwahati; Government Law College, Guwahati; Nowgong Law College, Nowgong, Assam; Tezpur Law College, Assam; Barpeta Law College, Barpeta, Assam; Dhubl Law College, Dhubrl, Assam; Diphu Law College, Diphu, Assam; AK Chanda Law College, Silchar, Assam

GUJARAT UNIVERSITY

Law Department, Sector 21, Plot 162, Gardhinagar, Ahmedabad, Gujarat State 380009, India

Courses offered

LLM
PhD

There are also the following law colleges: MS Bhagat and CS Sonawala Law College, Nadlad; Navgujarat Law College, Ahmedabad; People Edu-Society Law College, Bhuj; Sir LA Shaw Law College, Ahmedabad; Shri CV Shah Law College; Sarajanvik Law College, Godhra; IM Nanavati Law College, Ahmedabad; Motilal Nehru Law College, Ahmedabad; MN Law College, Ahmedabad

GURU GHASIDAS UNIVERSITY

Department of Law, Kaushalendra Rao Law College, Bilaspur Madhya Pradesh 495009, India

Course offered

LLB

DR HARISINGH GAUR, VISHWAVIDYALAYA (FORMERLY THE UNIVERSITY OF SAUGO SAGAR)

Gour Nagar, Sagar, Madhya Pradesh 47003, India
Tel: +91 22417

Courses offered

LLB
LLM
PhD

Affiliated colleges: DBC College, Panna; Government College, Bina; Government College, Tikamgarh

HEMVATI NANDAN BAHUGUNA GARHWAL UNIVERSITY

Department of Law, Sri Nagar, Garhwal Uttar Pradesh, India

Course offered

LLB

HIMACHAL PRADESH UNIVERSITY

Department of Law, Summer Hills, Shimla, Himachal Pradesh 171005, India
website: http://hpuniv.nic.in

Courses offered

LLB
LLM

INDORE UNIVERSITY

Law Department, Indore, Madhya Pradesh, India

Course offered

LLB

INSTITUTE OF JUDICIAL TRAINING AND RESEARCH
Tel: +91 522 300545; Fax: +91 522 300546
website: http://ijtr.nic.in

UNIVERSITY OF JAMMU
Department of Law, Canal Road, Jammu Tavi, Jammu and Kashmir 180001, India

Courses offered

LLB
LLM

JAI NARAIN VYAS UNIVERSITY
Faculty of Law, Jodhpur, Rajastan 34001, India
Tel: +91 291 31733

Courses offered

LLB
LLB (postgraduate course)
Diploma in Labour Law, Labour Welfare and Personnel Management
Postgraduate Diploma in Legislative Drafting
Postgraduate Diploma in Criminology with special reference to India
Postgraduate Diploma in Legal Science
LLM
PhD

Affiliated college: Ganga Singh College, Chapra

JIWAJI UNIVERSITY
Faculty of Law, Vidya Vihar, Gwalior, Madhya Pradesh, India
Tel: +91 341896

Course offered

LLB

JODHPUR UNIVERSITY
Faculty of Law, Jodhpur, Rajasthan, India

Course offered

LLB

KAKATIYA UNIVERSITY
Vidyarayanyapuri, Warangal 506 009, India

Course offered

LLM

Affiliated college: Adarshaw Law College, Hanamkonda

KANPUR UNIVERSITY

Law Department, Kalyanpur Kanpur, Uttar Pradesh, India

Course offered

LLB

KANNUR UNIVERSITY

Mangathupamba, Kalliaseri, Kannur 670562, India

Courses offered

LLB
LLM

Centre

Centre for Legal Studies, Thellecherry, Kerala, India

KARNATAKA UNIVERSITY

Department of Law, Pavate Nagar, Dharwad, Karnataka 580003, India

Courses offered

LLM
PhD

The following law colleges all offer a three-year LLB programme: University College of Law, Dharwar; JSS Sakri Law College, Hubil; SAM Evening Law College, Gadag; GK Evening Law College, Hubil; KPES Evening Law College, Dharwad; MES Law College, Sirsi; BVB Law College, Belgaum; Anjuman Law College, Bijapur; BVVS's Basaveshwar Law College, Bagalkot

UNIVERSITY OF KASHMIR

Department of Law, University Campus, Hazratbal, Srinagar 190006, India

Course offered

LLB
LLM

UNIVERSITY OF KERALA

Department of Law, Kerala University Campus, Kariavattom, Thiruvananthapuram, Kerala 695581, India
website: www.keralauniversity.edu

Courses offered

LLB
LLM
LLD
PhD
Postgraduate Diploma in Law

The following law colleges offer an LLB degree programme: Government Law College, Trivandrum; Kerala Law Academy, Peroorkada, Trivandrum

Journals

1 *Kerala University Journal of Legal Studies*
2 *Academy Law Review*

Centre

Centre for Advanced Legal Studies and Research

KUMAUN UNIVERSITY
Department of Law, Nainital, Uttar Pradesh 263001, India

Course offered

LLB

KURUKSHETRA UNIVERSITY
Law Department, Kurukshetra, Haryana 132119, India

Courses offered

LLB
LLM
PhD

KUVEMPU UNIVERSITY
Department of Law, Gnanasahyadri, Vishwaivyanilaya Karya Soudha BR Projects, Shimoga Dist, Karnataka 577451, India

Course offered

LLB

LALIT NARAYAN MITHILA UNIVERSITY
Department of Law, Kameshwaranagar, Darbhanga, Bihar 846008, India

Course offered

LLB

UNIVERSITY OF LUCKNOW

Department of Law, Badshah Bagh, Lucknow, Uttar Pradesh 226007, India

Courses offered

LLB
LLM
LLD
Postgraduate Diploma in Criminology (PGDC)

The LLB degree is an essential qualification for enrolment as an advocate. The LLM and LLD provide the necessary qualification for appointment to a university law school. The PGDC provides a qualification for appointment to the police, prisons and juvenile justice departments

UNIVERSITY OF MADRAS

Department of International Law and Constitution Law, Centenary Building, Chepauk, Chennai 600005, India
Tel/Fax: +91 44 538 9159
email: info@universityofmadras.edu
website: www.universityofmadras.edu

Courses offered

Bachelor of General Law
LLM (international and constitutional law)
LLD
PhD

MADURAI-KAMARAJ UNIVERSITY

Faculty of Law, Palkalai Nagar, Madurai, Tamil Nadu 625021, India

Course offered

Bachelor of General Law (under correspondence scheme)

MAGADH UNIVERSITY

Law Department, Bodh Gaya, Bihar 824234, India

Course offered

LLB

MAHARSHI DAYANAND SARASWATI UNIVERSITY

Faculty of Law, Ajmer, Rajastan 305001; Faculty of Law, Rohtak 124001, India

Courses offered

LLB
LLM
LLD

Affiliated college: Dunger College, Bikaner

Centre

Legal Aid and Advice Clinic

MAHATMA GANDHI UNIVERSITY

School of Indian Legal Thought, Nagambadom, Kottayam, Kerala, India

Courses offered

LLB
LLM
PhD

Government College, Ernakulam offering both three-year and five-year LLB courses

MANGALORE UNIVERSITY

Faculty of Law, Mangalagangothri, Karnataka 574199, India

Courses offered

LLB
LLM

Affiliated college: Dharmasthala Manjunatheshwara College, Mangalore

MANIPUR UNIVERSITY

School of Humanities and Social Sciences, Canchipur, Imphal, Manipur 795003, India

Course offered

LLB

MARATHWADA UNIVERSITY

Manikachand Pahade Law College, Aurangabad, Maharashtra 431004, India

Courses offered

LLB
Diploma in Taxation Law
Diploma in Labour Laws

The LLB degree is sufficient for legal practice

There are also the following law colleges: Dr Ambedker Law College, Mumbai; Dayanand College of Law, Latur; Shivaji Law College, Parbhani; Law College Nanded; Seth Balaram Kabra Shri GR Sikchi Law College, Jaina; Law College, Osmanabad. All offer a BA/LLB programme that is sufficient for entry into legal practice

MEERUT UNIVERSITY

Law Department, Meerut, Uttar Pradesh, India

Course offered

LLB

MS UNIVERSITY OF BARODA

Department of Law, Vadodara, Gujarat State 390002, India

Courses offered

LLB
LLM
BGL

UNIVERSITY OF MYSORE

Department of Studies in Law, Mysore Viswavidyanilaya, Karya Soudha, Crawford Hall, PB No 406, Mysore, Karnataka 570005, India

Courses offered

LLB
LLM

There are also the following law colleges: Sharadavilas Law College, Mysore; Vidyavardhaka Law College, Mysore; JSS Law College, Mysore; Gopi Law College, Arasikere; PES Law College, Mandya; H Hombegowda Memorial Law College, Mandya; M. Krishna Law College, Hassan. All colleges provide a three-year LLB course

NAGARJUNA UNIVERSITY

Nagarjuna Nagar, Guntur, Andhra Pradesh 522510, India
Tel: +91 25555

Course offered

LLM

Affiliated law college: DSR Hindu College of Law, Machilipatanam

NAGPUR UNIVERSITY

Faculty of Law, Ravindrinath Tagore Marg, Nagpur, Maharashtra 440001, India

Courses offered

LLM
LLD

The University College of Law, Nagpur and Dr Punjab Rao, Deshmukh College of Law, Amravati both provide a three-year LLB course

NALSAR UNIVERSITY OF LAW (NATIONAL ACADEMY OF LEGAL STUDIES AND RESEARCH UNIVERSITY)

Justice City, Shameerpet, Rangareddy Dist, Hyderabad 500 014, AP, India
Tel: +91 841 845159; Fax: +91 841 845161
email: director@nalsarlawuniv.org
website: www.nalsarlawuniv.org

Courses offered

BA/BL (Hons)
LLM
PhD
Postgraduate Diploma in Patents Law
Postgraduate Diploma in Media Laws
Postgraduate Diploma in Cyber Laws
Postgraduate Diploma in International Humanitarian Law

Journals

1   *NALSAR Law Review*
2   *Journal of Biotechnology and Law*
3   *Annual Survey of Andhra Law*

NATIONAL LAW SCHOOL OF INDIA UNIVERSITY

PO Bag 7201, Nagarbhavi, Bangalore 560 072, India
Tel: +91 80 3211303; Fax: +91 80 3217858
email: registrar@nls.ernet.in
website: www.nls.ac.in

Courses offered

BA/LLB (Hons)
LLM
MPhil
LLD

Centres

1   Centre for Child and the Law
2   Centre for Woman and Law
3   National Institute of Human Rights
4   Centre for Environmental Law, Education, Research and Advocacy
5   Institute for Law, Ethics and Medicine
6   Centre for Intellectual Property Law, Research and Advocacy

Journals

1   *National Law School Journal* (annually)
2   *March of the Law* (annually)

NATIONAL LAW UNIVERSITY

Administrative Block, JNV University, New Campus, Pali Road, Jodhpur 342001, India
Tel: +91 291 727883; Fax: +91 291 726682
email: nlu-jod@raj.nic.in
website: http://nlujodhpur.nic.in

Courses offered

BA/LLB (Hons)
BSc/LLB (Hons)
BBA/LLB (Hons)
LLM in Criminology, Criminal Law and Forensic Science
Masters in Constitutional Governance
Masters in Intellectual Property Rights
Masters in Law and Management
PhD

NATIONAL LAW INSTITUTE UNIVERSITY

Bhopal, Madhya Pradesh 462003, India
Tel: +91 755 234635

Courses offered

BA/LLB (Hons)
LLM

NORTH BENGAL UNIVERSITY

PO North Bengal University, Darjeeling, West Bengal 734430, India

Courses offered

BA Law
LLB
LLM

NORTH EASTERN HILL UNIVERSITY

Department of Law, Lower Lachaumiere, Shillong, Meghalaya 793001, India

Course offered

LLB

Affiliated colleges: Aizawl Law College, Aizawl; Shillong Law College, Shillong; Tura Law College, Tura

OSMANIA UNIVERSITY

University College of Law, Hyderabad, Andhra Pradesh 500007, India
Tel : +91 40 7682363; 7098043; Fax : +91 40 7090020
email: registrar@osmania.ac.in
website: www.osmania.ac.in

Courses offered

LLB
LLM
MPhil

Affiliated colleges: Andhra Mahila Sabha College of Law, Hyderabad; Anwarul Uloom College of Law, Hyderabad

PATNA UNIVERSITY

Faculty of Law, Patna, Bihar State 800005, India
Tel: +91 612 672941; Fax: +91 612 670877

Courses offered

LLM
PhD

PONDICHERRY UNIVERSITY

Faculty of Law, Nagar, Kalapet, Pondicherry 605014, India
Tel: +91 852177
website: www.pondiuni.org

Courses offered

LLB
LLM

Affiliated college: Dr Ambedkar Government Law College, Pondicherry

POORVANCHAL UNIVERSITY

Department of Law, Zafarbad Road Jaunpur, Uttar Pradesh, India

Course offered

LLB

UNIVERSITY OF PUNE (POONA)

Department of Law, Ganeshkind, Pune, Maharashtra 411007, India
Tel: +91 212 5692879; 5696061
email: vibhute@unipune.ernet.in
website: www.unipune.ernet.in

Courses offered

LLB
LLM
PhD

Diplomas in Women and Law; Environmental Law; Human Rights; Corporate Management

Affiliated college: Bharati Vidyapeeth's New Law College, Pune; ILS Law College (website: http://ilslaw.edu)

PUNJAB UNIVERSITY

Faculty of Law, Sector 14, Chandigarh 160014, India

Courses offered

BL
LLB
LLM
LLD
Advanced Diploma in Law
Advanced Diploma in Taxation

PUNJABI UNIVERSITY

Department of Law, Patiala, Punjab 147002, India
website: www.universitypunjabi.org

Courses offered

BL
LLB
LLM
Diploma in Taxation

UNIVERSITY OF RAJASTHAN

Department of Law, Jaipur, Rajasthan 302004, India

Courses offered

LLB
LLM
LLD
Diploma in Labour Law

Affiliated college: Baba Mungipaa Law College, Pilani

RANCHI UNIVERSITY

Chotanagour Law College, Ranchi, Bihar State 834008, India

Course offered

LLB

PANDIT RAVISHANKAR SHUKLA UNIVERSITY

Law Department, Raipur, Madhya Pradesh 492010, India
Tel: +91 533957

Courses offered

LLB
LLM

There are also the following law colleges: Kalyan Law College, Bhilai Nagar; Government Chattisgarh Law College, Raipur; SKTD Law College, Raipur; RCS Law College, Durg; Law College Rajnandigaon; Government College, Dhamtari; Government College, Baladabazar; Government College, Kanker; Government PG College, Jagdaipur. All provide a three-year LLB programme

ROHILKHAND UNIVERSITY
Faculty of Law, Bareilly, Uttar Pradesh 243123, India

Courses offered

LLB
LLM

Affiliated college: Bareilly College, Bareilly

SAMBALPUR UNIVERSITY
Faculty of Law College, Jyotivihar, PO Burla, Sambalpur, Orissa 768019, India

Courses offered

LLB
LLM
Postgraduate Diploma in Labour Law

SARDAR PATEL UNIVERSITY
Faculty of Law, Vidyanagar, Anand, Gujarat 388120, India

Courses offered

LLB
LLM
Diploma in Law and Practice

SAURASHTRA UNIVERSITY
Rajkot, Gujurat State 360005, India

Courses offered

LLB
LLM

There are several affiliated law colleges which offer the LLB degree: DD Kotiwala Municipal Law College, Porbandar; Municipal Law College, Gondal; Sangvi Law College, Rajkot

SHIVAJI UNIVERSITY

Shahaji Law College, Kolhapur, Vidyanagari, Kolhapur 416004, Maharashtra, India

Courses offered

LLB
Bachelor of Social Law and LLB (Special)
LLM
Diploma in Income Tax and Sales Tax
Diploma in Labour Law
Diploma in Mercantile Law

Affiliated college: Ismailsaheb Mulla Law College, Satara

SOUTH GUJARAT UNIVERSITY

Faculty of Law, PO Box 49, Surat, Gujarat State 395007, India

Courses offered

LLB
LLM

The following law colleges all offer an LLB programme: VTV Sarvajanik Law College, Surat; SKM Law College, Bulsar; VT Choksi Sarvajanik Law College, Surat; Dinshaw Daboo Law College, Navsari; Navyug Law College, Surat

SRI PADMAVATI MAHILA VISHWAVIDYALAYAM

Department of Law, Chittoor, Tirupati, Andhra Pradesh 517502, India

Courses offered

LLB
LLM
PhD

SRI KRISHNADEVARAYA UNIVERSITY

Faculty of Law, Anantapur, Andhra Pradesh 515003, India
Fax: +91 85 5422150
email: raghu_sku@yahoo.com

Courses offered

BL
LLM
Diploma in Labour Law
Diploma in Taxation
PhD

Affiliated college: Anantapur Law College, Anantapur

SRI VENKATESWARA UNIVERSITY
Department of Law, Tirupati, Andhra Pradesh 517502, India
Fax: +91 8574 24111

Courses offered

BL
LLM
PhD

Affiliated colleges: VR Law College, Nellore; Dr Ambedkar Law College, Tirupati

TAMIL NADU DR AMBEDKAR LAW UNIVERSITY
Poompozhil, 5 Greenways Road, Chennai 600028, India

Courses offered

LLB
BL
Bachelor of General Law
LLM
PhD

The following law colleges all offer a law programme: Government Law College, Chennai; Madurai Law College, Madurai; Government Law College, Tiruchy; Government Law College, Coimbatore; Central Law College, Salem; Government Law College, Thirunelveli

TRIPURA UNIVERSITY
Department of Law, PO Vani Vihar Bhubaneshwar, Orissa, India

Course offered

LLB

UTKAL UNIVERSITY
Law Department, Vani Vihar, Bhubaneswar, Dist Puri, Orissa 751004, India

Course offered

LLM

The following affiliated law colleges all offer an LLB degree programme: Athagarh Law College, Athargarh; Capital Law College, Bhubaneshwar; Madhusudan Law College, Cuttack; Mayur Bhanji Law College, Baripada, Mayurbhanj; Biswagura Law College, Cuttack; Gangadhar Mohapatra Law College, Puri

VIKRAM UNIVERSITY

Ujjain, Madya Pradesh 456010, India

Courses offered

LLB
LLM

The following law colleges all offer an LLB degree: Nagarpalika College, Raltam; Shri JL Nehru Law College, Mahavidyalaya, Mandsaur; Sandipani Law College, Ujjain

Notes:
1   Courses in law are also offered in the following universities, though there is no separate law department: Annamalal, Kakatiya, Kumaon, Maharishi Dayanand and Nagarjuna.
2   Jawaharlal Nehru University offers research facilities in its centre for Diplomacy, International Law and Economics in the School for International Studies (Tel: +91 11 6107676; 6167557; Fax +91 11 6165886; 6198234; website: www.jnu.ac.in).
3   Indian Law Institute, opp Supreme Court Building, New Delhi 110004 offers research facilities and conducts postgraduate diploma courses (website: www.ilidelhi.org).

Journal

Journal of Indian Law Institute

KENYA

In 1961, the first law faculty in East Africa was established at Dar-es-Salaarn as an external college of the University of London. The faculty was to produce law graduates for all the three East African countries. Later the Dar-es-Salaam College became a constituent College of the University of East Africa. Therefore, Kenyans could train as lawyers either at the Dar-es-Salaam College followed by one year of practical training at the Kenya School of Law, or through the articled clerk system at the School of Law.

In 1970, the University of East Africa was dissolved and each of the three countries established its own university. In the same year the articled clerk system of legal training in Kenya was phased out and a law faculty was established at the University of Nairobi with the Kenya School of Law providing the practical training for one year.

Today the University of Nairobi offers a four-year LLB degree and the Moi University offers a three-year LLB degree. The Kenya School of Professional Studies offers tuition for the external LLB degree from the University of London. The University of Nairobi also offers a parallel degree programme in law that aims to provide a cheap alternative for Kenyans who wish to study law.

The Kenya School of Law remains responsible for the completion of legal education of law graduates from the University of Nairobi as well as of law degree holders from recognised universities abroad wishing to be admitted to the Roll of Advocates in Kenya. The school provides a course of legal education of one year's duration, of which eight months is spent in an advocate's chambers and four months on a training programme. This is followed by an examination in subjects prescribed by the Council of Legal Education.

The CLEA country contact is William Musyoka of the University of Nairobi (address below) (Tel: +254 2 340477; Fax: +254 2 744284).

The system of law in Kenya is based on the common law. The superior court system comprises the Court of Appeal and the High Court.

The legal profession is fused. Practitioners from other common law systems may apply for the right of audience on an *ad hoc* basis in the Kenyan courts. Those from overseas jurisdictions who wish to practise in Kenya should contact the Law Society of Kenya, Professional Centre, Parliament Road, St John's Gate, PO Box 72219, Nairobi, Kenya (Tel: +254 2 229995; 225558; Fax: +254 2 223997; email: lsk@nbnet.co.ke).

LAW REPORTS

- *East African Court of Appeal Reports* I–XV (1934–48)
- *East Africa Law Reports* (1957–73)
- *Kenya Law Reports* (1976–80)
- *Kenya Appeal Reports* (1982–92)
- *The Law Reporter* (published by Librafile Books, PO Box 26663, Nairobi)
- *Lawafrica Law Reports* (LLR) (these provide online full text decisions of the Court of Appeal, Commercial Court and High Court: www.lawafrica.com (email: info@lawafrica.com)

LAW SCHOOLS

UNIVERSITY OF NAIROBI

Faculty of Law, Parklands Campus, PO Box 30197, Nairobi, Kenya
Tel: +254 2 340477; Fax: +254 2 744284
website: www.uonbi.ac.ke

Courses offered

LLB
LLM
PhD

Journal

University of Nairobi Law Journal

KENYA SCHOOL OF PROFESSIONAL STUDIES

Faculty of Law, PO Box 60550, Nairobi, Kenya
Tel: +254 2 7502558; Fax +254 2 750260
email: enquiries@swiftkenya.com
website: www.ksps.ac.ke

Courses offered

LLB (London External)
Diploma in Law (a bridging course for the LLB degree)

KENYA SCHOOL OF LAW

PO Box 30369, Nairobi, Kenya

Course offered

Diploma in Law

MOI UNIVERSITY

Faculty of Law, PO Box 3900, Eldoret, Kenya
Tel: +254 3 2143620; Fax: +254 3 2143047
website: www.mu.ac.ke

Course offered

LLB

LESOTHO

Legal education is conducted in the faculty of law of the National University of Lesotho. The faculty mounts two parallel programmes: a two tier six-year programme consisting of the Bachelor of Arts in Law degree (BA Law) which takes the first four years and the LLB degree which lasts for the other two years. This programme is tailored to meet the needs of those who intend to practise law in Lesotho. A three-year LLB programme is also offered, and this largely targets graduates from faculties other than law. The faculty of law has an internship programme for first year LLB students, in which they are attached to various legal practitioners both in Maseru and elsewhere. The object of the programme is to expose students to the problems and practice of the law in Lesotho.

The CLEA country contact is Umesh Kumar of the National University of Lesotho (address below) (email: u.kumar@nul.ls).

There is no local association of law teachers although some faculty members belong to the Society of Law Teachers of Southern Africa (SLTSA).

The system of law in Lesotho is mainly Roman-Dutch. The superior court system comprises the Court of Appeal which sits in Maseru and a High Court.

The legal profession is fused. Practitioners from other common law systems may apply to the courts for the right of audience on an *ad hoc* basis. Those from foreign jurisdictions who wish to practise in Lesotho should contact the Law Society of Lesotho, PO Box 2172, Maseru 102, Lesotho.

LAW REPORTS

- *Lesotho Law Reports* (1967–85)
- *Lesotho Law Reports and Legal Bulletin* (LLR-LB) (1991–date)
- Some decisions of the Court of Appeal are reported in the *South African Law Reports* and the *Law Reports of the Commonwealth*

LAW SCHOOL

NATIONAL UNIVERSITY OF LESOTHO
Faculty of Law, PO Roma 180, Lesotho
Tel: +266 340601; Fax: +266 340000
email: u.kumar@nul.ls
website: www.nul.ls

Courses offered

BA (law)
LLB (for law graduates)
LLB (for non-law graduates)

Journal

Lesotho Law Journal (a journal of law and development)

MALAWI

Legal education in Malawi is conducted in the faculty of law at the University of Malawi which is based in Zomba. The faculty offers a four-year honours degree in law for students who have already completed one year of general education at any college of the University, or at some other approved university. The faculty also admits applicants into its four-year programme if they have a degree or diploma from the University of Malawi or some other recognised university. Holders of the degree are entitled to practise subject to a one-year pupillage requirement.

The system of law is based on the common law, although customary law is important in some areas.

The superior court system comprises the Supreme Court of Appeal and a High Court.

The legal profession is fused. Practitioners from common law systems may apply for a right of audience on an *ad hoc* basis to the Malawian courts. Those from foreign jurisdictions wishing to practise in Malawi should contact the Malawi Law Society, Room 23, Elber House, PO Box 1712, Blantyre, Malawi (Tel: +265 623599; Fax: +265 625010).

LAW REPORTS

- *Malawi Law Reports* (formerly known as *African Law Reports (Malawi)*) (1958–89 (vols 1–12))
- Currently there is no series of local law reports, although some decisions of the Supreme Court of Appeal appear in the *Law Reports of the Commonwealth*

LAW SCHOOL

UNIVERSITY OF MALAWI

Faculty of Law, Chancellor College, PO Box 280, Zomba, Malawi
Tel: +265 524222; Fax: +265 524046
email: law@chirunga.sdnp.org.mw
website: www.unima.mw

Course offered

LLB

MALAYSIA

Legal education in Malaysia is conducted in the law faculties of the University of Malaya (UM), International Islamic University Malaysia (ILUM), Universiti Kebangsaan Malaysia (UKM) and Universiti Technologi MARA. All are located around the Klang Valley near Kuala Lumpur, the capital of Malaysia. Following the LLB degree, those wishing to practise must successfully complete the Certificate in Legal Practice and then undertake six months of chambers/practical work.

The CLEA country contact is Mohd Darbi Hashim of Universiti Teknologi Mara (address below) (email: darbi@salam.uitm.edu.my).

The legal profession in Malaysia is fused and, once admitted, practitioners discharge the functions of both solicitors and advocate. The superior courts consist of the High Court of Malaya, the High Court of Sebah and Sarawak, the Court of Appeal and the Federal Court.

Law graduates from approved UK universities wishing to practise in Malaysia must have obtained the Malaysian Certificate of Legal Practice before doing their pupillage. Law degrees from Singapore, Australia and New Zealand are also recognised. All overseas graduates must comply with the requirements set out by the Legal Profession Qualifying Board of Malaysia (LPQB). Further information can be obtained from the Bar Council of Malaysia, 5 Jalan Tun Perak, Pen Surat 12478, Kuala Lumpur 50050, Malaysia (email: council@malaysianbar.org.my; website: www.malaysianbar.org.my) or the LPQB (Fax: +60 3 2910142).

LAW REPORTS

- *Malaysia Law Journal*
- *All Malaysia Law Reports*
- *Current Law Journal*

LAW SCHOOLS

UNIVERSITY OF MALAYA

Faculty of Law, Kuala Lumpur 50603, Malaysia
Tel: +60 3 79676500; Fax: +60 3 795732239; 79558650
email: law@um.edu.my
website: www.um.edu.my

Courses offered

Bachelor of Jurisprudence (BJuris)
Bachelor of Jurisprudence (BJuris) (external)
Bachelor of Laws (LLB)
Master of Comparative Law (MCL)

Master of Criminal Justice (MCJ)
Master of Laws (LLM)
PhD
Certificate in Legal Practice

Journals

1   *Journal of Malaysian and Comparative Law* (JMCL) (publishes contributions from scholars all over the world. Its articles in both English and Bahasa Malaysia reflect its dual character as a Malaysian and comparative law journal
2   *Survey of Malaysian Law*

INTERNATIONAL ISLAMIC UNIVERSITY MALAYSIA

Kuliyyah of Laws, Jalan Gombak 53100, Kuala Lumpur, Malaysia
Tel: +60 6 20564000; Fax: +60 3 20564854
email: nahmad@iiu.edu.my
website: www.iiu.edu.my/laws

Courses offered

LLB
LLB Shari'ah (Bachelors of Laws in Shari'ah)
Master of Comparative Laws (MCL)
PhD
Diploma in Shari'ah Law and Practice (DSLP)

Diploma in Administration and Islamic Judiciary (DAIJ) (the Diploma courses are used to help upgrade the knowledge and skills of practising lawyers, Kadis and legal officers)

Centre

Law Centre
Objectives:

- To offer specialised courses on developing areas of law such as intellectual property, international trade, marine insurance, shipping, new financial instruments, Islamic financing, Takaful, building and construction law and cyberspace law.
- To undertake research in the field of Islamic financing and Islamic capital market.
- To administer the two diploma courses, DSLP and DAIJ, and to introduce new diploma and certificate courses.
- To publish legal materials.

UNIVERSITI TEKNOLOGI MARA

Faculty of Administration and Law, 40450 Shah Alam, Selangor Darul Ehsan, Malaysia
Tel: +60 3 55164123; Fax: +60 3 55108107
email: darbi@salam.uitm.edu.my
website: www.uitm.edu.my

Courses offered

LLB
Certificate in Legal Practice

MIT is an institution especially set up for the Bumiputeras

Journal

Universiti Technologi MARA Law Review (website: www.uitm-ejournal.edu.my)

UNIVERSITI KEBANGSAAN MALAYSIA

Faculty of Laws, 46300 Bangi, Selangor Darul Ehsan, Malaysia
Tel : +60 3 89213895; 89215338; Fax: +60 3 89252976
email: dpps@pkrisc.cc.ukm.my
website: www.ukm.my

Courses offered

LLB
LLM
PhD

MALTA

The faculty of law at the University of Malta is one of the oldest faculties in one of the oldest universities in Europe. Those wishing to practise must complete the three-year BA in Legal and Humanistic Studies and the one-year Diploma of Legal Procurator. They must also serve a period of one year in chambers.

The CLEA country contact is Elisa Demicoli of the University of Malta (address below) (email: elisa.demicoli@um.edu.mt).

The Maltese legal system is a reflection of the cross-currents which have influenced Malta's history and also European history as a whole. The civil law and common law systems have interacted to shape the Maltese legal system. There is a particular common law influence in the field of public law (for example, the Criminal Procedure Code), and also in commercial and maritime law.

The superior court system consists of the Constitutional Court and Court of Appeal. The official language of all legal proceedings is Maltese.

Practitioners from foreign jurisdictions who wish to practise in Malta should contact the Malta Chamber of Advocates, Law Courts, Republic Street, Valletta, Malta (Tel: +356 23231).

LAW REPORTS

- There is no regular series of local law reports
- Constitutional Court decisions are available online at www.home.um.edu.mt/laws

LAW SCHOOL

UNIVERSITY OF MALTA

Faculty of Laws, Block A, New Humanities Building, University of Malta, Msida, Malta
Tel: +356 21 333998; 23402780; Fax: +356 21 324478
email: laws@um.edu.mt
website: www.home.um.edu.mt/laws

Courses offered

BA (Legal and Humanistic Studies)
Master of Arts (MA) in Financial Services
Magister Juris (MJur) in European Union and Comparative Law
MA in Human Rights and Democratisation
Magister Juris (MJur) in International Law
Master of Philosophy (MPhil)

Doctor of Philosophy (PhD)
Doctor of Laws (LLD)
Diploma in Competition Law and Economics
Diploma of Legal Procurator
Diploma of Notary Public

Journals

1   *ID-DRITT Law Journal*
2   *Mediterranean Journal of Human Rights*

MAURITIUS

Legal education is carried out in two stages: the academic stage and the vocational stage. The law department of the University of Mauritius provides academic training through its LLB degree. In order to practise, a person must also pass a vocational course organised by the Council of Legal Education.

The CLEA country contact is Rosario Domingue of the University of Mauritius (address below) (email: rdomingu@uom.ac.mu).

The system of law in Mauritius is influenced by both French civil law and the common law. The French Civil Code, Commercial Code and Penal Code are all in force with local modifications. Criminal and civil procedure and the rules of evidence are modelled on English practice.

The superior court system comprises the Supreme Court for Mauritius and Courts of Appeal (Court of Civil Appeal and Court of Criminal Appeal). An appeal lies from the Supreme Court or Courts of Appeal to the Judicial Committee of the Privy Council. In some cases this is a matter of right, eg, on questions of the interpretation of the Constitution, and, in others, only with leave of the Court. The official language in proceedings before the Supreme Court is English.

The legal profession is divided into barristers, attorneys and notaries.

Practitioners from foreign jurisdictions who wish to practise in Mauritius should contact the Mauritius Bar Association, 102 Chancery House, Lislet Geoffroy Street, Port Louis, Mauritius (Tel: +230 2082958; Fax: + 230 2122558; email: yab@chambers.sirhamid.intnet.mu).

LAW REPORT

Mauritius Reports (MR) (1860–date) (a collection of selected decisions of the Supreme Court) (website: www.angelfire.com)

LAW SCHOOL

UNIVERSITY OF MAURITIUS

Department of Law, Faculty of Law and Management, Reduit, Mauritius
Tel: +230 4541041 ext 1414 or 1427; Fax: +230 4656906
email: rdomingu@uom.ac.mu
website: www.uom.ac.mu

Courses offered

LLB (Hons)
BA (Hons) Law and Management
BSc (Hons) Finance with Law
BSc Police Studies
LLM (there are plans to run this programme jointly with the University of Kent, UK)

Diploma in Legal Studies (with specialisation in business law, criminal law or civil law)

Journal

University of Mauritius Research Journal

Centre

Law Clinic

MOZAMBIQUE

Legal education is conducted in the faculty of law at the Eduardo Mondlane University in Maputo, the capital city. The five-year *Licenciatura* provides entry into the legal profession. Teaching is undertaken in Portuguese.

The CLEA country contact is Taibo Caetano Mucobora of Eduardo Mondlane University (address below) (email: mucobora@zebra.uem.mz).

The law is based on that of the former colonial power, Portugal.

The Supreme Court sits as a trial court as well as having an appeal jurisdiction. There is also an Administrative Court. The official language of the courts is Portuguese.

Practitioners from foreign jurisdictions who wish to apply for a right of audience in the Mozambiquan courts, or who wish to practise there, can obtain details from the Ordem dos Advogados de Mozambique, Avenue Vladimir Lenin 691-10, Andar Nos 2 and 3, CP 1796, Maputo, Mozambique (Tel: +258 1 431634; Fax: +258 1 431635).

LAW SCHOOL

EDUARDO MONDLANE UNIVERSITY

Faculty of Law, Kenneth Kaunda Avenue 960, PO Box 257, Maputo, Mozambique
Tel: +258 1 494630; 490768; Fax: +258 1 494631
email: fdireito@zebra.uem.mz
website: www.uem.mz

Course offered

Licenciatura (degree in law)

Journal

Revista da Faculade de Direito (*Faculty Law Review*)

Published in Portuguese, it contains articles and materials on all aspects of local and regional legal issues

Centres

Practical Legal Training Centre
Commercial Studies Centre

NAMIBIA

Legal education is conducted in the law faculty of the University of Namibia which is situated in the capital city of Windhoek. In 1993, a new degree structure was introduced. The degree of BJuris is obtained after three years of study and the LLB degree after a further two years. The BJuris qualifies the holder, after a period of practical training, for entry into the magistracy, the prosecution service (in the lower courts) and into those areas that do not require a full legal professional qualification.

For entry into full membership of the legal profession and the practice of law in Namibia, a degree in law is required either from the University of Namibia or a comparable educational institution situated outside Namibia which has been prescribed by the Minister of Justice. In addition, a person must have satisfactorily undergone practical legal training with the Justice Training Centre for one year and have passed the Legal Practitioners Qualifying Examination.

There is no local society of law teachers although some are members of the Society of Law Teachers of Southern Africa.

The system of law is largely based on South African Roman-Dutch law, although customary law remains important in some areas.

The superior court system comprises the High Court and a Supreme Court that sits in Windhoek. Since 1995, Namibia has had a fused profession, although the Society of Advocates of Namibia operates a *de facto* Bar. Such members are also members of the Law Society of Namibia (PO Box 714, Windhoek, Namibia; Fax +264 61 2302233). Practitioners from foreign jurisdictions who wish to practice in Namibia should contact the Society of Advocates of Namibia, PO Box 1323, Windhoek, Namibia (Tel: +264 61 231151; Fax: +264 61 230162; email: socadv@mweb.com.na).

LAW REPORTS

- *The Namibian Reports* (NR) (1990–date)
- Some cases are also reported in the *South African Law Reports*
- Recent unreported decisions are available on www.orusovo.com/socanam/unreport.htm

LAW SCHOOL

UNIVERSITY OF NAMIBIA

Faculty of Law, Private Bag 13301, 340 Mandume Ndemufayo Avenue, Windhoek, Namibia
Tel: +264 61 2063522; Fax: +264 61 3072286
email: lawfac@unam.na; shbukurura@unam.na
website: www.unam.na

Courses offered

BJuris
LLB

Centres

1   Justice Training Centre (Tel: +264 061 206 3989; Fax: +264 061 206 3988)
    The Centre offers the following courses:
    - Legal Professional Training course for persons in possession of an LLB degree (or an approved degree supplemented by a bridging course) who wish to qualify for admission to practise law in Namibia. The course runs for nine months.
    - The bridging course in basic principles and tenets of Roman-Dutch law for graduates holding law degrees from non-common law countries.
    - Pre-service (induction) and in-service (capacity building) training courses for magistrates, prosecutors, interpreters, court clerks, police, defence force personnel, immigration and prison officials and other law administration and enforcement personnel. The induction courses run for a minimum of one month whilst the capacity building courses run for up to three months.
    - Training courses for non-degree magistrates and prosecutors.
    - Training courses for community court justices.

2   Human Rights and Documentation Centre (HRDC)
    The mandate of the HRDC is to create and cultivate a sustainable culture of human rights and democracy in Namibia

NEW ZEALAND

Legal education leading to a degree of Bachelor of Laws and admission as a barrister and solicitor of the High Court of New Zealand is provided by the law faculties or law schools at the University of Auckland, University of Waikato, Victoria University of Wellington, University of Canterbury and University of Otago.

All five universities offer both undergraduate (LLB and LLB (Hons)) degrees and postgraduate degrees (LLM and PhD) in law. All are recognised by the New Zealand Council of Legal Education.

After completing the LLB degree at a law school in New Zealand, persons wishing to be admitted as barristers and solicitors are required to complete a 13-week practical Professional Legal Studies Course with the Institute of Professional Legal Studies (IPLS). The Institute can be contacted as follows: The National Administrator, Institute of Professional Legal Studies, PO Box 56491, Wellington, New Zealand (email: ipls@netlink.co.nz; website: www.ipls.org.nz).

Once the degree and the IPLS course are completed, and a person is found to be of suitable good character to be admitted as a barrister and solicitor, such a person may seek admission.

The CLEA representative for the Australasia region is Ros MacDonald of the Queensland University of Technology (address under Australia) (email: r.macdonald@qut.edu.au).

There is no formal society of New Zealand law teachers as such; however most law teachers in New Zealand belong to the Australasian Law Teachers Association (ALTA) of which there is a New Zealand Executive. The Secretary is currently based at the Victoria University of Wellington (details below).

The legal system is based on the common law. The superior court system comprises the Court of Appeal which is, in most cases, the court of final jurisdiction and the High Court. In some circumstances appeals still lie to the Privy Council.

The legal profession in New Zealand is fused and practitioners are admitted as barristers and solicitors. Even so, many lawyers in the main city centres choose to practise as barristers only.

The overall control of legal education in New Zealand, leading to admission as a barrister and solicitor of the High Court of New Zealand, is vested in the Council of Legal Education. One of the responsibilities of the Council is to decide what will be required in the way of further education by lawyers qualified in foreign jurisdictions who wish to be admitted in New Zealand. The Council can be contacted through the Secretary at PO Box 5041, Wellington, New Zealand. The New Zealand Law Society can also be contacted at the following address: Law Society Building, PO Box 5041, Wellington, New Zealand (Tel: +64 4 4727837; Fax +64 4 9151284; email: lawtalk@nz-lawsoc.org.nz; website: www.nz-lawsoc.org.nz).

LAW REPORTS

There is a well developed series of local law reports including:

- *New Zealand Law Reports* (NZLR) (1840–date)
- *New Zealand District Court Reports* (1981–date)

- There are some 20 other series of law reports (for details see the University of Waikato's web pages (below))
- All the decisions of the New Zealand courts of general jurisdiction (Court of Appeal, High Court, and District Court) are becoming available on the AUSTLII web pages (www.austlii.edu.au)
- Useful websites on all aspects of law in New Zealand are www.findlaw.co.nz; and www.knowledge-basket.co.nz
- Decisions from the Maori Land Court and Appellate Court are available free of charge on www.bennion.co.nz/mlr

The five New Zealand law schools all publish law reviews. These (along with the *Maori Law Review*) are all listed at http://library.canterbury.ac.nz/law/reviews.shtml

LAW SCHOOLS

UNIVERSITY OF AUCKLAND

School of Law, Private Bag 92019, Auckland, New Zealand
Tel: +64 9 3737599 ext 5970; Fax +64 9 3737473
email: h.smeeton@auckland.ac.nz
website: www.law.auckland.ac.nz

Courses offered

BA/LLB (Hons)
Bcom/LLB (Hons)
BHSc/LLB (Hons)
BSc/LLB (Hons)
Bprop/LLB (Hons)
LLM
PhD

Centres

1   New Zealand Centre for Environmental Law (NZCEL) (Fax: +64 09 93737473; email: k.bosselmann@auckland.ac.nz)
    The Centre's objectives include:
    - Developing mono-disciplinary and multi-disciplinary research programmes in the various fields of environmental law and policy.
    - Exploring the relationship between environmental law and the Treaty of Waitangi and developments in environmental law in relation to the aims, aspirations and rights of Maori and other indigenous peoples.
    - Developing programmes to encourage and support graduate research on environmental law and policy.
    - Establishing links with relevant research centres and environmental law associations in New Zealand and other countries.

2   The Legal Research Foundation (Inc) (Fax: +64 09 3737471; email: n.campbell@auckland.ac.nz)
    The Foundation promotes legal education, research, and law reform and publishes the *New Zealand Law Review*

Journals

1   *New Zealand Journal of Environmental Law* (NZJEL) (provides an outlet for longer analytical and comparative legal writing in the area of environmental and natural resources law) (contact The Editor, New Zealand Journal of Environmental Law, Faculty of Law, University of Auckland Fax: +64 09 373 7440; email: ka.palmer@auckland.ac.nz)
2   *New Zealand Law Review* (quarterly) (includes refereed articles by leading New Zealand and international scholars, along with annual and biennial reviews of the major areas of the law, written by specialist contributing editors)

UNIVERSITY OF CANTERBURY

School of Law, Private Bag 4800, Christchurch, New Zealand
Tel: +64 3 3642602; Fax: +64 3 3642757
email: enquiries@laws.canterbury.ac.nz
website: www.laws.canterbury.ac.nz

Courses offered

LLB
LLM

Centre

Centre for Commercial and Corporate Law (acts as a forum for the exchange of information, views and expertise relating to corporate and commercial law. As such the Centre aims to bridge the gap between academic lawyers, practitioners in law and accountancy and those working in finance and industry)

Journal

Canterbury Law Review (email: e.toomey@laws.canterbury.ac.nz)

UNIVERSITY OF OTAGO

Faculty of Law, PO Box 56, Dunedin, New Zealand
Tel: +64 3 4798857; Fax: +64 3 4798855
email: law@otago.ac.uk
website: www.otago.ac.nz/law

Courses offered

LLB
LLM
Master of Bioethics and Health Law (MBHL)
Master of International Studies (MINTS)
PhD

Journal

Otago Law Review (annually) (contains articles and shorter notes on the study and practice of law)

VICTORIA UNIVERSITY OF WELLINGTON

Faculty of Law, PO Box 600, Wellington, New Zealand
Tel: +64 4 4636366; Fax: +64 4 4636365
email: law-enquiries@vuw.ac.nz
website: www.lawschool.vuw.ac.nz

Courses offered

LLB
LLM
PhD
Diploma in Law (for practitioners)

Centres

1   New Zealand Centre for Conflict Resolution
    The objectives of the Centre are:
    • To promote the study and practice of dispute resolution, with particular emphasis on negotiation, mediation and arbitration.
    • To promote the comparative, empirical and theoretical study of conflict and its resolution in both domestic and international contexts.

2   New Zealand Centre for Public Law (email: law-centres@vuw.ac.nz)

Journal

Victoria University of Wellington Law Review

UNIVERSITY OF WAIKATO

School of Law, Private Bag 3105, Hamilton, New Zealand
Tel: +64 7 8384167; Fax +64 7 8384417
email: lawrecp@waikato.ac.nz
website: www.waikato.ac.nz/law

Courses offered

LLB
BA/LLB
BSocSc/LLB
BSc/LLB
BMS/LLB (Management studies)
LLM (linked with the University of Papua New Guinea)

Journal

Waikato Law Review – Taumauri (annually)

The Law School also organises the South Pacific Mooting Competition

NIGERIA

The Legal Education Act 1962 introduced a two tier structure of legal education. The first tier involves academic training in accredited universities whilst the second tier involves vocational training at the Nigerian Law School. Following a major curriculum reform in 1989 by the National Universities Commission (a federal agency that lays down minimum standards for all universities in the country), the period spent at a university in Nigeria for the study of law was extended to five years (and six years in the case of part time study). In 1990/91 the new curriculum was implemented, designed to introduce more compulsory and optional non-law courses into law degree programmes so as to make legal education at the first tier more liberal and interdisciplinary.

About 4,000 law students graduate each year with an LLB degree from both federal and State universities in Nigeria. Almost all of them then proceed to the second tier, training at the Nigerian Law School (NLS) which was established in 1962 to provide vocational training necessary for a fused profession. In December 1997, the NLS moved from its previous home in Lagos to Abuja. It has now been decentralised with additional campuses being established in Lagos, Enugu and Kano. The Council of Legal Education runs a one-year professional course at the NLS for law graduates from approved universities, and awards a qualifying Certificate for Call to the Bar to students who successfully complete the course and pass the examination.

Generally, a law degree (including the core subjects) awarded to full time students from another common law country will suffice for admission to the law school. It is compulsory for all prospective lawyers to attend the NLS and pass a written examination before being presented to the Body of Benchers for admission as a barrister and solicitor of the Supreme Court of Nigeria. All such legal practitioners are members of the Nigerian Bar Association.

The Nigerian Institute of Advanced Legal Studies is the premier research centre and undertakes a wide range of research projects on both legal issues in Nigeria and in sub-Saharan Africa.

The CLEA country contact is Toyin Doherty of the Nigerian Law School (address below) (Fax: +234 9 5231570; 5231571).

The system of law in Nigeria is based largely on common law and Sharia law. The Federal courts comprise the Supreme Court of Nigeria (which also acts as the Constitutional Court), the Court of Appeal, the Federal High Court, the High Court of the Federal Capital Territory, Abuja, the Sharia Court of Appeal of the Federal Capital Territory, Abuja and the Customary Court of Appeal of the Federal Capital Territory, Abuja. The State courts comprise customary courts, magistrates' courts, Area Courts, a High Court, Sharia Court of Appeal and a Customary Court of Appeal.

The legal profession is fused. Practitioners from other Commonwealth countries may apply for the right of audience on an *ad hoc* basis. Those from foreign jurisdictions who wish to practise in Nigeria should contact the Nigerian Bar Association, Ozumba Mbadiwe Street, Victoria Island, PMB 12023, Lagos 21083, Nigeria (Tel: +234 1 461 8287; Fax: +234 1 470 7432; email: nba@nova.net.ng).

LAW REPORT

Although there are many series of law reports in Nigeria, the most regular are the *Nigerian Weekly Law Reports* (NWLR) which report appellate decisions. They are published by Nigerian Law Publications Ltd, 90 Lewis Street, Lagos, Nigeria (Tel: +234 1 263006)

LAW SCHOOLS

ABIA STATE UNIVERSITY

College of Legal Studies, PMB 2000, Uturu, Abia State, Nigeria
Tel: +234 88 220785; 220330
email: registrar@abiasu.edu.ng

Course offered

LLB

UNIVERSITY OF ABUJA

Bwagwalada, PMB 117, Garki, Abuja, Nigeria
Tel: +234 9 8812380; 8821393; 8821891; Fax: +234 9 8821605
email: registrar@uniabuja.edu.ng

Course offered

LLB

UNIVERSITY OF ADO EKITI

Faculty of Law, PMB 5363, Ado-Ekiti, Ondo State, Nigeria
Tel: +234 30 240370; 240711; Fax: +234 30 240301

Course offered

LLB

AHMADU BELLO UNIVERSITY

Faculty of Law, PMB 1013, Zaria, Nigeria
Tel: +234 69 51292; 50591; 50691; Fax: +234 69 50022; 50891; 51575
email: registrar@abu.edu.ng

Courses offered

LLB
LLB with specialisation in Islamic law
LLM
PhD

AMBROSE ALLI UNIVERSITY
Faculty of Law, PMB 14, Ekpoma, Edo State, Nigeria
Tel: +234 55 98446; 98448
email: registrar@edosu.edu.ng

Courses offered

LLB
LLM
PhD

BAYERO UNIVERSITY
Faculty of Law, New Campus, PMB 3011, Kano, Nigeria
Tel: +234 64 666021; 666023; Fax: +234 64 665904
email: registrar@buk.edu.ng

Course offered

LLB

UNIVERSITY OF BENIN
Faculty of Law, Benin-Lagos Expressway, Ugbowo, PMB 1154, Benin City, Nigeria
Tel: +234 52 600678; 600568; 600443; Fax: +234 52 602366
email: registrar @uniben.edu.ng

Courses offered

LLB
LLM

BENUE STATE UNIVERSITY
Faculty of Law, PMB 102119, Makurdi, Nigeria
Tel: +234 44 533811
email: registrar@bensu.edu.ng

Course offered

LLB

UNIVERSITY OF CALABAR
Faculty of Law, PMB 1115, Calabar, Nigeria
Tel: +234 87 221086; 222790; Fax: +234 87 230595; 221766
email: registrar@unical.edu.ng

Course offered

LLB

DELTA STATE UNIVERSITY

Faculty of Law, PMB 1, Abraka, Delta State, Nigeria
Tel +234 54 66027; 66024
email: registrar@desu.edu.ng

Course offered

LLB

ENUGU STATE UNIVERSITY OF SCIENCE AND TECHNOLOGY

PMB 01160, Enugu, Nigeria
Tel: +234 42 451264; 451319; Fax: +234 42 455705
email: registrar@esut.edu.ng

Course offered

LLB

UNIVERSITY OF IBADAN

Department of Law, Oyo Road, Ibadan, Nigeria
Tel: +234 2 8101100; Fax: +234 2 8103043
email: registrar@kdl.ui.edu.ng

Course offered

LLB

UNIVERSITY OF ILORIN

Department of Law, Tanke Road, PMB 1515, Ilorin, Nigeria
Tel: +234 31 225299; 221552; Fax: +234 31 222561; 221593
email: registrar@ulorin.edu.ng

Course offered

LLB

IMO STATE UNIVERSITY

Sarnek Road, off Okigwe Road, PMB 2000, Owerri, Nigeria
Tel: +234 83 231433; 233055; Fax: +234 83 232716
email: registrar@imosu.edu.ng

Course offered

LLB

UNIVERSITY OF JOS

Faculty of Law, PMB 2084, Jos, Plateau State, Nigeria
Tel: +234 73 53724; 44952; 610514; Fax: +234 73 610514
email: unijos@aol.com
website: www.uiowa.edu/intlinet/unijos

Courses offered

LLB
LLM
MA (law and diplomacy)
PhD (law and diplomacy)

UNIVERSITY OF LAGOS

Faculty of Law, Akoka, Yaba, Lagos, Nigeria
Tel: +234 1 823260; Fax: +234 1 822644

Courses offered

LLB
LLM
Masters in International and Diplomacy Law
PhD
Diploma in Commercial and Industrial Law

LAGOS STATE UNIVERSITY

Faculty of Law, Lagos-Badagry Expressway, Ojo, PMB 1087, Apapa, Lagos, Nigeria
Tel/Fax: +234 1 5884048
email: lasu@alpha.linkserve.com

Course offered

LLB

UNIVERSITY OF MAIDUGURI

Faculty of Law, Bama Road, PMB 1069, Maiduguri, Nigeria
Tel: +234 76 232424; Fax: +234 76 236314; 231639
email: registrar@unimaid.edu.ng

Courses offered

LLB
Diploma in Sharia Law

UNIVERSITY OF NIGERIA

Faculty of Law, Nsukka, Enugu State, Nigeria
Tel: +234 42 770644; 770095; Fax: +234 42 771977; 771500
email: registrar@unn.edu.ng

Courses offered

LLB
LLM
PhD

NIGERIAN INSTITUTE OF ADVANCED LEGAL STUDIES

University of Lagos Campus, Akoka, Yaba, PMB 12820, Lagos, Nigeria
Tel: +234 1 821109; 821223; 821753; Fax: +234 1 825558
email: bowa@infoweb.abs.net

The Institute provides facilities for postgraduate research in Nigerian and African law

NIGERIAN LAW SCHOOL

PMB 170, Garki, Bwari, Abuja, Federal Capital Territory, Nigeria
Tel: +234 9 803296; 804316

Course offered

Legal Practice Certificate

NNAMDI AZIKIWE UNIVERSITY

PMB 5025, Awka, Nigeria
Tel: +234 46 550180; Fax: +234 46 550082
email: registrar@nauni.edu.ng

Course offered

LLB

OBAFEMI AWOLOWO UNIVERSITY

Faculty of Law, Ile-Ife, Osun State, Nigeria
Tel: +234 36 2302909; 231822; Fax: +234 36 233128; 232401; 231822
email: registrar@oauife.edu.ng

Courses offered

LLB
LLM
MPhil

OGUN STATE UNIVERSITY

Faculty of Law, PMB 2002, Ago-Iwoye, Ogun State, Nigeria
Tel: +234 39 390149; 390147
email: registrar@ogunsu.edu.ng

Course offered

LLB

ONDO STATE UNIVERSITY

PMB 5363, Ado-Ekiti, Ondo State, Nigeria
Tel: +234 30 240711; 240370; Fax: +234 30 240188

Course offered

LLB

RIVERS STATE UNIVERSITY OF SCIENCE AND TECHNOLOGY

Faculty of Law, Nkpolu Oroworukwo, PMB 5080, Port Harcourt, Nigeria
Tel: +234 84 333288; 334838; Fax: +234 84 230720
email:registrar@rsustech.edu.ng

Course offered

LLB

UNIVERSITY OF SOKOTO

Faculty of Law, PMB 2346, Sokoto, Nigeria

Course offered:

LLB (Common Law and Islamic Law)

UNIVERSITY OF UYO

Faculty of Law, PMB 1017, Uyo, Akwa Ibom State, Nigeria
Tel: +234 85 201111; 202694; Fax: +234 85 20294
email: registrar@uniuyo.edu.ng

Course offered

LLB

USMAN DANFODIO UNIVERSITY

Faculty of Law, PMB 2346, Sokoto, Nigeria
Tel: +234 60 236688; 234042; Fax: +234 60 235519; 234042
email: registrar@udosok.edu.ng

Course offered

LLB

Note:

There are also three approved private universities that offer law degree programmes:

1   Madonna University, Okija, Anambra State, Nigeria
2   Igbinedion University, Edo State, Nigeria
3   Benson Idahosa University, Benin, Nigeria

PAKISTAN

All the main provincial universities in Pakistan have law faculties which offer the LLB degree. In addition to State universities there are numerous private law colleges which also offer the LLB. Law colleges were traditionally part of the (State funded) university system and there was one law college to one university. Over the past 15 years, with demand for legal education soaring and university colleges not being able to expand proportionally, 'private' law colleges (ie, owned and run by private individuals and without State funding) have sprung up all over the country. These request an affiliated status with a university, usually the university of the Province in which the college is physically located.

All law colleges offer an LLB degree programme that since 1995 has moved from a two-year to a three-year programme. The LLB syllabus contains, in addition to the core subjects of the common law, a substantial section on various areas of Islamic law. It is both an academic as well as a professional degree and law graduates are issued with a licence to practice after a six-month apprenticeship period with a senior lawyer having 10 years' experience as a lawyer of the High Court. Thereafter they undertake a test and interview and, if successful, they are issued licences to appear before all the courts and tribunals in the Province except the High Court and Supreme Court of Pakistan. After two years, they are enrolled as advocates of the High Court. It takes another 10 years to be eligible to become an advocate of the Supreme Court. Those wishing to practise before the Federal Shariat Court must have practised for at least five years as an advocate of the High Court.

Some colleges also offer higher degrees, ie, LLM and PhD. There is no local association of law teachers.

The CLEA country contact is Mir Aurangzeb of University Law College, Quetta (address below) (email: miraurangzeb@yahoo.com).

Pakistan has a fused legal profession. Legal practitioners, called advocates, must become members of the Bar Association established at the respective courts. The Legal Practitioners and Bar Councils Act 1973 provides for the establishment of provincial Bar Councils at each High Court and a supervising central Pakistan Bar Council. The Bar Councils admit advocates on their rolls and hold examinations for this purpose. The Pakistan Bar Council supervises the provincial Bar Councils and lays down the standard of legal education in consultation with the universities of Pakistan. The Pakistan Bar Council recognises universities whose degrees in law qualify them for enrolment as an advocate. In order to qualify as an advocate, a person must be a citizen of Pakistan, have attained the age of 21 years, have obtained a Bachelor's degree in a non-law subject from a recognised university and an LLB degree.

Pakistan's legal system is marked by a substantial body of codified laws inherited from British India. Pakistani law is therefore still in many respects based on British Indian law and therefore ultimately on English common law. Islamic law has now become an important source of law and there are very few areas of law that have not been affected by the jurisdiction of the Federal Shariat Court.

The superior court system comprises the High Court, the Federal Shariat Court, the Supreme Court and the Shariat Appeal Bench of the Supreme Court.

Practitioners from overseas jurisdictions who wish to practise in Pakistan should contact the Pakistan Bar Council, Old Supreme Court Building, Peshawar Road, Rawalpindi, Pakistan (Tel: +92 51 562539; Fax: +92 51 517022).

LAW REPORTS

There is a well established series of law reports including:

- *Pakistan Legal Decisions* (PLD)
- *Supreme Court Monthly Review* (SCMR)
- *Pakistan Supreme Court Cases* (PSC)
- *Monthly Law Digest* (MLD)
- *Civil Law Cases* (CLC)
- *Shariat Decisions* (SD)
- *Pakistan Criminal Law Journal* (PCrLJ)
- *National Law Reports* (NLR)
- *Karachi Law Reports* (KLR)
- *Pakistan Law Journal* (PLJ)
- *Annual Law Digest* (ALD)
- The Advanced Legal Studies Institute (www.nyazee.com) is in the process of putting online the judgments of the higher courts as well as major statutes

LAW SCHOOLS

ADVANCED LEGAL STUDIES INSTITUTE

749, Street 17, Sector G-10-1, Islamabad, Pakistan
website: www.nyazee.com

The Institute promotes research into Islamic law and into the laws prevailing in Muslim countries, especially in Pakistan. The Institute provides online a series of databases covering:

- Islamic law
- Islamic banking
- Pakistan law

INTERNATIONAL ISLAMIC UNIVERSITY

Faculty of Shariah and Law, PO Box 1243, Islamabad, Pakistan
Tel: +92 854 370
Telex: 54068 IIU PK

Courses offered

BA/LLB (Hons) (Shariah and law)
LLM (Shariah and law)

KARACHI UNIVERSITY

The following law colleges offer the LLB and LLM: SM Law College, Karachi (Karachi University); Islamia Law College, Karachi (Karachi University); Federal Urdu Law College (Karachi University)

The following colleges offer an LLB degree: Hamdard Law College, Hamdard University, Karachi; Government Law College Hyderabad, Hyderabad City (Sind); Khairpur Law College, Khairpur (Sind); Islamia Law College, Bhawalpur; Bhawalpur University, Bhawalpur; Government Law College, Multan (Punjab)

PAKISTAN COLLEGE OF LAW

46-A Tipu Block, New Garden Town, Lahore, Pakistan
Tel: +92 42 5831801; 5831838; Fax: +92 42 5832041
email: hum@brain.net.pk; info@pcl.edu.pk
website: www.pcl.edu.pk

Courses offered

LLB (Punjab University degree-graduate course)
LLM
Diploma in Environmental Law

Certificate courses in competitive jurisprudence; family law; Law skills and advocacy; legal research and writing; international law and trade; international human rights

Journal

Pakistan Law Review (contains articles and comment on the law, legal profession and the judiciary in Pakistan) (email: paklawreview@yahoo.com)

Centres

1   Women Law Centre (acts as a liaison between female students, the faculty and the legal profession. Its primary goal is to provide educational support structure and research opportunities for female law students. The group serves as a forum for developing discourse on issues affecting women pertaining to their rights, careers, families, etc. It conducts short workshops regarding law issues relating to women)
2   Human Rights Centre
3   Alternate Dispute Resolution Centre

UNIVERSITY OF PESHAWAR

Faculty of Law, Peshawar, Pakistan
Tel: +92 91 844082; Fax: +92 91 41979
email: ahmad@fol.psw.erum.com.pk

Course offered

LLB

Journal

Journal of Law and Society (biannually)

Centres

1   Legal Research Centre
2   Human Rights Institute

Affiliated law colleges: Islamia Law College, University Road, Peshawar (Tel: +92 91 41942); Peshawar Law College, Peshawar Saddar, Peshawar; Frontier Law College, Peshawar Cantt (Tel: +92 91 277115; 27796); Kohat Law College, Kohat; Mardan Law College, Yadgar Chowk, Mardan Cantt; Swat Law College, Mingora, Swat; Abbott Law College, Abbotabad (Hazara); Justice Law College, Abbotabad (Hazara)

PUNJAB UNIVERSITY

University Law College, New Campus, Lahore, Pakistan

Courses offered

LLB
LLM
PhD
Diploma in Labour Law

The Punjab Law College has affiliated law colleges in Lahore, Faisalabad and Rawalpindi and the Quaid-e-Azam Law College, Lahore

UNIVERSITY LAW COLLEGE, QUETTA

Khojak Road, PO Box 75, Quetta, Balochistan 87300, Pakistan
Tel: +92 81 821810; Fax: +92 81 826492
email: miraurangzeb@yahoo.com

Course offered

LLB

SIND UNIVERSITY

Faculty of Law, Jamschoro, Pakistan
Fax: +92 221 771372

Affiliated law colleges: Jinnah Law College, Jamshoro University, Hyderabad, Sind; Government Law College, Larkana, Sind

Course offered

LLB

PAPUA NEW GUINEA

Legal education is conducted at the faculty of law at the University of Papua New Guinea. The holder of an LLB degree can enter practice following the successful completion of the Practical Training Course at the Legal Training Institute and then six months in Chambers.

The CLEA regional representative is Ros Macdonald of the Queensland University of Technology (address under Australia) (email: r.macdonald@qut.edu.au).

The Constitution of Papua New Guinea provides that the laws of the country consist of the Constitution, the organic laws, Acts of Parliament, emergency regulations and provincial laws as well as 'laws made or adopted by or under the Constitution and the underlying laws'. Amongst the 'underlying laws' are the rules of common law and equity. The organic laws in general relate to the organisation of certain government institutions such as the Judicial and Legal Services Commission and the Ombudsman Commission. The Constitution of Papua New Guinea and the organic laws represent the 'supreme' law of the country and all Acts inconsistent with them are invalid and ineffective.

The National Judicial System consists of the Supreme Court, National Court of Justice and other courts (for example, district, local and village courts). The official language of the superior courts is English.

Practitioners from other common law countries who wish to apply for a right of audience on an *ad hoc* basis in the courts or who wish to practise in Papua New Guinea should contact the Papua New Guinea Law Society Inc, PO Box 2004, Port Moresby, Papua New Guinea (Tel: +675 3 217344; 217348; Fax: +675 3 217634; email: lawsoc@daltron.com.pg).

LAW REPORT

Papua New Guinea Law Reports (1963–96)

LAW SCHOOLS

LEGAL TRAINING INSTITUTE
PO Box 6961, Boroko, Papua New Guinea
Tel: +675 3 257522; Fax: +675 3 253408

Course offered

Legal Practice Certificate

UNIVERSITY OF PAPUA NEW GUINEA

School of Law, PO Box 317, University Post Office, Waigani, Papua New Guinea
Tel: +675 3 267481; 267646; 267336; Fax: +675 3 267187
email: law.school@upng.ac.pg
website: www.upng.ac.pg

Courses offered

LLB
LLM
PhD
Diploma in Law (prosecutions)
Diploma DMS (magisterial studies)
Diploma in Clinical Studies

SIERRA LEONE

Legal education is conducted in the department of law at the University of Sierra Leone which is situated in Freetown, the capital of Sierra Leone. The LLB degree entitles the holder to practise.

The CLEA regional representative is Seth Bimpong-Buta (email: sethbb@hotmail.com).

The system of law is based on the common law which comprises 'the rules of law generally known as the common law, the rules of law generally known as the doctrines of equity, and the rules of customary law including those determined by the Superior Court of Judicature' (Constitution of Sierra Leone, s 170(2)).

The legal profession is fused and a person can, after enrolment, practise as a barrister or solicitor, or both. Practitioners from foreign jurisdictions who wish to practise in Sierra Leone should contact the Sierra Leone Bar Association, 84 Dundas Street, Freetown, Sierra Leone (Tel: +232 22 224702; Fax +232 22 224439; email: slba@slonline.net).

LAW REPORTS

- *African Law Reports* (Sierra Leone) (1964–73)
- *Sierra Leone Law Reports* (1960–63 (vols 1–3))
- Currently there is no series of local law reports

LAW SCHOOL

UNIVERSITY OF SIERRA LEONE

Law Department, Fourah Bay College, Mount Aureol, Freetown, Sierra Leone
Tel: +232 22 227924; 224260; Fax: +232 22 224260
email: fbcadmin@sierratel.sl; vesking@hotmail.com

Course offered

LLB

SINGAPORE

Legal education is conducted in the law faculty of the National University of Singapore (NUS). The four-year LLB (Hons) degree is the principal route of entry into the legal profession in Singapore. After the LLB degree, graduates proceed directly to practical training. This involves completing the Postgraduate Practice Law Course and six months of pupillage. After that, they are eligible to petition for admission as an advocate and solicitor of the Supreme Court of Singapore.

The faculty also runs a special course, the Diploma in Singapore Law, for graduates from certain universities in the United Kingdom who wish to practice law in Singapore.

The CLEA country contact is Kumar Amirthalingam (email: lawka@nus.edu.sg).

The system of law in Singapore is based on the common law. The superior courts system comprises the High Court and the Court of Appeal.

Practitioners from other common law systems may apply for the right of audience on an *ad hoc* basis in the Singaporean courts. Those from overseas jurisdictions who wish to practise in Singapore must take a one-year course at the Singapore Academy of Law. For details, they should contact the Law Society of Singapore (email: lawsoc@singnet.com.sg; website: www.lawsoc.org.sg).

LAW REPORT

- *Singapore Law Reports* (1992–date)

LAW SCHOOL

NATIONAL UNIVERSITY OF SINGAPORE

Faculty of Laws, Kent Ridge, Singapore 119260
Tel: +65 775 6666; Fax: +65 779 0979
email: lawweb@nus.edu.sg
website: www.nus.edu.sg

Courses offered

LLB (Hons)
Dip Business Law
Graduate Diploma in Singapore Law
Master of Laws (coursework, by research, or a combination of both)
Joint Master in International Commercial Law (with the University of Nottingham)
PhD

Centres

1   Asia-Pacific Centre for Environmental Law (APCEL) (promotes capacity building
in environmental legal education)
Its projects and programmes include:
- Online Environmental Law Database comprising international and regional
instruments, and national legislation from the ASEAN Member States and the
region.
- Capacity-Building in Environmental Legal Education in the Asia-Pacific
Training programmes for law educators at the tertiary level in the Asia-Pacific
region with the aim of developing and enhancing their skills in teaching
environmental law.
- Study of Environmental Law in ASEAN Countries.

Contact details:
Asia-Pacific Centre for Environmental Law, Faculty of Laws, National University
of Singapore, as above
Tel: +65 874 6246; Fax: +65 872 1937; 779 0979
email : lawapcel@nus.edu.sg

2   Centre for Commercial Law Studies
Objectives:
- To provide a focal point for comparative and regional commercial law
research and dialogue which would be of practical value to practitioners,
legislators and businessmen.
- To contribute to the reform of commercial law in Singapore.
- To disseminate information on and stimulate interest in comparative
commercial law.

Contact details:
Centre for Commercial Law Studies, Faculty of Law, National University of
Singapore, as above
Tel: +65 6874 3644; Fax: +65 6779 0979
email: lawccls@nus.edu.sg

Journals

1   *Singapore Journal of Legal Studies*
2   *Singapore Journal of International and Comparative Law* (biannually)
3   *Singapore Law Review* (publishes articles and comments on topics of international
legal and comparative interest) (email: lawsjicl@nus.edu.sg; the journal is
available online though WESTLAW)

SOUTH AFRICA

Legal education in South Africa is conducted at 21 law faculties and six postgraduate schools for legal practice. In 1998 the majority of law faculties at South African universities introduced a new undergraduate four-year law degree to replace the existing BProc and five-year LLB degrees as the standard academic requirement for admission to all branches of the legal profession. The object of the new degree was to eliminate the perception that certain academic legal qualifications were inferior or superior to others, and it also brings South Africa into line with most other Commonwealth countries. The legal content of the new degree is at least the same as, and at some universities more than, that of the old LLB degree which was usually done over two or three years as a postgraduate degree. In most cases the new degree contains more legal skills training and outcomes based education than the old.

Successful completion of the six-month course at the School for Legal Practice (SLP) of the Law Society of South Africa (email: pltdir@lssa.org.za) entitles a student to a reduction in articles or community service from two years to one year and to sit for the attorneys admission examination without having served articles. The Centres of the SLP are at Bloemfontein, Cape Town, Durban, East London, Johannesburg, Pietersburg, Port Elizabeth and Pretoria.

The CLEA Southern African Chapter President and country representative is Philip Iya of the University of Fort Hare (address below) (email: philiya@hotmail.com). Most law teachers in South Africa belong to the Society of Law Teachers of Southern Africa (SLTSA). The current President is Shadreck Gutto who may be contacted at the Faculty of Law, University of Witswatersrand (address below).

The system of law in South Africa is based on Roman-Dutch law, with some influences from the common law and customary indigenous law. The court system comprises the Constitutional Court, the Supreme Court of Appeal, the High Courts and the magistrates' courts. The legal profession is divided between advocates (barristers) and attorneys (solicitors), although some of the latter now have a right of audience in the High Courts.

Practitioners from other Commonwealth countries may apply for the right of audience as advocates (barristers) on an *ad hoc* basis in the South African courts. Those from foreign jurisdictions who wish to practise as barristers in South Africa should contact the General Council of the Bar of South Africa, PO Box 2260, Johannesburg 2000, South Africa (Tel: +27 11 3363976; Fax: +27 11 3368970; email: gcb@mweb.co.za; website: www.sabar.co.za). Those wishing to practise as solicitors should contact the Law Society of South Africa (email: mklsa@lmweb.co.za).

LAW REPORTS

- *South African Law Reports* (SALR)
- *All South African Law Reports* (All SALR)
- *Butterworths Constitutional Law Reports* (BCLR)
- *South African Criminal Law Reports* (SACLR)
- *South African Constitutional Law Reports* (SACR)

- Decisions of the Constitutional Court are available free of charge on www.concourt.gov.za
- JUTASTAT is a fee based database of several series of law reports on www.jutastat.com

LAW SCHOOLS

UNIVERSITY OF CAPE TOWN

Faculty of Law, Private Bag, Rondebosch 7700, Cape Town, South Africa
Tel: +27 21 6503087; Fax: +27 21 6505662
email: corder@law.uct.ac.za
website: www.uct.ac.za/law

Courses offered

LLB
LLM (without specialisation by thesis or coursework and minor dissertation)
LLM (in any of the following specialist areas: commercial law; constitutional and administrative law; criminal justice; international law; labour law; marine law and environmental law; shipping law; public law; tax law)
MPhil
PhD
LLD

Centres

1   School for Legal Practice
2   School for Advanced Legal Studies
3   Institute for Development and Labour Law (email: devlab@uct.ac.za)
4   Legal Aid Clinic
5   Institute of Marine and Environmental Law (website: www.uctshiplaw.com)
6   Environmental Law Unit
7   Institute of Criminology
8   Centre for Socio-Legal Research Law, Race and Gender Unit

Journals

1   *Sea Changes* (monitors international developments in marine and environmental law)
2   *Acta Juridica*
3   *Responsa Meridiana* (annually) (published under the auspices of the Law Student Councils of the Universities of Cape Town, Stellenbosch and the Western Cape. Contains articles of general legal interest)
4   *On Trial* (formerly *Bona Fide*)
5   *Development and Labour Monographs* (quarterly)

UNIVERSITY OF DURBAN-WESTVILLE

Faculty of Law, Private Bag X54001, Durban 4000, South Africa
Tel: +27 31 8205036; Fax: +27 31 8204848
email: law@udw.ac.za
website: www.udw.ac.za

Courses offered

LLB
BA Law
Bachelor of Criminology
Bachelor of Criminal Justice Administration
Bachelor of Arts (law)
Master of Child Care and Protection
Master of Law (public health law)
Master of Law (international and African regional law)
Master of Criminology
Doctor of Criminology

Centre

Legal Aid Clinic

UNIVERSITY OF FORT HARE

Nelson Mandela School of Law, Private Bag X1314, Alice 5700, South Africa
Tel: +27 40 6022122; Fax: +27 40 6532334
email: lpiyo@ufh.ac.za; mlaw@ufh.ac.za
website: www.ufh.ac.za

Courses offered

LLB
LLM
LLD

Centre

Oliver Tambo Centre (focuses on human rights problems for marginalised
communities) (email: nrembe@ufh.ac.za)

UNIVERSITY OF NATAL

Faculty of Law, Howard College School of Law, PO Box X10, King George V
Avenue, Dalbridge, Durban 4001, South Africa
Tel: +27 31 2602487; Fax: +27 31 2602559
email: louw@nu.ac.za
website: www.und.ac.za

Faculty of Law, Pietermaritzburg School of Law, Private Bag X01, Scottsville 3209,
Pitermaritzburg, South Africa
Tel: +2733 2605778; Fax: +27 33 2605015
email: cowling@nu.ac.za
website: www.und.ac.za

Courses offered

LLB
LLM (general coursework)
LLM (specialist maritime law; labour law; business law; medical law environmental law; trial advocacy and clinical law; constitutional law)
PhD
LLD

Centres

1   Centre for Socio-Legal Studies (UND)
2   Community Law and Rural Development Centre (UND)
3   Campus Law Clinic (UND)
4   Centre For Criminal Justice (UNP)
5   Legal Aid Clinic (UNP)
6   School for Legal Practice (UNP)

UNIVERSITY OF THE NORTH

Faculty of Law, Private Bag X1106, Sovenga, near Pietersburg 0727, South Africa
Tel: +27 15 2682686; Fax: +27 15 2682897
email: okpaluba@mweb.co.za

Courses offered

LLB
LLM in Management and Development
LLM in Environmental Law
LLM in Labour Law
LLD

UNIVERSITY OF THE NORTH-WEST

Faculty of Law, Private Bag X2046, Mmabatho 27355, South Africa
Tel: +27 14 892111; Fax: +27 14 25775

Courses offered

B Criminal Justice
LLB
LLM
LLD

Centres

1   Institute of Development Research
2   Institute of African Studies
3   Institute of Education

UNIVERSITY OF THE ORANGE FREE STATE

Faculty of Law, PO Box 339, Bloemfontein 9301, South Africa
Tel: +27 514012451; 4019111; Fax: +27 51 4480381
email: henningj@unovs.ac.za
website: www.uovs.ac.za

Courses offered

LLB
LLM
LLD

Centres

1   Centre for Business Law
2   Centre for Human Rights Studies
3   Legal Aid Clinic
4   Centre for Financial Planning Law
5   School for Legal Practice

Journal

Journal for Juridical Science

UNIVERSITY OF PORT ELIZABETH

Faculty of Law, PO Box 1600, Port Elizabeth 6000, South Africa
Tel: +27 41 5042190; Fax: +27 41 5042818
email: law@upe.ac.za
website: www.upe.ac.za/law

Courses offered

LLB
LLM
LLM in Criminal Justice
LLM in Taxation
LLM in Labour Law
LLM in Tourism Law
LLD

Journals

1   *OBITER* (publishes articles on topical legal issues)
2   *Commercial Law Bulletin* (bimonthly) (summarises recent developments in commercial and labour law in South Africa and select international commercial law developments)

Centres

1   School for Legal Practice (provides practical legal training at the postgraduate level) (email: lwains@upe.ac.za)

2   Bureau for Mercantile Law (monitors new developments in the field of commercial law and labour law) (email: mercantile@upe.ac.za)
3   Tourism Law Unit (undertakes research on tourism law and gaming laws in southern Africa) (email: tourismlaw@upe.ac.za)
4   Centre for Street Law
5   Legal Clinic (email: legal@upe.ac.za)

POTCHEFSTROOM UNIVERSITY

Faculty of Law, Private Bag X6001, Potchefstroom 2520, South Africa
Tel: +27 18 2991920; Fax: +27 18 2991923
email: drthadb@puknet.puk.ac.za
website: www.puk.ac.za

Courses offered

LLB
LLM
LLD

Journal

Potchefstroom Electronic Law Journal (email@ prfeam@puknet.ac.za)

UNIVERSITY OF PRETORIA

Faculty of Law, Pretoria 0002, South Africa
Tel: +27 12 4204266; Fax: +27 12 3422638
email: cnel@hakuna.up.ac.za
website: www.up.ac.za

Courses offered

LLB
LLM
LLD
PhD

Journal

De Jure

Centres

1   Centre for Child Law
2   Centre for Practical and Continuing Legal Education
3   Centre for Advanced Corporate and Insolvency Law
4   Centre for Human Rights
5   Law Clinic

RAND AFRIKAANS UNIVERSITY

Faculty of Law, PO Box 524, Kingsway, Auckland Park, Johannesburg 2006, South Africa
Tel: +27 11 4892132; Fax: +27 11 4892049
email: mcuw@rau3.rau.ac.za;mh@regte.rau.ac.za
website: www.rau.ac.za

Courses offered

BA Law
LLB
LLM
LLD

Journal

Tydskrif vir die Suid-Afrikaanse Reg (*Journal of South African Law*)

Centres and Units

1   Centre for International and Comparative Labour Law
2   Research Unit for Banking Law
3   Centre for Insurance Law
4   Centre for Sports Law
5   Centre for Economic Law
6   Research Unit for Tax Law

RHODES UNIVERSITY

Faculty of Law, PO Box 94, Grahamstown 6140, South Africa
Tel: +27 46 6038225; Fax: +27 46 6222845
email: d.pyle@ru.ac.za
website; www.rhodes.ac.za

Courses offered

LLB
LLM
PhD

Centre

Legal Aid Clinic

UNIVERSITY OF SOUTH AFRICA

Faculty of Law, PO Box 392, Pretoria, South Africa
Tel: +27 12 4298739; Fax: +27 12 4293393; 4298587
email: wwykdh@unisa.ac.za
website: www.unisa.ac.za

Courses offered

LLB
LLM
LLD

Journals

1   *Codicillus* (the faculty's in-house journal)
2   *Juta's Business Law*
3   *SA Mercantile Law Journal*
4   *Comparative and International Law Journal of Southern Africa* (CILSA)
5   *South African Yearbook of International Law* (SAYIL)
6   *Journal for Contemporary Roman-Dutch Law* (THRHR)

Centres

1   Centre for Business Law
2   Centre for Indigenous Law
3   Centre for Legal Terminology in African Languages
4   The VerLoren van Themaat Centre for Public Law Studies
5   Institute of Foreign and Comparative Law
6   Legal Aid Clinic
7   Unit for Legal Historical Research
8   Centre for Human Rights

UNIVERSITY OF STELLENBOSCH

Faculty of Law, Stellenbosch, South Africa
Tel: +27 21 8084853; Fax: +27 21 8866235
email: eis@sun.ac.za; law@sun.ac.za
website: www.sun.ac.za/law

Courses offered

BComm (law)
BA (law)
BAcc/LLB
LLB
LLM
LLD

Centres and Units

1   Trade Law Centre for Southern Africa (www.tralac.org)
2   The Research Unit for Legal and Constitutional Interpretation (RULCI)
3   Legal Aid Clinic

Journals

1   *Responsa Meridiana* (published under the auspices of the University of Stellenbosch and the University of Cape Town)
2   *Stellenbosch Law Review*

UNIVERSITY OF TRANSKEI

Faculty of Law, Private Bag X1, Unitra 5117, South Africa
Tel: +27 47 5022111; Fax: +27 47 5326820
email: postmaster@getafix.utr.ac.za
website: www.utr.ac.za

Courses offered

LLB
LLM
PhD

Centre

Legal Aid Clinic

Journal

Transkei Law Journal

UNIVERSITY OF VENDA

School of Law, Private Bag X5050, Thohoyandou, South Africa
Tel: +27 15 9628313; 9628504; Fax: +27 15 9628407
email: Modie@univen.ac.za
website: www.univen.ac.za

Courses offered

BA (law)
LLB
Master of Human Rights Law
PhD

Centre

Ismail Mahomed Centre for Human and Peoples' Rights

VISTA UNIVERSITY

Faculty of Law

The university has campuses as follows:

Bloemfontein: PO Box 380, Bloemfontein 9300
Mamelodi: Private Bag X1311, Silverton 0127
Port Elizabeth: Private Bag X613, Port Elizabeth 6000
Soweto: Private Bag X09, Bertsham 2013
Tel: +27 51 5051386; Fax: +27 51 5051422
email: bloro-j@blenny.ac.za
website: www.vista.ac.za

Courses offered

LLB
LLM

UNIVERSITY OF THE WESTERN CAPE

Faculty of Law, Private Bag X17, Bellville 7535, South Africa
Tel: +27 21 9592911; Fax: +27 21 9592960
email: law@uwc.ac.za
website: www.uwc.ac.za

Courses offered

LLB
BComm
LLM
MPhil
PhD

Centres

1   Community Law Centre (seeks to protect and promote the human rights and democratic norms that have been enshrined in the 1996 Constitution and in international human rights instruments. The Centre pays particular attention to the position of women, children and other vulnerable groups such as persons with disabilities) (email: clc@sn.apc.org)
2   Legal Aid Clinic
3   The Social Law Project (SLP) (seeks to contribute to sustainable economic upliftment, socio-economic justice and access to social security benefits in both the formal and existing informal sectors, with particular emphasis on women and other disadvantaged groups)

UNIVERSITY OF THE WITSWATERSRAND

School of Law, Private Bag 3, Jan Smuts Avenue, Johannesburg 2001, South Africa
Tel: +27 11 7165530; Fax: +27 11 3373427
email: law@wits.ac.za
website: www.law.wits.ac.za

Courses offered

LLB
LLM
Master of Laws (by dissertation)
Masters Degree in Tax Law
Masters Degree in Labour Law
PhD

Journals

1   *Annual Survey of South African Law*

2   *South African Journal on Human* Rights (the journal welcomes submissions dealing with human rights, legal philosophy; constitutional and administrative law; freedom of information; law and development and public international law. Submissions taking an interdisciplinary and/or empirical approach are particularly encouraged) (Fax: +27 11 4032341; email: sajhr@law.wits.ac.za)

3   *De Minimis*

Centres

1   The Mandela Institute (develops policy and offers advanced teaching in areas of law that connect South Africa to the world global economy. These include: intellectual property law; banking law; company law; and international arbitration)

2   Centre for Applied Legal Studies (areas of interest include: human rights; public interest litigation; law reform; competition and trade law) (Tel: +27 11 7178654; Fax: +27 11 4034321; email: timolt@law.wits.ac.za)

3   Campus Law Clinic

UNIVERSITY OF ZULULAND

Faculty of Law, Private Bag X1001, Kwa-Dlangezwa 3886, South Africa
Tel: +27 35 9026029; 9026628
email: rsoni@pan.uzulu.za
website: www.uzulu.ac.za

Courses offered

LLB
LLM

SOUTH PACIFIC

Legal education is undertaken at the University of the South Pacific (USP). Students undertake their first year of studies towards the LLB degree either at the Laucala Campus of USP in Suva, the Fiji Islands, or at the Emalus Campus, Port Vila, Vanuatu. They then proceed to the Emalus Campus to complete years II, III and IV. The Law School also offers the LLB degree programme by extension studies. USP covers 12 different jurisdictions.

The Institute of Justice and Applied Legal Studies (IJALS), which is located on the Laucala Campus in the Fiji Islands, offers the six-month post-degree, Professional Diploma in Legal Practice (PDLP). A person who holds both the USP LLB degree and the PDLP is entitled to apply for admission as a legal practitioner in the countries of the USP region.

The CLEA country contact for the region is Ros Macdonald of the Queensland University of Technology (address under Australia) (email: r.macdonald@qut.edu.au).

The countries of the USP region have justice systems that are based on the common law system. Several countries (eg, Tonga) have expatriate, senior legal officers and judges, usually from Australia, New Zealand or the UK. All of the countries have a magistrates' court and a superior court which may be designated a High Court or a Supreme Court. In addition there may also be local village or island courts, in which matters relating to customary law are determined (particularly in relation to land and family matters). In addition there is a third tier of courts that operate at a local level and have limited territorial and procedural jurisdiction. These may exist as island courts, village courts or something similar.

None of the USP countries has a permanent Court of Appeal. In each country a visiting Court of Appeal is convened once or twice a year; its members are drawn from the member countries and/or Australia, New Zealand and Papua New Guinea.

The legal profession in the countries of the region is fused in nature. Generally, the legal profession is small. The Fiji Islands has the largest legal profession and there is a relatively sizeable profession in Vanuatu, owing to its status as an offshore financial centre.

Rules for admission into legal practice vary from country to country within the region:

- *Cook Islands*: admission in Australia, New Zealand, or any other Commonwealth country prescribed by the Minister. Alternatively candidates must have passed a suitable examination in law and demonstrated satisfactory knowledge.
- *Fiji Islands:* course of study approved by the Board of Legal Education (BLE) followed by a programme of practical legal training approved by the BLE.
- *Kiribati*: admission as a barrister or solicitor in England and Wales or any other common law country.
- *Nauru*: admission in Australia, New Zealand, the UK or any other country prescribed by the Minister. Alternatively candidates must hold a degree approved by the Minister. In addition, a pupillage, practical training course or a period of post-admission experience is required.
- *Niue and Tokelau*: rights of audience and practice if admitted in New Zealand or with the leave of the High Court.

- *Samoa*: prescribed qualification to be approved by the Council of the Law Society, which must be equivalent to an academic and/or professional qualification of a jurisdiction similar to Samoa.
- *Solomon Islands*: admission in another Commonwealth country plus five years' practical experience, immediately preceding the date of the application. Provisional admission (subject to a period of supervision) is available to persons who are entitled to be admitted, or have been admitted but do not have the requisite practical experience.
- *Tonga*: demonstration of adequate professional knowledge, training and experience in a common law jurisdiction.
- *Tuvalu*: the prescribed countries where admission as barrister, solicitor or law agent will fulfil local requirements are: Australia, Canada, the Fiji Islands, India, Ireland, New Zealand and the UK.
- *Vanuatu*: the Law Council under delegated legislation determines admission rules. A law degree approved by the Council is required. Vanuatu applicants may be admitted if they have been admitted in a Commonwealth jurisdiction; other applicants are required to have two years' continuous practical experience.

Contact details for the relevant Law Society/Bar Association are available www.vanvatu.usp.ac.fj.

LAW REPORTS

- *Solomon Islands Law Reports* (published by the University of the South Pacific) (Fax: +678 27785; email: lawsales@vanuatu.usp.ac.fj)
- The Pacific Islands Legal Information Institute (www.paclii.org) has a wide range of full text cases from around the region. This has been produced from data developed and published by the University of the South Pacific as follows:
  - Cook Islands:
    High Court (1998–date)
  - Fiji Islands:
    Supreme Court of Fiji (1962–date)
    Court of Appeal of Fiji (1962–date)
    High Court (1967–date)
    Magistrate's Court Decisions (1998–date)
    Fiji Law Reports
  - Kiribati:
    Court of Appeal of Kiribati (1975–date)
    High Court of Kiribati (1998–date)
    Digest of Selected Cases (1966–72)
  - Nauru:
    Supreme Court of Nauru (1974–date)
  - Samoa:
    Supreme Court of Samoa (1961–date)
    Court of Appeal of Samoa (1962–date)
    High Court of Samoa (1907–date)
    Index to Western Samoa Law Reports (1921–93)
  - Solomon Islands:
    Solomon Island Cases

- ○ Tonga:
  Supreme Court of Tonga (1990–date)
  Court of Appeal of Tonga (1992–date)
  Tonga Land Court decisions (1984–date)
- ○ Vanuatu:
  Supreme Court of Vanuatu (1981–date)
  Court of Appeal of Vanuatu (1982–date)
  Vanuatu Senior Magistrate's Court decisions (1999–date)
  Index to Vanuatu Law Reports (1980–94)

LAW SCHOOLS

UNIVERSITY OF THE SOUTH PACIFIC

School of Law, PO Box 1168, Suva, Fiji Islands
Tel: +679 313900; Fax: +679 314274
email: hughes_r@vanuatu.usp.ac.fj
website: www.vanuatu.usp.ac.fj

Courses offered

LLB
LLB/BA
LLM (in co-operation with Waikato University, School of Law, New Zealand)
PhD

Centres

1   Institute of Justice and Applied Legal Studies, Suva, Fiji Islands (Fax: +679 314274; email: pulea_mp@usp.ac.fj)
- • Provides the professional practice course (Diploma in Legal Practice).
- • Runs a variety of continuing legal education courses.
2   Law Clinic (Tel: +679 313900; Fax: +679 314274; email: pulea_mp@usp.ac.fj; website: www.vanuatu.usp.ac.fj/ijals/ijals_main.html)

Journals

1   *Journal of South Pacific Law* (publishes legal research with a focus on laws of the South Pacific region) (website: www.vanvatu.usp.ac.fj)
2   *South Pacific Law Bulletin* (IJALS)
3   *South Pacific Law listserve* (IJALS)

UNIVERSITY OF SOUTH PACIFIC

School of Law, PO Box 12, Port Vila, Vanuatu
Tel: +678 22748; Fax: +678 27785
email: law@vanuatu.ac.fj
website: www.vanuatu.ac.fj

Course offered

LLB

BAR ASSOCIATIONS AND LAW SOCIETIES

Many of the countries do not have a legal profession sufficiently large or active to support a Law Society or Bar Association. Addresses for professional societies in some of the USP countries are as follows:

COOK ISLANDS

Cook Island Law Society
PO Box 144, Avarua, Rarotonga
Tel: +682 24567; Fax: +682 21567

FIJI ISLANDS

Fiji Law Society
PO Box 1296, Suva, Fiji Islands

KIRIBATI

Attorney-General's Chambers, PO Box 62, Bairiki, Tarawa Island, Kiribati
Tel: +686 21242; Fax: +686 21025

NAURU

Nauru Law Society
PO Box 54, Nauru

NIUE

Attorney-General of Niue, Office of the Attorney-General of Niue, PO Box 40, Alofi, Niue
Tel: +683 4208; Fax: +683 4228

SAMOA

Samoa Law Society
PO Box 2949, Apia, Samoa
Tel: +685 21751

SOLOMON ISLANDS

Solomon Islands Law Society
c/o Attorney-General's Chambers, Honiara, Guadicanal, Solomon Islands
Tel: +677 22263; 21616; Fax: +677 21608

Solomon Islands Bar Association
PO Box 729, Honiara, Solomon Islands

TONGA

Tonga Law Society
PO Box 2185, Nuku'alofa, Tonga

TUVALU

Attorney-General, Government Offices, Funafuti, Tuvalu
Tel: +688 823; Fax: +688 800

VANUATU

The Law Society
PO Box 166, Port Vila, Vanuatu

SRI LANKA

Legal education is conducted in the law faculties of the Universities of Colombo, the Open University of Sri Lanka at Nugegoda, a suburb of Colombo, and in the Sri Lanka Law College which is managed by the Council of Legal Education.

The University of Colombo and the Open University of Sri Lanka offer four-year LLB degrees. Holders of the degree must pass the final examination of the Council of Legal Education and serve six months of apprenticeship under a senior lawyer and undergo practical training conducted by the Sri Lanka Law College to enrol as attorneys-at-law.

The CLEA country contact is Joe Silva of the Sri Lanka Law College (address below) email: locwal@slt.lk). A local CLEA Chapter was also established in 2002.

The Sri Lanka Law College is managed by the Council of Legal Education and established under Ordinance No 2 of 1900. There are two types of students, namely: (1) the direct entrants selected after a competitive examination, who follow a three-year course; and (2) the LLB graduates of the two universities and barristers of the United Kingdom who are required to take the final examination conducted by the College. Approximately 350 law students graduate each year and 500 (LLB graduates and Law College students) qualify as legal practitioners each year.

The main system of law in Sri Lanka is based on the common law and Roman-Dutch law. The superior court system comprises the Supreme Court (the apex court) and the Court of Appeal which sit in Colombo.

The legal profession is fused, although there is an informal grouping of advocacy specialists practising out of chambers in Colombo.

Practitioners from foreign jurisdictions who wish to practise in Sri Lanka should contact the Bar Association of Sri Lanka, 153 Mihindu Mawartha, Colombo 12, Sri Lanka (Tel: +94 1 447134; 331697; 387477; Fax: +94 1 4488090; email: basl@eureka.lk; website: www.slbar.org).

LAW REPORTS

- *Sri Lankan Law Reports*
- Local law reports are also available free of charge from: www.lawnet.lk and www.justiceministry.gov.lk

LAW SCHOOLS

UNIVERSITY OF COLOMBO

Faculty of Law, College House, PO Box 1490, Cumaratunga Munidasa Mawatha, Colombo 03, Sri Lanka
Tel: +94 1 500942; Fax: +94 1 502001
email: law@cmb.ac.lk
website: www.cmb.ac.lk

Courses offered

LLB
LLM (by coursework and extended essay)
MPhil (by research)
PhD

Journals

1   *Colombo Law Review*
2   *Sri Lanka Journal of International Law*

OPEN UNIVERSITY OF SRI LANKA

Department of Legal Studies, PO Box 21, Nawala, Nugegoda, Sri Lanka
Tel: +94 1 853777; Fax: +94 1 436858
email: hdlaw@ou.ac.lk
website: www.ou.ac.lk

Courses offered

LLB
BA in Legal Policy

SRI LANKA LAW COLLEGE

Faculty of Law, 244 Hulftsdorp Street, Colombo 12, Sri Lanka
Tel: +94 1 323759; Fax: +94 1 436040
email: locwal@slt.lk
website: www.lankika.com/law/lawcollege.htm

Courses offered

Course leading to admission to the Bar
Diploma courses (as part of the continuing legal education programme)

SWAZILAND

Legal education is conducted in the department of law in the Faculty of Social Sciences at the University of Swaziland. The degree structure consists of the BA (law) degree which is studied for a minimum of four years, followed by a two-year LLB degree. The LLB degree qualifies the holder for admission to practise.

The system of law in Swaziland is mainly Roman-Dutch, whilst customary law is important in some respects.

The superior courts are the Court of Appeal and the High Court.

There is no local society of law teachers, although some are members of the Society of Law Teachers of Southern Africa. The CLEA Southern Africa Chapter President is Philip Iya of the University of Fort Hare (address under South Africa) (email: philiya@hotmail.com).

Swaziland has a fused legal profession. Practitioners from foreign jurisdictions wishing to practise in Swaziland should contact the Law Society of Swaziland, PO Box 512, Mbabane, Swaziland.

LAW REPORTS

- *Swaziland Law Reports* (SLR) (1963–81)
- Currently there is no formal law reporting system in operation

LAW SCHOOL

UNIVERSITY OF SWAZILAND

Faculty of Social Science, Department of Law, Private Bag 4, Kwaluseni, Swaziland
Tel: +268 5184011; 5185108; Fax: +268 5185276
email: uniswapgs@uniswa.sz
website: www.uniswa.sz

Courses offered

BA
LLB
Certificate in Law
Diploma in Law

UNITED REPUBLIC OF TANZANIA

Legal education in Tanzania is undertaken at the University of Dar-es-Salaam (which offers a four-year LLB degree programme) and the Open University of Tanzania (which offers a six-year, distance learning LLB degree programme). Holders of an approved law degree wishing to practise must obtain the Postgraduate Diploma in Law which is the accepted practising qualification by the Council of Legal Education.

There is no association of law teachers. The CLEA regional representative is Lillian Tibatemwa-Ekirikubinza (email: litbatemwa@muklaw.bushnet.net). The local CLEA representative is Sifuni Mchome (email: sm@mailclient1.ddsm.ac.tz).

The system of law in Tanzania is based on the common law. The superior court system comprises the Court of Appeal which sits in Dar-es-Salaam and the High Court. There is also a specialist Commercial Court.

Practitioners from other common law systems may apply for the right of audience on an *ad hoc* basis in the Tanzanian courts. Those from foreign jurisdictions who wish to practise in Tanzania should contact the Law Society of Tanzania, PO Box 2148, Dar-es-Salaam, Tanzania (Tel/Fax: +255 51 21907; email:tanglaw.society@twiga.com).

LAW REPORTS

- *Tanganyika Territory Law Reports* (1921–47)
- *Law Report Supplements to the Official Gazette* (1948–70)
- *Law Reports of Tanzania* (1973–79)
- *High Court Digest*
- *Tanzania Law Reports* (1980–date) (published by Jutastat (www.jutastat.com))

LAW SCHOOLS

UNIVERSITY OF DAR ES SALAAM

Faculty of Law, PO Box 35093, Dar-es-Salaam, Tanzania
Tel: +255 22 2410254
email: dean@law.udsm.ac.tz
website: http://law.udsm.ac.tz

Courses offered

LLB
LLM
PhD
LLD
Postgraduate Diploma in Law (for holders of the LLB degree)
Specialised Postgraduate Diploma in Law (for the holders of degrees other than the LLB)

Centre

Centre for the Study of Forced Migration (CSFM)
- Provides academic programmes on refugees studies, human rights and international humanitarian law.
- Provides short term training to those working in the areas of refugees.
- Conducts research on forced migration with an emphasis on East Africa.
- Engages in outreach activities and dissemination of information relevant to forced migration.

Journal

East African Law Review

OPEN UNIVERSITY OF TANZANIA

PO Box 23409, Dar-es-Salaam, Tanzania

Course offered

LLB (by distance learning)

UGANDA

Legal education is conducted in the faculty of law at Makerere University, Uganda Christian University, Mukono, and at the Law Development Centre (LDC). Those holding an LLB degree and wishing to practise must take the Postgraduate Bar Course offered by the LDC.

The CLEA country contact is Lillian Tibatemwa-Ekirikubinza of Makerere University (address below) (email: ltibatemwa@muklaw.ac.ug).

The system of law in Uganda is based on the common law. The superior court system comprises the Supreme Court (the apex court), the Court of Appeal and the High Court. The Court of Appeal also serves as the Constitutional Court. The legal profession is fused.

Practitioners from other common law systems may apply for the right of audience on an *ad hoc* basis. Those from foreign jurisdictions wishing to practise in Uganda should contact the Law Society of Uganda, Plot 69 Nkrumah Road, PO Box 426, Kampala, Uganda (Tel: +256 41 251054; Fax: +256 41 242460; email: legalaid@imul.com).

LAW REPORTS

- *Uganda Law Reports* (1904–57)
- *East African Law Reports* (1957–73)
- *Lawafrica Law Reports* (provide full text online decisions of the Supreme Court, Court of Appeal and High Court (www.lawafrica.com))

LAW SCHOOLS

MAKERERE UNIVERSITY

Faculty of Law, PO Box 7062, Kampala, Uganda
Tel: +256 41 542284; Fax: +256 41 532956
email: lawdean@muklaw.bushnet.net
website: www.muklaw.ac.ug

Courses offered

LLB
LLM
LLD

Journals

1   *Makerere Law Journal*
2   *Journal of Peace and Human Rights*

Centres

1   Human Rights and Peace Centre (HURIPEC) (Fax: +256 41 543110)
2   Law Development Centre (Makerere Hill, PO Box 7117, Kampala, Uganda)

Courses offered

Diploma in Legal Practice
Diploma in Law

UGANDA CHRISTIAN UNIVERSITY

Department of Law, PO Box 4, Mukono, Uganda
Tel: +256 41 290231; Fax: +256 41 290139
email: ucu@ucu.ac.ug

Course offered

LLB

UNITED KINGDOM

(including other parts of the British islands and the overseas territories)

Legal education in the UK is conducted in the faculties of 69 universities and other institutions of higher education in England and Wales, 10 in Scotland and two in Northern Ireland. A wide range of degrees is offered at undergraduate level (including LLB, BA in Law and Law in combination with other subjects) and at postgraduate level (LLM, MA, BCL, etc), brief details of which can be found under individual entries below.

The CLEA UK contact is Selina Goulbourne of the University of Greenwich (address below) (Tel: +44 208 3318727; Fax: +44 208 3318473; email: s.goulbourne@greenwich.ac.uk).

There are two associations for law teachers:

1   Society of Legal Scholars in the UK and Ireland (formerly the SPTL)
    The Hon Secretary is Nick Wikeley, Faculty of Law, University of Southampton (address below) (Fax: +44 23 80593416; email: njw@soton.ac.uk).

2   The Association of Law Teachers (ALT)
    The contact is Mike Cuthbert, University of Northampton (address below) (Fax: +44 1604 721214; email: mike.cuthbert@northampton.ac.uk).

Other legal education bodies include:

- British and Irish Legal Education Technology Association (BILETA) which promotes technology in legal education throughout the UK and Ireland (www.bileta.ac.uk).
- Clinical Legal Education Organisation Network (CLEO) is designed to enable academics to share experiences of running clinical programmes in law schools (www.ukcle.ac.uk/resources/cleo/index.html).
- Learning in Law Initiative Network (LILI) (www.ukcle.ac.uk/lili/index.html).
- Socio-Legal Studies Association (www.ukc.ac.uk/slsa/index.htm).
- Consortium for Access to Legal Education Consortium (CALE) members are committed to providing access to high quality law degree programmes for a wide range of students choosing to study part time. Their focus is on promoting and sharing best practice in the delivery of face to face courses (www.ukcle.ac.uk/resources/cale.html).
- Global Alliance for Justice Education (GAJE) (www.gaje.org).

There are three separate legal systems in the UK: England and Wales; Scotland; and Northern Ireland. The House of Lords is the final court of appeal from decisions of the superior courts of England and Wales, Northern Ireland and (except criminal appeals) Scotland. The European Court of Justice exercises jurisdiction in respect of the interpretation and application of the law of the European Union. Apart from Scotland, which has its own system of private civil law, the legal systems of the UK are based on the common law. Under devolution legislation implemented in 1998, certain legislative powers have been devolved to a Scottish Parliament and more limited devolution to the Northern Ireland and Welsh Assemblies.

The Channel Islands and the Isle of Man each have their own legal systems and, as dependencies of the Crown, are not strictly part of the UK. However, for convenience, they are dealt with below.

LEGAL EDUCATION IN ENGLAND AND WALES

Law schools in England and Wales offer degrees recognised by the Law Society and the Bar Council as 'qualifying law degrees'. These provide exemptions from the academic stage of legal training, known as the Common Professional Examination (CPE) (also known as the Postgraduate Diploma in Law). Non-law graduates are required to sit the CPE which is a one-year full time course (or two years part time or by distance learning). Those wishing to qualify as barristers or solicitors then proceed to the vocational stage of training.

Entry into the legal profession

The legal profession is divided into solicitors and barristers. However, under current legislation, solicitors and barristers no longer enjoy a monopoly in respect of practice in their own fields. Thus, for example, a solicitor with an advocacy certificate enjoys the right of audience in the superior courts.

Solicitors

For those wishing to practise as a solicitor in England and Wales, the vocational stage of legal education, the Legal Practice Course (LPC), is conducted in a number of specialised institutions. Some of these are independent (such as the College of Law and BPP Law School) whilst others are attached to universities. Currently there are 28 institutions offering the LPC, most as either a one-year full time course or two years part time course, in preparation for the Law Society's Final Examination. Further details are published by the Law Society of England and Wales (email: www.lawsociety.org.uk). This is followed by undertaking a training contract for two years and completion of a Professional Skills Course.

Practitioners from foreign jurisdictions wishing to gain admission as a solicitor in England and Wales may be required to undertake the Qualified Lawyers Transfer Test: details can be obtained from the Law Society of England and Wales (as above).

Foreign legal consultants are permitted to practise in England and Wales under their home title without requalifying. The areas of work reserved for solicitors (as well as barristers) in England and Wales include rights of audience, property transfers and succession. Foreign lawyers do not have rights of audience unless the lawyer, being here temporarily, is exercising special rights under EU law.

Barristers

Those wishing to practise as a Barrister in England and Wales must become a member of an Inn of Court and complete the Bar Vocational Course (BVC) which runs for one academic year, full time, or for two years, part time. It is offered by eight institutions. Full information can be obtained from the Bar Council/General Council of the Bar (www.barcouncil.org.uk). There is also a requirement for pupillage.

Applications for temporary membership of the Bar may be made by common law practitioners for the purpose of conducting a particular case or cases. A 'common law practitioner' is defined as: (i) a member of the Hong Kong Bar of not less than three years' standing; and (ii) a practitioner in other common law jurisdictions who has a period of not less than three years' regularly exercised rights of audience in superior courts which administer law which is substantially equivalent to the common law of England and Wales. Members of the Bar of Northern Ireland and of the Faculty of Advocates in Scotland are likewise eligible for temporary admission in the same way as common law practitioners.

Practitioners from other jurisdictions wishing to practise in England and Wales should contact the Secretary of the Joint Regulations Committee (JRC) of the General Council of the Bar of England and Wales (as above).

LEGAL EDUCATION IN SCOTLAND

Legal education in Scotland involves obtaining a qualifying law degree at a Scottish university which permits direct entry onto the Diploma in Legal Practice (DLP). Those law degrees recognised by both the Law Society of Scotland and the Faculty of Advocates are offered at: the University of Aberdeen, University of Dundee, University of Edinburgh, University of Glasgow and the University of Strathclyde.

Those wishing to seek qualification as a solicitor, but who do not hold a qualifying law degree, must take the Law Society of Scotland's professional training course prior to studying for the DLP.

Entry into the legal profession

The legal profession is divided into solicitors and advocates.

After completion of the LLB qualifying degree, students seeking admission as either a solicitor or advocate are required to take the DLP. This is offered by the University of Aberdeen, University of Dundee, University of Edinburgh and the Glasgow Graduate School of Law.

Advocates

Every candidate for admission must first present a petition to the Court. The Court thereafter remits to the Faculty of Advocates for matriculation of the candidate as an Intrant. Once the Intrant has passed or been exempted from the educational and training requirements, he or she may apply to the Clerk of the Faculty for admission to the Faculty. The final stage in the process is admission by the Court to the public office of advocate.

There are no special provisions for admission of members of other Commonwealth Bars to the Scottish Bar (except for members of the English Bar and members of the Bar of Northern Ireland). There are, however, general provisions in the Regulations as to Intrants giving the power to grant exceptions.

Full details can be obtained from the Faculty of Advocates (Fax: +44 131 2253642).

Solicitors (who may also take the title of Writers to the Signet)

Following completion of the DLP, intending solicitors serve a two-year training contract with a solicitor and must attend a two-week Professional Competence Course and, from 2003, pass a Test of Professional Competence.

The Council of the Law Society of Scotland is responsible for issuing certificates of qualification which the applicant produces to the Court of Session for admission.

Full details can be obtained from the Law Society of Scotland (website: www.lawscot.org.uk).

Foreign legal consultants are permitted to practise in Scotland under their home title without requalifying, and are entitled to provide advice about the law of the country in which they are qualified. A foreign legal consultant may not prepare: (a) any writ relating to property; (b) any writ relating to any action or proceeding in any court; (c) any papers relating to probate (called confirmation).

LEGAL EDUCATION IN NORTHERN IRELAND

The academic stage of legal education in Northern Ireland involves the completion of a qualifying law degree from Queen's University Belfast or University of Ulster. Law degrees from the Republic of Ireland are also accepted as qualifying law degrees. Non-law graduates may also study for a two-year Bachelor of Legal Science at Queen's University Belfast, after which they may continue onto the professional training course.

Entry into the legal profession

The legal profession is divided into solicitors and barristers.

A one-year postgraduate vocational training course for both intending barristers and solicitors, and known as the Certificate in Professional Legal Studies (CPLS), is offered by the Institute of Professional Legal Studies at Queen's University Belfast.

Those wishing to qualify as a solicitor must serve an apprenticeship for two years under a supervising solicitor known as a Master.

Those wishing to qualify as a barrister must undertake a 12-month pupillage after completion of the CPLS.

There is now reciprocal recognition of qualifications between England and Wales and Northern Ireland. As such, it is possible for a solicitor admitted to the Roll in England and Wales to be admitted to the Roll in Northern Ireland without further examination. Applications from Scottish solicitors are considered on an *ad hoc* basis.

Practitioners from other jurisdictions wishing to practise in Northern Ireland should contact the Law Society of Northern Ireland (website: www.lawsoc-ni.org).

Foreign legal consultants are permitted to practise in Northern Ireland under their home title without requalifying. They are subject to the same statutory restrictions as anyone else who is not a qualified solicitor.

Any practising member of the Bar of England and Wales may be called to the Bar of Northern Ireland. Otherwise there are no provisions made for the admission of Commonwealth practitioners unless the applicant is a national of a Member State of the European Union.

Foreign legal consultants are permitted to practise in Northern Ireland under their home title without requalifying. If they wish to practise as barristers they must apply for temporary membership of the Bar by contacting the Under Treasurer, Royal Courts of Justice, Chichester Street, Belfast BT1 3J, Northern Ireland.

CHANNEL ISLANDS AND THE ISLE OF MAN

Guernsey

Practitioners from an overseas jurisdiction wishing to practise in Guernsey must produce a Certificate of Admission either as a Barrister or as a Solicitor in England and Wales, or Northern Ireland or Scotland, together with either a Diploma stating that the applicant is a 'Bachelier' of one of the faculties of law of France or a 'Certificat d'Etudes Juridiques Francaises et Normande' from Caen University. The applicant must also serve pupillage and pass the relevant examinations on the laws of Guernsey. Foreign legal consultants are allowed to practise in Guernsey under their home title without requalifying but do not enjoy rights of audience and are not permitted to draft documents for presentation to the Court nor carry out local property transfers or prepare wills.

Further information can be obtained from the Guernsey Bar Council, PO Box 212, St Peter Port, Guernsey, Channel Islands. (Fax: +44 1481 701435)

Jersey

There is no automatic admission of overseas practitioners in Jersey. The system involves a combination of educational qualifications which may be obtained overseas and local examinations in the laws and customs of Jersey. This applies to both advocates and solicitors. Foreign legal consultants are permitted to practise in Jersey under their home title without requalifying but are not allowed to undertake any work involving Jersey law.

Further details can be obtained from the Honorary Secretary, Jersey Law Society, Vibert and Valpy, 8 Duchamel Place, St Helier, Jersey, Channel Islands.

Isle of Man

A person may be articled in the Isle of Man if he or she: (1) has been called to the Bar in England and Wales, Northern Ireland or any of the Channel Islands; or (2) is a Counsel of the Irish Bar; or (3) is admitted as a member of the Faculty of Advocates in Scotland; or (4) has been admitted as a solicitor in any part of the British Isles of the Republic of Ireland. Foreign legal consultants are not permitted to practise in the Isle of Man under their home title without requalifying.

Further details can be obtained from the Isle of Man Law Society, 27 Hope Street, Douglas, Isle of Man (Tel: +44 1624 662910; Fax: +44 1624 679232; email: iomlawsoc@advsys.co.uk).

UNITED KINGDOM OVERSEAS (FORMERLY KNOWN AS DEPENDENT) TERRITORIES

The remaining Overseas Territories are as follows: Anguilla; Bermuda; British Antarctic Territory; British Indian Ocean Territory; British Virgin Islands; Cayman Islands; Falkland Islands; Gibraltar; Montserrat; Pitcairn; Henderson; Ducie and Oeno Islands; St Helena; Ascension; and Tristan da Cunha; South Georgia and South Sandwich Islands; and Turks and Caicos Islands. All have their own legal systems based on English law, with varying degrees of legislative autonomy, for example, the

Sovereign Base Areas of Akrotiri and Dhekelia (Cyprus) apply Cyprus law as modified. In all cases, appeals from local courts lie ultimately to the Judicial Committee of the Privy Council.

An organised Bar exists in all the territories except the British Antarctic Territory, British Indian Ocean Territory, Pitcairn and the Sovereign Base Areas. There may be local admission requirements. Only the Cayman Islands has its own law school and this is listed in the section on the Caribbean.

LAW REPORTS

- Each jurisdiction has its own series of law reports and there are numerous specialist series dealing with, for example, tax, immigration, criminal and admiralty matters
- The British and Irish Legal Information Institute (BAILII) contains full text judgments (free of charge) of all recent cases in the superior courts in the UK (website: www.bailii.org)
- Privy Council decisions (full text and free of charge 1996 onwards) are also available on www.bailii.org
- *Times Law Reports*

LAW SCHOOLS

UNIVERSITY OF ABERDEEN

School of Law, Taylor Building, Regent Walk, Aberdeen AB24 3UB, UK
Tel: +44 1224 272420; Fax: +44 1224 272442
email law095@abdn.ac.uk
website: www.abdn.ac.uk

Courses offered

LLB/LLB (Hons)
BLE
BLE (Hons)
LLM
PhD
Diploma in Legal Education
Diploma in Legal Practice

Centres

1   Civil Law Centre
The aims of the Centre are:
- To research the Classical Roman law, its second life in Europe, and the means by which it was transmitted into modern legal systems.
- To research the law of modern civil or mixed legal systems.

- To research Scots law where it shows the influence of the civil law tradition.
- To promote, where appropriate, the functional solutions offered by the civil law tradition to the problems of Scots law.
- To promote and expand the teaching of Roman and civil law.

2 Centre for Property Law
- The aims of the Centre are to focus and co-ordinate the activities of a number of specialists working in different areas of the wide field of property. The Centre's primary area of work is the property law of Scotland. The major areas of land law, corporeal moveable property, commercial property and intellectual property are all represented. A second area of expertise and research is the property law of South Africa, both in its own right and as a source potentially relevant to the development of Scots law.

UNIVERSITY OF ABERTAY DUNDEE

Dundee Business School, Bell Street, Dundee DD1 1HG, UK
Tel: + 44 1382 308486; Fax: +44 1382 308400
email: dbs@abertay.ac.uk
website: www.abertay.ac.uk

Courses offered

BA (Hons) in European Business Law
BA (Hons) in Law
LLM in World Trade Law
Diploma in Conveyancing and Executry Law

ANGLIA POLYTECHNIC UNIVERSITY

Anglia Law School, Bishop Hall Lane, Chelmsford CM1 1SQ, UK
Tel: +44 1245 493131; Fax: +44 1245 493134
email: l.m.murkin@anglia.ac.uk
website: www.anglia.ac.uk

Courses offered

LLB (Hons)
BA/BSc (Combined Hons) Law
BA/BSc (Combined Hons) Criminology
BA (Hon) Business Law
BA (Hons) Investigative Studies
LLM/MA in International and European Business Law
LLM/MA International Sports Law
LLM Legal Practice
MBA Legal
MPhil
PhD
Common Professional Examination
Legal Practice Course

UNIVERSITY OF BIRMINGHAM

School of Law, PO Box 363, Edgbaston, Birmingham B15 2TT, UK
Tel: +44 121 4143637; Fax: +44 121 4143585
email: law@bham.ac.uk
website: www.law.bham.ac.uk

Courses offered

LLB
LLB (law and politics)
LLB (law and business studies)
LLB (law with French)
LLB (law with German)
MJur (comparative legal research by thesis)
LLM
LLM (commercial law)
PhD
Diploma in Legal Studies – Common Professional Examination qualification
Legal Practice Course (in association with De Montfort University)

Centres

1   Institute of Judicial Administration (the aims of the Institute are to initiate, co-ordinate and develop teaching and research in all aspects of the administration of justice in England and Wales. Teaching and research is conducted on a comparative and inter-disciplinary basis)
2   Institute of European Law

Journal

Civil Justice Quarterly (published in association with the Institute of Judicial Administration) (principal focus is on the UK but it covers a wide range of issues relating to civil justice from an international and comparative perspective)

BOURNEMOUTH UNIVERSITY

School of Finance and Law, Talbot Campus, Fern Barrow, Poole, Dorset BH12 5BB, UK
Tel: +44 1202 595187; Fax: +44 1202 595261
email: fandl@bournemouth.ac.uk
website: www.bournemouth.ac.uk

Courses offered

LLB Business Law
BA/LLB Taxation Law
LLB Law with Finance
BA Accounting and Law
MA Law
MPhil
PhD
Common Professional Examination
Legal Practice Course

BPP LAW SCHOOL

68–70 Red Lion Street, London WC1R 4NY, UK
Tel: +44 207 4302304; Fax: +44 207 4041389
email: louiseeaston@bpp.com
website: www.bpp.com

Courses offered

Common Professional Examination
Bar Vocational Course
Legal Practice Course

BRADFORD COLLEGE

Bradford Law School, Great Horton Road, Bradford, West Yorkshire BD7 1AY, UK
Tel: +44 1274 753333; Fax: +44 1274 753241
email: admissions@bilk.ac.uk
website: www.bilk.ac.uk

Courses offered

BA Law and European Business
BA Marketing and Law
LLB
BA Accountancy and Law

UNIVERSITY OF BRIGHTON

Brighton Business School, Mithras House, Lewes Road, Brighton BN2 4GJ, UK
Tel: +44 1273 642987; Fax: +44 1273 642980
email: j.e.lucas@brighton.ac.uk
website: www.bus.brighton.ac.uk

Courses offered

BA Law with Accountancy
Common Professional Examination

UNIVERSITY OF BRISTOL

Faculty of Law, Wills Memorial Building, Queens Road, Bristol BS8 1RJ, UK
Tel: +44 117 9545329; Fax: +44 117 9251870
email: law-dept@bris.ac.uk
website: www.law.bris.ac.uk

Courses offered

LLB
LLB (European Legal Studies)
LLB (law and French)
LLB (law and German)
LLB (law with study abroad)

BSc Chemistry and Law
MA in Legal Studies
LLM
PhD
Diploma in Intellectual Property Law and Practice

Centres

1   Centre for Law and Gender
2   Centre for the Study of Administrative Justice
3   Centre for Criminal Justice Research Centre for International Legal Studies
4   Intellectual Property Centre
5   Norton Rose Centre for Commercial and Banking Law

BRUNEL UNIVERSITY

Department of Law, Faculty of Social Sciences, Uxbridge, Middlesex UB8 3PH, UK
Tel: +44 1895 274000; Fax: +44 1895 810476
email: adrienne.obrien@brunel.ac.uk
website: www.brunel.ac.uk

Courses offered

LLB
LLB (business and finance law)
MA/LLM in Criminal Justice
MA/LLM in Child Law and Policy
MA/LLM in Law and Politics of the European Union
MPhil
PhD

Centres

1   Centre for Consumer and Commercial Law Research
2   Centre for Criminal Justice Research
3   Centre for the Study of Law, the Child and the Family

UNIVERSITY OF BUCKINGHAM

School of Law, Buckingham, Bucks MK18 1EG, UK
Tel: +44 1280 814080; Fax: +44 1280 822245
email: andrew.durand@buckingham.ac.uk
website: www.buck.ac.uk

Courses offered

LLB
LLB (law and politics)
LLB (law, biology and environment)
LLB (English and European law)
LLM
LLM (international and commercial law)

MPhil
DPhil

Journal

Denning Law Journal (annually)

UNIVERSITY OF CAMBRIDGE
Faculty of Law, 10 West Road, Cambridge CB3 9DZ, UK
Tel: +44 1223 330033; Fax: +44 1223 330055
email: admin@law.cam.ac.uk
website: www.law.cam.ac.uk

Courses offered

BA
Double Maîtrise: Paris II – Cambridge
LLM
MLitt
PhD
MPhil (Criminology)
LLD
Diploma in Legal Studies
Diploma in International Law

Centres

1   The Institute of Criminology
2   The Lauterpacht Research Centre for International Law
3   The Centre for European Legal Studies
4   Centre for Corporate and Commercial Law
5   Centre for Public Law
6   Intellectual Property Unit
7   The ESRC Centre for Business Research

Journals and other periodicals

1   *The Cambridge Law Journal*
2   *International Law Reports*
3   *Iran-United States Claims Tribunal Reports*
4   *Cambridge International Document Series*
5   *Clarendon Studies in Criminology*
6   *Cambridge Studies in English Legal History*
7   *ICSID Reports*
8   *International Environmental Law Reports*

UNIVERSITY OF CENTRAL ENGLAND
Faculty of Law and Social Science, Perry Bar, Birmingham B42 2SU, UK
Tel: +44 121 3316600; Fax: +44 121 3315640
email: law@uce.ac.uk
website: www.uce.ac.uk

Courses offered

LLB
BA
LLM European Legal Studies
LLM International Human Rights
Common Professional Examination
Legal Practice Course

UNIVERSITY OF CENTRAL LANCASHIRE

Lancashire Law School, Harris Building, Corporation Street, Preston PR1 2TQ, UK
Tel: +44 1772 893062; Fax: +44 1772 892908
email: rdtaylor@uclan.ac.uk
website: www.uclan.ac.uk

Courses offered

LLB
LLB with French
LLB with German
LLB with Criminology
LLM in Environmental Law
LLM in Employment Law
LLM in European Law
LLM in Medical Law and Bioethics
MA in International Law and Business
MPhil
PhD
Common Professional Examination Course
Legal Practice Course

CITY UNIVERSITY

Institute of Law, Northampton Square, London EC1V OHB, UK
Tel: +44 20 70408301; Fax: +44 20 70408578
email: law@city.ac.uk
website: www.city.ac.uk

Note:
On 1 August 2001, the Inns of Court School of Law became part of City University,
joining with the Department of Law at City to form the new Institute of Law

Courses offered

LLB
LLM
LLM Criminal Litigation
Diploma in Law (Common Professional Examination)
Bar Vocational Course

COLLEGE OF LAW

50–52 Chancery Lane, London WC2A 1SX, UK
Tel: +44 1483 460200; Fax: +441483 460305
email: susan_drury@lawcol.co.uk
website: www.lawcol.org.uk

Courses offered

Common Professional Examination
Bar Vocational Course
Legal Practice Course

The College has the following branches:

Chester:
Christleton Hall, Christleton, Chester CH3 7AB, UK
Tel: +44 1244 335291; Fax: +44 1244 332081

Guildford:
Braboeuf Manor, Guildford GU3 1HA, UK
Tel: +44 1483 460200; Fax: +44 1244 460305

London:
2 Bream's Building, Chancery Lane, London EC4A 1DP, UK
Tel: +44 207 6117460; Fax: +44 207 6117444

14 Store Street, Bloomsbury, London WC1E 7DE, UK
Tel: +44 207 2911200; Fax: +44 207 2911305

York:
Bishopthorpe Road, York YO2 1QA, UK
Tel: +44 1904 682000; Fax: +44 1904 682099

COVENTRY UNIVERSITY

School of International Studies and Law, Priory Street, Coventry CV1 5FB, UK
Tel: +44 24 76888256; 7688176; Fax: +44 24 76888679
email: isladmin@coventry.ac.uk
website: www.coventry-isl.org.uk

Courses offered

LLB
LLB (business law)
LLB (criminal justice)
LLB (European law with French/Italian/German/Russian/Spanish)
BA Law
LLM in Human Rights
LLM in Criminal Justice
MA in Diplomacy Law and Global Change

Centre

Criminal Justice Research Centre

DE MONTFORT UNIVERSITY

Department of Law, The Gateway, Leicester LE1 9BH, UK
Tel: +44 116 2577177; Fax: +44 116 2577186
email: rwward@dmu.ac.uk
website: www.dmu.ac.uk

Courses offered

LLB
LLB (law with French/German)
LLB Law and Criminal Justice
LLM Business Law
LLM Countryside and Agriculture Law
LLM Food Law
LLM Environmental Law
MPhil
PhD
Common Professional Examination
Legal Practice Course

Centre

Environmental Law Institute

Journals

1   *Environmental Liability Journal*
2   *Encyclopædia of Environmental Health and Practice*

UNIVERSITY OF DERBY

School of Education, Human Sciences and Law, Division of Law, University of
Derby, Kedleston Road, Derby DE22 1GB, UK
Tel: +44 1332 591446; Fax: +44 1332 597754
email: t.wragg@derby.ac.uk
website: www.derby.ac.uk

Courses offered

LLB
LLB with a Modern Language
LLB with European Studies
LLB with Politics
BA Law

UNIVERSITY OF DUNDEE

Department of Law, Scrymgeour Building, Park Place, Dundee DD1 4HN, UK
Tel: +44 1382 344461; Fax: +44 1382 226905
email: f.j.clark@dundee.ac.uk
website: www.dundee.ac.uk

Courses offered

LLB
LLB (Hons)
LLM
LLM Corporate Government
LLM Environmental Regulation
PhD
Diploma in Legal Practice (CPLP)

Centres

1   The Centre for Energy, Petroleum and Mineral Law and Policy (CEPMLP)
2   The International Water Law Research Institute (IWLRI) (promotes academic research, postgraduate teaching, advisory services and professional training in the area of international and national law of water resources)
3   Centre for Professional Legal Practice
4   Charity Law Research Unit

Journal

The CEPMLP Internet Journal (website: www.dundee.ac.uk/cepmlp/journal)

UNIVERSITY OF DURHAM

Department of Law, 50 North Bailey, Durham DH1 3ET, UK
Tel: +44 191 3742041; Fax: +44 191 3742044
email: g.r.sullivan@durham.ac.uk
website: www.durham.ac.uk

Courses offered

LLB, LLB (Hons)
LLB, BA (law and economics)
LLB, BA (law and politics)
LLB, BA (law and sociology)
LLB (ELS)
LLM
MJur
PhD
Legal Studies Course (Certificate)
Legal Studies Course (Diploma)

Centres

1   Centre for Law and Computing
2   Durham European Law Institute
3   Human Rights Centre

UNIVERSITY OF EAST ANGLIA

School of Law, University Plain, Norwich NR4 7TJ, UK
Tel: +44 1603 592520; Fax: +44 1603 250245
email: law@uea.ac.uk
website: www.uea.ac.uk/law

Courses offered

LLB
LLB Law with European Legal Systems
LLB Law with French Law and Language
LLB Law with German Law and Language
LLB Law with American Legal Studies
LLM International Trade Law
LLM Employment Law
LLM International Commercial and Business Law
MPhil
PhD

Centres

1   Centre for Family Law and Family Policy
2   Centre for European Law and Practice

UNIVERSITY OF EAST LONDON

School of Law, Longbridge Road, Dagenham RM8 2AS, UK
Tel: +44 208 2232113; Fax: +44 208 2232927
email: p.berwick@uel.ac.uk
website: www.uel.ac.uk

Courses offered

LLB
BA in Criminology and Criminal Justice
LLM in International Legal Studies
MPhil
PhD

Centre

Encountering Legal Cultures Research Group (particularly concerned with post-colonial theory, feminist theory and critical race theory)

UNIVERSITY OF EDINBURGH

Faculty of Law, Old College, South Bridge, Edinburgh EH8 9YL, Scotland
Tel: +44 131 6502006; Fax: +44 131 6506317
email: law.faculty@ed.ac.uk
website: www.law.ed.ac.uk

Courses offered

LLB
LLM in Innovation, Technology and the Law
LLM in European Law
MSc in Criminology
MPhil
PhD
Diploma in Legal Practice

Centres

1   Centre for Law and Society
2   Legal Practice Unit
3   Shepherd and Wedderburn Centre for Research in Intellectual property and Technology (SCRIPT)
4   Edinburgh Europa Centre
5   Joseph Bell Centre for Forensic Statistics and Legal Reasoning
    Set up to evaluate, present and interpret evidence
6   David Hume Institute (set up to consider legal and economic aspects of public policy)

Journal

Edinburgh Law Review

UNIVERSITY OF ESSEX

School of Law, Wivenhoe Park, Colchester CO4 3SQ, UK
Tel: +44 1206 872558; Fax: +44 1206 873627
email: law@essex.ac.uk
website: www.essex.ac.uk

Courses offered

LLB
LLB in English and French Law with Maitrise
LLB in English and European Laws
LLB Law and Philosophy
LLB Law and Human Rights
LLB Law and Politics
BA Law and Human Rights
LLM
MA in the Theory and Practice of Human Rights
MA in European Integration
MEnv Environment, Science and Society
MPhil
PhD

Centres

1   Human Rights Centre (email: hrc@essex.ac.uk)
2   Centre for the Environment and Society
3   Pan European Institute

UNIVERSITY OF EXETER

School of Law, Amory Building, Rennes Drive, Exeter EX4 4RJ, UK
Tel: +44 1392 263265; Fax: +44 1392 263196
email: law@exeter.ac.uk
website: www.ex.ac.uk

Courses offered

LLB
LLB European with (French)/Maîtrise or (German)/Magister
LLB with European Study
LLM
MPhil
PhD
Diploma in Law
Legal Practice Course

Centres

1   Centre for European Legal Studies (CELS) (promotes research into questions of EU law)
2   Centre for Legal Practice (delivers the Legal Practice Course)

Journals

1   *Bracton Law Journal* (annually)
2   *Exeter Papers in European Law*

UNIVERSITY OF GLAMORGAN

Law School, Pontypridd, Mid-Glamorgan CF37 1DL, Wales
Tel: +44 1443 483005; Fax: +44 1443 483002
email:law@glam.ac.uk
website: www.glam.ac.uk

Courses offered

LLB
BA Law
LLM Commercial Dispute Resolution
LLM Employment Law and Practice
LLM European Union Law
Common Professional Examination
Legal Practice Course

UNIVERSITY OF GLASGOW

School of Law, 5–9 Stair Building, Glasgow G12 8QQ, Scotland
Tel: +44 141 3304507; Fax: +44 141 3304900
email: enquiries@law.gla.ac.uk
website: www.law.gla.ac.uk

Courses offered

LLB
LLM in Commercial Law
MPhil
PhD
Diploma in Legal Practice

Centres and Units

1   Glasgow Graduate School of Law (runs the Diploma in Legal Practice and has a collaborative arrangement with the University of Strathclyde)
2   Institute of Law and Ethics in Medicine
3   Lockerbie Trial Briefing Site (website: www.ltb.org.uk)

GLASGOW CALEDONIAN UNIVERSITY

Department of Law and Public Administration, City Campus, Cowcaddens Road, Glasgow G4 0BA, Scotland
Tel: +44 141 3313430; Fax: +44 141 3313005
email: J.Charlton@gcal.ac.uk
website: www.fob.gcal.ac.uk

Courses offered

BA Law with Administrative Studies
LLM/Postgraduate Diploma in European and International Trade Law
MPhil
PhD
Diploma in Legal Studies

UNIVERSITY OF GREENWICH

Law Department, School of Social Science and Law, Maritime Campus, 30 Park Row, Greenwich, London SE10 9LS, UK
Tel: +44 208 3318727; Fax: +44 208 3318473
email: s.goulbourne@greenwich.ac.uk
website: www.gre.ac.uk

Courses offered

LLB
BA Law
BA Legal Studies
Common Professional Examination
Bar Vocational Course

UNIVERSITY OF HERTFORDSHIRE

Faculty of Law, St Albans Campus, 7 Hatfield Road, St Albans, Herts AL1 3RR, UK
Tel: +44 1707 284000: Fax: +44 1707 286205
email: r.m.martin@herts.ac.uk
website: www.herts.ac.uk/law

Courses offered

LLB
LLM in International, Commercial, Email Commerce and Maritime Law
Legal Practice Course

Centre

Centre for International Law

HOLBORN COLLEGE

200 Greyhound Road, London W14 9RY, UK
Tel: +44 207 3853377; Fax: +44 207 3813377
email: hlt@holborncollege.ac.uk
website: www.holborncollege.ac.uk

Courses offered

LLB
LLM

UNIVERSITY OF HUDDERSFIELD

Huddersfield University Business School, Department of Law, Queensgate,
Huddersfield HD1 3DH, UK
Tel: +44 1484 422288; Fax: +44 1484 472279
email: postmaster@hud.ac.uk
website: www.hud.ac.uk

Courses offered

LLB
LLM (by distance learning)
Common Professional Examination
Legal Practice Course

UNIVERSITY OF HULL

Law School, Cottingham Road, Hull HU6 7RX, UK
Tel: +44 1482 465857; Fax: +44 1482 466388
email: law@law.hull.ac.uk
website: www.law.hull.ac.uk

Courses offered

LLB
LLB Law with French/German Law and Language
LLB with Philosophy
LLB Law and Politics
LLM (with Washington College of Law)
LLM International Law
LLM Human Rights Law
LLM International Business Law
LLM European Public Law
MJuris
PhD

Centres and Groups

1   Information Law and Technology Unit
2   Institute of European Public Law (IEPL)
3   McCoubrey Centre for International Law

Journals

1   *European Public Law Journal*
2   *Hull Student Law Journal*

INNS OF COURT SCHOOL OF LAW
See City University

KEELE UNIVERSITY

School of Law, Keele, Staffs ST5 5BG, UK
Tel: +44 1782 583218; Fax: +44 1782 583228
email: m.thomson@keele.ac.uk
website: www.keele.ac.uk

Courses offered

LLB
LLB and BA/BSc
LLM in International and European Law
MA in Environmental Law and Policy
MA in Child Care Law and Practice
LLM in General Legal Studies and Research
LLM in Child Law
MA in Medical Ethics
MPhil
PhD
Common Professional Examination

Group

Gender, Sexuality and Law Research Group

UNIVERSITY OF KENT

Kent Law School, Canterbury CT2 7NS, UK
Tel: +44 1227 827832; Fax: +44 1227 827831
email: kls-office@akv.ac.uk
website: www.ukc.ac.uk

Courses offered

BA
BA Law and French/German/Spanish/Italian Law
LLM Criminal Justice
LLM European Law
LLM Environmental Law and Policy
LLM International Commercial Law
LLM Medical Law
MA in European Integration
MPhil
PhD

Centres

1   Kent Criminal Justice Centre
2   Kent Law Clinic

KINGSTON UNIVERSITY

School of Law, Kingston Hill, Kingston KT2 7LB, UK
Tel: +44 208 5472000; Fax: +44 208 5477038
email: m.beard@kingston.ac.uk
website: www.law.kingston.ac.uk

Courses offered

LLB
Common Professional Examination
LLM in Dispute Resolution
LLM in Business Law
LLM
MA in Legal Studies

UNIVERSITY OF LANCASTER

Law School, Lancaster LA1 4YF, UK
Tel: +44 1524 65201 ext 2463; Fax: +44 1524 848137
email: law@lancaster.ac.uk
website: www.lancs.ac.uk

Courses offered

LLB
LLB (European Legal Studies)
LLB (International)
LLM in European and International Legal Studies
LLM in International Human Rights and Humanitarian Law
LLM/MA in International Law and International Relations
LLM/MA in History of Law and Society
LLM/MA in Socio-Legal Studies
MRes in Socio-Legal Studies
PhD

UNIVERSITY OF LEEDS

Department of Law, 20 Lyddon Terrace, Leeds LS2 9JT, UK
Tel: +44 113 2335033; Fax: +44 113 2335056
email: lawvls@leeds.ac.uk
website: www.leeds.ac.uk

Courses offered

LLB
LLB with French/Chinese/Japanese
BA Accounting and Law
LLM
MA
MPhil
PhD

Centres

1   Centre for Business Law and Practice
2   Centre for Criminal Justice Studies
3   Centre for the Study of Law in Europe
4   Human Rights Research Unit
5   Cyberlaw Research Unit

LEEDS METROPOLITAN UNIVERSITY

School of Law, Cavendish Hall, Beckett Park, Leeds LS6 3QS, UK
Tel: +44 113 2837549; Fax: +44 113 2833206
email: law@lmu.ac.uk
website: www.lmu.ac.uk

Courses offered

LLB
BA (Hons) Law with Information Technology
LLM
MPhil
Diploma in Law (Common Professional Examination)

UNIVERSITY OF LEICESTER

Faculty of Law, University Road, Leicester LE1 7RH, UK
Tel: +44 116 2522363; Fax: +44 116 2525023
email: law@le.ac.uk
website: www.le.ac.uk

Courses offered

LLB
LLB (European Union)
LLB (International)
LLB in Law with French Law and Language
BA Economics and Law
LLM/MA
MPhil
PhD

Centres

1   Centre for European Law and Integration
2   International Centre for Management, Law and Industrial Relations (website: http://iclaw-web.co.uk)

INSTITUTE OF LEGAL EXECUTIVES

Kempston Manor, Kempston, Bedfordshire MK42 7AB, UK
Tel: +44 1234 841000; Fax: +44 1234 840373
email: info@ilex.org.uk
website: www.ilex.org.uk

Course offered

ILEX membership qualification

UNIVERSITY OF LINCOLN

Faculty of Social Sciences and Law, Brayford Pool, Lincoln LN6 7TS, UK
Tel: +44 1522 882000
email: efitzpatrick@lincoln.ac.uk
website: www.lincoln.ac.uk

Course offered

LLB

UNIVERSITY OF LIVERPOOL

Liverpool Law School, Liverpool L69 7ZS, UK
Tel: +44 151 7942807; Fax: +44 151 7942829
email: law@liverpool.ac.uk
website: www.liv.ac.uk

Courses offered

LLB
LLB with English and French Laws
LLB with English and German Laws
BA Legal and Business Studies
LLM
PhD

Centres and Units

1   Centre for the Study of the Child, the Family and the Law
2   Institute of Medicine, Law and Bioethics
3   Charity Law Unit
4   Feminist Legal Research Unit
5   International and European Law Unit
6   Criminal Justice Unit

LIVERPOOL JOHN MOORES UNIVERSITY

School of Law and Applied Social Studies, Josephine Butler House, 1 Myrtle Street,
Liverpool L7 4DN, UK
Tel: +44 151 2313911; Fax: +44 151 2313908
email: law@livjm.ac.uk
website: http://cwis.livjm.ac.uk

Courses offered

LLB
LLM in European Law
MPhil
PhD
Legal Practice Course

Journal

Liverpool Law Review (biannually)

Centre

Centre for Social Welfare Law Research

UNIVERSITY OF LONDON EXTERNAL PROGRAMME

Senate House, London WC1E 7HU, UK
Tel: +44 207 8628317; Fax: +44 207 8628315
email: adam.dawkins@lon.ac.uk
website: www.londonexternal.ac.uk

Courses offered

LLB
LLM

UNIVERSITY OF LONDON

Schools of the University:

1 Birkbeck College
2 King's College London
3 London School of Economics and Political Science
4 Queen Mary and Westfield College
5 School of Oriental and African Studies
6 University College London

Note:
Each college/school offers a separate LLB programme. At present the LLM programme is run as an inter-collegiate programme. A full listing of subjects can be obtained from: http://ials.sas.ac.uk

BIRKBECK COLLEGE

School of Law, Malet Street, London WC1E 7HX, UK
Tel: +44 207 6316507; Fax: +44 207 6316506
email: admin@law.bbk.ac.uk
website: www.bbk.ac.uk

Courses offered

LLB
Master's in Research (Law) (MRes)
MPhil
PhD

INSTITUTE OF ADVANCED LEGAL STUDIES

Charles Clore House, 17 Russell Square, London WC1B 5DR, UK
Tel: +44 207 8625800; Fax: +44 207 8625850
email: ials.lib@sas.ac.uk
website: http://ials.sas.ac.uk

Courses offered

MPhil
PhD

The Institute's International and Professional Training Unit (IPTU) also provides a variety of short courses

Journal

Amicus Curiae (monthly)

KING'S COLLEGE LONDON

School of Law, Strand, London WC2R 2LS, UK
Tel: +44 207 8365454; Fax: +44 207 8732465
email: enq.genlaw@kcl.ac.uk
website: www.kcl.ac.uk

Courses offered

LLB
LLB (English and French law)
LLB (law with German law)
LLB (law with European legal studies)
LLM
MA (medical ethics and law)
MPhil
PhD

Centres and Groups

1   Centre of Medical Law and Ethics (CMLE)
2   Centre of European Law (CEL)
3   British Institute of Human Rights (BIHR)
4   Centre for Crime and Justice Studies
5   Child Studies Unit
6   International Centre for Prison Studies (ICPS)
7   Centre of British and Constitutional Law and History
8   Trust Law Committee
9   Coroners' Law Resource (has links to information relating to coroners' law and practice)
10 Human Rights Act Research Unit (HRARU)
11 Civil Liberties Research Unit (CLRU)

Journals

1   *King's College Law Journal*
2   *Dispatches*
3   *Criminal Justice Matters*
4   *British Journal of Criminology*

LONDON SCHOOL OF ECONOMICS AND POLITICAL SCIENCE

Law Department, Houghton Street, London WC2A 2AE, UK
Tel: +44 207 4057686; Fax: +44 207 9557366
email: r.baldwin@lse.ac.uk
website: www.lse.ac.uk

Courses offered

LLB
LLB with French Law
LLM
MSc in Law and Accounting
MPhil
PhD

Centre

Centre for Environmental Law and Policy

Journals

1 *Modern Law Review*
2 *Public Law*

QUEEN MARY AND WESTFIELD COLLEGE

Department of Law, Mile End Road, London E1 4NS, UK
Tel: +44 207 8823282; Fax: +44 208 9818733
email: law-enquiries@qmul.ac.uk
website: www.laws.qmw.ac.uk

Courses offered

LLB
LLB (English and European law)
LLB (law with German language)
BA (law and German)
BA (law and politics)
BA (law and economics)
LLM
MSc in Management of Intellectual Property
MPhil
PhD

Centre

Centre for Commercial Law Studies (website: www.ccls.edu)

Journal

Queen Mary Law Journal

SCHOOL OF ORIENTAL AND AFRICAN STUDIES

Department of Law, Thornhaugh Street, Russell Square, London WC1H OXG, UK
Tel: +44 207 4197655; Fax: +44 207 6365615
email: kd16@soas.ac.uk
website: www.soas.ac.uk/law

Courses offered

LLB
BA Law (with another discipline)
LLM
MA International and Comparative Legal Studies
MPhil
PhD

Centres

1   Centre of Islamic and Middle East Law (promotes the study and understanding of Islamic law and modern Middle East legal systems)
2   East Asian Law Centre (promotes the study and understanding of laws and legal traditions in East Asia)
3   Group for Ethnic Minority Studies (focuses on the current issues in the study of ethnic minorities)
4   Malaysian Legal Studies Group

Journal

Journal of African Law (two parts annually) (website: www.journals.cambridge.org)

UNIVERSITY COLLEGE LONDON

Faculty of Laws, Bentham House, Endsleigh Gardens, London WC1H 0EG, UK
Tel: +44 207 6792000; Fax: +44 207 3879597
email: j.jowell@ucl.ac.uk
website: www.ucl.ac.uk

Courses offered

LLB
LLB Law with Advanced Studies
LLB Law with French/German/Italian Law
BA Law and History
LLM
MA in Legal and Political Theory
MPhil
PhD

Centres

1   Centre for Politics Law and Society (concentrates on issues in political and legal philosophy, intellectual history, law and politics)
2   The Constitution Unit (specialises in constitutional reform and comparative constitutional studies)
3   London Shipping Law Centre (undertakes research into shipping law)

LONDON GUILDHALL UNIVERSITY

Department of Law, 84 Moorgate, London EC2M 6SQ, UK
Tel: +44 207 3201500; Fax: +44 207 3201523
email: webb@lgu.ac.uk
website: www.lgu.ac.uk

Courses offered

LLB
LLB (business law)
Common Professional Examination
Legal Practice Course

MPhil
PhD

UNIVERSITY OF LUTON

Luton Business School, Department of Law, Vicarage Street, Luton LU1 3JU, UK
Tel: +44 1582 489030; Fax: +44 1582 743466
email: law@luton.ac.uk
website: www.luton.ac.uk

Courses offered

LLB
LLB/BA
LLM

UNIVERSITY OF MANCHESTER

Manchester School of Law, Oxford Road, Manchester M13 9PL, UK
Tel: +44 161 2753560; Fax: +44 161 2753579
email: tom.gibbons@man.ac.uk
website: www.man.ac.uk

Courses offered

LLB
LLB English Law and French Law
BA Accounting and Law
BA Law and Politics
BSc in Health Care, Ethics and Law
LLM International Business Law
LLM Law and Economics
MPhil
PhD

Centres

1   Centre for Law and Business
2   Institute for Law, Medicine and Bioethics

MANCHESTER METROPOLITAN UNIVERSITY

School of Law, Elizabeth Gaskell Campus, Hathersage Road, Manchester M13 0JA,
UK
Tel: +44 161 2473049; Fax: +44 0161 2476309
email: law.cse@mmu.ac.uk
website: www.did.cse.mmu.ac.uk

Courses offered

LLB
LLB with French

LLM
MA Medicine, Law and Ethics
MA Sport and the Law
MPhil
PhD
Common Professional Examination
Bar Vocational Course

Research units

1 Sport and the Law
2 Fiscal and Corporate Affairs
3 Law and Social Justice

Journal

Journal of the British Association of Sport and the Law

MIDDLESEX UNIVERSITY

Law School, Middlesex University Business School, The Burroughs, London NW4 4BT, UK
Tel: +44 208 3625000; Fax: +44 208 3626498
email: s.homewood@mdx.ac.uk
website: http://mubs.mdx.ac.uk

Courses offered

BA Law
LLB
LLM Employment Law
Common Professional Examination

Centre

Centre for Legal Research

NAPIER UNIVERSITY

Department of Law, Sighthill Court, Edinburgh EH11 4BN, Scotland, UK
Tel: +44 131 4553488; Fax: +44 131 4553500
email: j.dickson@napier.ac.uk
website: www.napier.ac.uk

Courses offered

BA
BA Criminal Justice
LLM International Law

UNIVERSITY OF NEWCASTLE UPON TYNE

Newcastle Law School, 21–24 Windsor Terrace, Newcastle upon Tyne NE1 7RU, UK
Tel: +44 191 2227624; Fax: +44 191 2610064
email: newcastle.law-school@ncl.ac.uk
website: www.ncl.ac.uk

Courses offered

LLB
BA Law with French
LLM in International Legal Studies
LLM in International Trade
LLM in Environmental Studies
MPhil
PhD

Centres

1   Centre for Corporate Governance and Financial Market Regulation
2   Newcastle Centre for Family Studies

Journal

Web Journal of Current Legal Issues (website: http://webjcli.ncl.ac.uk)

UNIVERSITY OF NORTHAMPTON

School of Accounting Information Systems and Law, Park Campus, Boughton Green
Road, Northampton NN2 7AL, UK
Tel: +44 1604 735500; Fax: +44 1604 721214
email: Mike.Cuthbert@nene.ac.uk
website: www.nene.ac.uk

Courses offered

LLB
LLM

UNIVERSITY OF NORTH LONDON

School of Law, Governance and Information Management, 62–66 Highbury Grove,
London N5 2AD, UK
Tel: +44 207 6072789; Fax: +44 207 7535403
email: j.mppn@unl.ac.uk
website: www.unl.ac.uk

Courses offered

LLB
LLM in European and International Law
MA in Legal Practice
Common Professional Examination

UNIVERSITY OF NORTHUMBRIA

Northumberland Road, Newcastle upon Tyne NE1 8ST, UK
Tel: +44 191 2274494; Fax: +44 191 2274557
email: linda.landels@unn.ac.uk
website: www.law.unn.ac.uk

Courses offered

LLB
LLM (Advanced Legal Practice)
Common Professional Examination
Bar Vocational Course

Journals

1   *International Journal of Clinical Education*
2   *Journal of Obligations and Remedies*
3   *Journal of Mental Health Law*

UNIVERSITY OF NOTTINGHAM

Department of Law, University Park, Nottingham NG7 2RD, UK
Tel: +44 115 9515700; Fax: +44 115 9515696
email: law-enquiries@nottingham.ac.uk
website: www.nottingham.ac.uk/law

Courses offered

BA (law)
BA (law and politics)
LLB
BA (law with French)
BA (law with German)
LLM International Law
MPhil
PhD

Centres

1   Centre for Environmental Law (email: cel@nottingham.ac.uk)
2   Human Rights Law Centre (email: David.Harris@nottingham.ac.uk)
3   Institute for the Study of Genetics, Biorisks & Society (email: iqbis@nottingham.ac.uk)
4   Treaty Centre (conducts research into the law of treaties and the practice of treaty making)
5   Public Procurement Research Group

NOTTINGHAM TRENT UNIVERSITY/NOTTINGHAM LAW SCHOOL

Belgrave Centre, Chaucer Street, Nottingham NG1 5LP, UK
Tel: +44 115 8484270; Fax +44 115 8486489
email: peter.kunzlik@ntu.ac.uk
website: www.nls.ntu.ac.uk

Courses offered

LLB
LLB
LLM in Corporate Law
LLM in Health Law

Common Professional Examination
Bar Vocational Course
Legal Practice Course

Centres

1   The Centre for Legal Research
2   Centre for Health Law

Journal

Nottingham Law Journal (biannually)

OPEN UNIVERSITY

Briggs Building, Walton Hall, Milton Keynes MK7 6AA, UK
Tel: +44 1908 652738; Fax: +44 1908 655898
email: g.j.slapper@open.ac.uk
website: www.ou.ac.uk

Courses offered

LLB
BA

UNIVERSITY OF OXFORD

Chairman of the Board, Law Faculty Office, St Cross Building, St Cross Road, Oxford
OX1 3UR, UK
Tel: +44 1865 271490; Fax: +44 1865 271560
email: lawfac@ox.ac.uk
website: www.law.ox.ac.uk

Courses offered

BA Jurisprudence
Bachelor of Civil Law (BCL)
Magister Juris (MJur)
Master of Studies in Legal Research (MStud)
Master of Letters (MLitt)
DPhil

Centres

1   Centre for Criminological Research
2   Centre for Socio-Legal Studies
3   Institute of European and Comparative Law
4   Oxford Intellectual Property Centre

Journals

1   *Oxford Journal of Legal Studies*
2   *Oxford University Commonwealth Law Journal*
3   *Electronic   Journal   of   Intellectual   Property   Rights*   (website:
     www.oiprc.ox.ac.uk/EJINDEX.html)

OXFORD BROOKES UNIVERSITY

School of Social Sciences and Law, Gipsy Lane Campus, Headington, Oxford OX3 OBP, UK
Tel: +44 1865 484901; Fax: +44 1865 819073
email: ssl@brookes.ac.uk
website: http://sss.brookes.ac.uk

Courses offered

LLB
BA/BSc
LLM in Criminal Justice
LLM in International Law
Common Professional Examination

Centre

Centre for Legal Research and Policy Studies (undertakes research into the part played by the courts in the implementation of policy by government and its agents and the inter-relationship between politicians, judges and citizens in policy formulation)

OXFORD INSTITUTE OF LEGAL PRACTICE

King Charles House, Park End Street, Oxford 0X1 1JD, UK
Tel: +44 1865 722619; Fax: +44 1865 722408
website: www.oxilp.ac.uk

Course offered

Legal Practice Course (a joint venture between the University of Oxford and Oxford Brookes University)

UNIVERSITY OF PLYMOUTH

Business School, Drake Circus, Plymouth PL4 8AA, UK
Tel: +44 1752 232000; Fax: +44 1752 232853
email: enquiry@pbs.plym.ac.uk
website: www.pbs.plym.ac.uk

Courses offered

LLB (Hons) Law
BSc (Hons) Law with Business Studies
BSc Maritime Business with Maritime Law
Postgraduate Diploma in Law

UNIVERSITY OF PORTSMOUTH

Department of Accounting and Management Science, Portsmouth Business School, Milton Site, Loclsway Road, Southsea, Hans PO4 8JF
Tel: +44 23 92844076; 92844095; Fax: +44 23 92844059; 92844093
email: suzanne.longden@pport.ac.uk
website: www.port.ac.uk

Courses offered

BA Law with Accounting
MA Business Law
LLM Business Law

QUEEN'S UNIVERSITY OF BELFAST

School of Law, 28 University Square, Belfast BT7 1NN, Northern Ireland, UK
Tel: +44 28 90273451; Fax: +44 28 90273376
email: law-enquiries@qub.ac.uk
website: www.law.qub.ac.uk

Courses offered

LLB
LLB (law and accountancy)
LLB (law and politics)
LLB Common and Civil Law with French
LLB Common and Civil Law with Hispanic Studies
Bachelor of Legal Science
LLM in Human Rights Law
LLM/MSSc in Criminal Justice
LLM in Computers and the Law
MPhil/PhD

Centres

1   Institute of Governance, Public Policy and Social Research
2   Human Rights Centre
3   Institute of Criminology and Criminal Justice

Journals

1   *Northern Ireland Legal Quarterly*
2   *Bulletin of Northern Ireland Law*
3   *Digest of Northern Ireland Law*
4   *International Commentary on Evidence: A Journal of Law and Theory in Electronic Format* (website: www.law.qub.ac.uk/ice)

UNIVERSITY OF READING

Department of Law, Old Whiteknights House, Whiteknights, PO Box 217,
Reading RG6 6AH, UK
Tel: +44 118 9875123; Fax: +44 118 9753280
email: law@rdg.ac.uk
website: www.rdg.ac.uk

Courses offered

LLB
LLB with French Law
LLB with Legal Studies in Europe

LLM
MPhil
PhD

Centre

Centre for Property Law

ROBERT GORDON UNIVERSITY

School of Public Administration and Law, Garthdee, Aberdeen AB10 7QE, UK
Tel: +44 1224 262908; Fax: +44 1224 262929
email: spal_info@mailbox.rgu.ac.uk
website: www.rgu.ac.uk

Courses offered

BA in Law and Management
LLB
MSc/LLM in Construction Law and Arbitration
LLM in Employment Law and Practice
LLM in International Commercial Law
MSc/LLM in International Trade
LLM in Information, Communication and Technology Law

Centre

Institute for Employment Law

UNIVERSITY OF SHEFFIELD

Department of Law, Crookesmoor Building, Conduit Road, Sheffield S10 1FL, UK
Tel: +44 114 2226770; Fax: +44 114 2226832
email: l.bloodworth@sheffield.ac.uk
website: www.shef.ac.uk

Courses offered

LLB
LLB (European, comparative and international law)
BA (law) Law and Criminology
BA (law) Law with French/German/Spanish
MA (law)
MA in International Criminology
MA in Biotechnological Law and Ethics
MPhil
PhD
Legal Practice Course

Centres

1   Centre for Criminological and Legal Research (CCLR)
2   Centre for Socio-Legal Studies (CSLS)
3   Centre for International, Comparative and European Law (CICEL)

4   Institute for Commercial Law Studies (ICLS)
5   Institute for the Study of the Legal Profession (ISLP)
6   Sheffield Institute for Biotechnological Law and Ethics (SIBLE)

SHEFFIELD HALLAM UNIVERSITY

School of Social Science and Law, 51/3 Broomsgrove Road, Sheffield S10 2BP, UK
Tel: +44 114 2252518; Fax: +44 114 2252591
email: k.m.williams@shu.ac.uk
website: www.shu.ac.uk

Courses offered

BA Criminology
BA Law and Business
BA Law and Criminology
LLB
MA Criminal Justice
LLM Law and Ethics in Healthcare
LLM European Law and Policy

UNIVERSITY OF SOUTHAMPTON

Faculty of Law, Highfield, Southampton SO17 1BJ, UK
Tel: +44 23 80593632; Fax +44 23 80593024
email: law@soton.ac.uk
website: www.soton.ac.uk

Courses offered

LLB
LLB (European legal studies)
LLB (international legal studies)
LLM
MA (criminal justice)
LLM (maritime law/international law/commercial law/European law)
MPhil
PhD

Centres

1   Institute of Maritime Law (focuses on maritime and international trade law)
2   Institute of Criminal Justice (examines issues relating to the balance between order and control of crime and the protection of civil liberties)
3   Behaviour Science and Law Network
4   Centre for Environmental Law

SOUTHAMPTON INSTITUTE

The Law School, East Park Terrace, Southampton SO14 0YN, UK
Tel: +44 23 80319501; Fax: +44 23 8035948
email: si.law@solent.ac.uk
website: www.solent.ac.uk

Courses offered

LLB
BA Legal Studies
LLM

Centres

1 Law Research Centre (especially disability law, energy law, environmental law and military law)
2 Disablement Policy and Law Research Unit

Journal

Mountbatten Journal of Legal Studies (website: www.solent.ac.uk/law/mjls)

SOUTH BANK UNIVERSITY

Law Division, South Bank Business School, 103 Borough Road, London SE1 0AA, UK
Tel: +44 207 8155733; Fax: +44 207 8157808
email: molanm@sbu.ac.uk
website: www.sbu.ac.uk/sbbslaw

Courses offered

LLB
Common Professional Examination
Legal Practice Course

UNIVERSITY OF STAFFORDSHIRE

Law School, Leek Road, Stoke-on-Trent ST4 2DF, UK
Tel: +44 1782 294550; Fax: +44 1782 294335
email: c.j.barton@staffs.ac.uk
website: www.staffs.ac.uk

Courses offered

LLB
LLM
Common Professional Examination
Legal Practice Course

Centre

Centre for the Study of the Family, Law and Social Policy

UNIVERSITY OF STIRLING

Department of Accountancy, Finance and Law, Stirling FK9 4LA, UK
Tel: +44 1786 467280; Fax: +44 1786 467308
email: accountancy@stir.ac.uk
website: www.stir.ac.uk

Course offered

BA Business Law

Journal

Scottish Law Gazette

UNIVERSITY OF STRATHCLYDE

Law School, Stenhouse Building, 173 Cathedral Street, Glasgow G4 ORQ, Scotland, UK
Tel: +44 141 5483738; Fax: +44 141 551546
email: contact-law@strath.ac.uk
website: www.law.strath.ac.uk

Courses offered

LLB
LLB (European)
LLB (law and a modern language)
BA (business law)
LLM in Construction Law
LLM in Information Technology
LLM Human Rights Law (with the University of Glasgow)
MSc in Criminal Justice
PhD
Diploma in Legal Practice

Centres

1   Centre for Professional Legal Studies (CPLS)
2   Centre for Law, Computers and Technology
3   Centre for Sentencing Research

UNIVERSITY OF SURREY

Department of Linguistic and International Studies, Guildford, Surrey GU2 5XH, UK
Tel: +44 1483 686200; Fax: +44 1483 686201
email: r.malcolm@surrey.ac.uk
website: www.surrey.ac.uk

Courses offered

LLB Law with French/German/Russian/Spanish
LLB in Law and European Studies
LLB

Centre

Surrey European Law Centre

UNIVERSITY OF SUSSEX

School of Legal Studies, Falmer, Sussex BN1 9SN, UK
Tel: +44 1273 678562; Fax: +44 1273 678466
email: enquiries.sls@sussex.ac.uk
website: www.sussex.ac.uk

Courses offered

LLB
BA Law
BA with North American Studies
LLB European Commercial Law
Common Professional Examination
LLM
MPhil
DPhil

SWANSEA INSTITUTE OF HIGHER EDUCATION

Swansea Law School, Mount Pleasant, Swansea SA1 6ED, West Glamorgan, Wales, UK
Tel/Fax: +44 1792 4811169
email: law@sihe.ac.uk
website: www.sihe.ac.uk

Courses offered

LLB
LLB Law with Languages

UNIVERSITY OF TEESSIDE

School of Social Sciences and Law, Middlesborough, Tees Valley TS1 3BA, UK
Tel: +44 1642 342306; Fax: +44 1642 384099
email: H.A.Taylor@tees.ac.uk
website: www.tees.ac.uk/schools/socialsciences

Course offered

LLB

Centre

Centre for Applied Social-legal Studies

THAMES VALLEY UNIVERSITY

Department of Law, Ealing Campus, St Mary's Road, Ealing, London W5 5RF, UK
Tel: +44 208 5795000; Fax: +44 208 5661353
email: law@tvu.ac.uk
website: www.tvu.ac.uk

Courses offered

LLB
Common Professional Examination
Legal Practice Course

UNIVERSITY OF ULSTER

School of Public Policy, Economics and Law, Shore Road, Newtownabbey, Co
Antrim, Northern Ireland BT37 0QB, UK
Tel: +44 28 90368240; Fax: +44 28 90366847
email: eru@ulst.ac.uk
website: www.busmgt.ulst.ac.uk

Courses offered

LLB/BA in Law and Government
LLB/BA in Law and Economics
LLB/BA Law and Business Studies
LLM European Law and Policy

The University of Ulster has four campuses in Northern Ireland

Centre

Public Policy Group (focuses on governance and regulation)

UNIVERSITY OF WALES, ABERYSTWYTH

Faculty of Law, Hugh Owen Building, Penglais, Aberystwyth, Ceredigion SY23 3DY,
Wales, UK
Tel: +44 1970 622712; Fax: +44 1970 622729
email: enquiries@uk.ac.aber
website: www.aber.ac.uk

Courses offered

LLB
LLB with French/German/Spanish/Italian
BA Law with French/German/Spanish/Welsh/Italian
BA Law with Maths/Economics/ Politics/Accounting and Finance/Business
Studies/Marketing/Information Management
LLM
LLM in Business Law
LLM in Environmental Law and Management
MPhil
PhD

Centres

1   Centre for Law in Rural Areas (CLARA)
2   The Centre for Welsh Legal Affairs

Journals

1   *Public Procurement Law Review*
2   *Cambrian Law Review*

UNIVERSITY OF WALES, CARDIFF

Cardiff Law School, PO Box 427, Law Building, Museum Avenue, Cardiff CF10 1XJ, Wales, UK
Tel: +44 29 20874348; Fax: +44 29 20874097
email: law@cardiff.ac.uk
website: www.cf.ac.uk

Courses offered

LLB
LLB (law and criminology)
LLB (law and sociology)
LLB (law and politics)
LLB Law and French/German/Spanish/Italian/Japanese
LLM
MPhil
PhD
Legal Practice Course
Bar Vocational Course

Centres and Groups

1   Centre for International Family Law Studies
2   Cardiff Centre for Crime Law and Justice
3   Centre for Medico-Legal Studies
4   Centre for Law and Religion
5   Centre for Contemporary Civil Law Studies
6   Cardiff Crime Study Group

Journal

Journal of Law and Society (quarterly)

UNIVERSITY OF WALES, SWANSEA

Law Department, Singleton Park, Swansea, Wales SA2 8PP, UK
Tel: +44 1792 295831; Fax: +44 1792 295855
email: ebms.admin@swansea.ac.uk
website: www.swan.ac.uk/law

Courses offered

LLB
Law and Modern Languages
BSc Joint Honours in Law and Psychology (three years)
LLM in Commercial and Maritime Law
MPhil
PhD

Centres

1   Centre for Instalment Credit Law
2   Institute of International Shipping and Trade Law

Journals

1   *Wales Law Journal*
2   *Journal of International Commercial Law*

UNIVERSITY OF WARWICK

School of Law, Coventry CV4 7AL, UK
Tel: +44 24 76523075; Fax +44 76524105
email: barbara.gray@warwick.ac.uk
website: www.law.warwick.ac.uk

Courses offered

LLB
LLB European Law
BA Law and Sociology
BA Law and Business
LLM
MPhil
PhD

Centres

1   CTI Law Technology Centre (email: CTILaw@warwick.ac.uk)
2   National Centre for Legal Education (email: ncle@warwick.ac.uk)
3   Legal Research Institute (email: lee.bridges@warwick.ac.uk)

Journals

1   *CTI Law Technology Centre Newsletter* (quarterly)
2   *National Centre for Legal Education Newsletter* (quarterly)
3   Book series *Law in its Social Setting*
4   *Journal of Information, Law and Technology* (email: jilt@warwick.ac.uk; website: http://elj.warwick.ac.uk/Jilt)

Centre

Centre for Capital Punishment Studies

UNIVERSITY OF WESTMINSTER

School of Law, 4–12 Little Titchfield Street, London W1W 7UW, UK
Tel: +44 207 9115000; Fax +44 207 9115152
email: boona@westminster.ac.uk
website: www.wmin.ac.uk

Courses offered

LLB
MPhil
PhD
Common Professional Examination
Legal Practice Course

Centre

Centre for Capital Punishment Studies

UNIVERSITY OF THE WEST OF ENGLAND

Faculty of Law, Frenchay Campus, Coldharbour Lane, Bristol BS16 1QY, UK
Tel: +44 117 3442604: Fax +44 117 3442268
email: law@uwe.ac.uk
website: www.uwe.ac.uk

Courses offered

LLB
LLB Law with French/German/Spanish
BA Law
LLM
MPhil
PhD
Common Professional Examination
Bar Vocational Course
Legal Practice Course

Centres

1   The Centre for Criminal Justice
2   The Human Rights Unit
3   The Comparative, International and European Law Unit
4   The Legal Education and Professional Skills Research Unit
5   British Institute of Legal Practice (provides tuition for the Common Professional
     Examination; Bar Vocational Course; Legal Practice Course)

UNIVERSITY OF WOLVERHAMPTON

School of Legal Studies, Arthur Storer Building, Molineux Street, Wolverhampton
WV1 1SB, UK
Tel: +44 1902 821515; Fax: +44 1902 322696
email: sls-staff@wlv.ac.uk
website: www.wlv.ac.uk

Courses offered

LLB
BA with Law as a major or minor (combined studies)
LLM
MPhil
PhD
LLDip (CPE) Common Professional Examination
Legal Practice Course

ZAMBIA

The law faculty of the University of Zambia offers a four-year LLB degree. Those wishing to qualify as legal practitioners must have completed the LLB degree, or its equivalent, from any recognised university to qualify as legal practitioners and then take the nine-month Legal Practitioners Qualifying Examination Course at the Zambia Institute of Advanced Legal Education. After successful completion of the course, students are recommended for admission to the Zambian Bar.

The CLEA country contact is Eva Mukelabai of the Zambia Institute of Advanced Legal Education (address below) (email: ziale@zamnet.zm).

The system of law is based on the common law, although customary law remains important in some areas. The superior court system comprises the High Court and a Supreme Court which sits in Lusaka, Kabwe and Ndola. The legal profession is fused.

Practitioners from other common law jurisdictions may apply for the right of audience on *an ad hoc* basis in the Zambian courts. Those from other jurisdictions who wish to practise in Zambia should contact the Law Association of Zambia, LAZ House, No 1 Lagos Road, Rhodes Park, PO Box 35271, Lusaka 10101, Zambia (Tel: +260 1 254401; Fax: +260 1 254428).

LAW REPORTS

- *Law Reports of Northern Rhodesia* (1931–58 (vols 1–6))
- *Rhodesia and Nyasaland Law Reports* (1956–64)
- *Zambia Law Reports* (1965–97)
- Some judgments from the superior courts are available free online from the Zambia Legal Information Institute (ZamLII) (www.zamnet.zm)

LAW SCHOOLS

UNIVERSITY OF ZAMBIA

School of Law, PO Box 32379, Lusaka, Zambia
Tel: +260 1 290733 (direct); 2917778 ext 2203 and 2198; Fax: +260 1 290733
email: achanda@law.unza.zm
website: www.zamnet.zm

Courses offered

LLB
LLM
Postgraduate Diploma in International Law
Postgraduate Diploma in Human Rights Law

Centre

Zambian Legal Information Institute

The Institute was established by the Law School of the University of Zambia in 1996. Its aim is to improve access to judgments, statutes and other legal materials of the Republic of Zambia both within Zambia and elsewhere and to connect lawyers, judges, academics, students and others within Zambia with the growing collection of legal information available via the internet. Its website is www.zamnet.zm.

ZamLII provides online research of Zambian and foreign legal information and general information about Zambia. The collection of legal information includes the Constitution of Zambia, rules and selected decisions of the courts, selected Acts, legal commentary, a legal directory and information about the University of Zambia School of Law. The email address is zamlii@zamnet.zm

Journal

Zambia Law Journal (annually) (covers legal issues of national, regional and international significance of relevance to Zambia)

ZAMBIA INSTITUTE OF ADVANCED LEGAL EDUCATION

Plot 9/11 Andrew Mwenya Road, Rhodes Park, PO Box 30690, Lusaka, Zambia
Tel: +260 1 254557; Fax: +260 1 254620
email: ziale@zamnet.zm
website: www.ziale.org.zm

Courses offered

Legal Practitioners Qualifying Examination Course
Diploma in Legislative Drafting (six months)
Practical Gender and the Law
Practical Advanced Human Rights and the Law

The Institute also provides advanced training for prosecutors, magistrates and judges

ZIMBABWE

Legal education in Zimbabwe is conducted in the faculty of law at the University of Zimbabwe in Harare, the capital city.

The faculty offers a four-year Bachelor of Laws honours degree, holders of which are automatically entitled to register as legal practitioners. The faculty also offers a masters degree in law by coursework and an MPhil and DPhil degree by research.

The system of law in Zimbabwe is largely based on Roman-Dutch law, although common law has relevance in some areas. The superior court system comprises the High Court, which sits in Harare and Bulawayo, and the Supreme Court, which sits in Harare.

The legal profession is fused although there are two *de facto* Bars practising out of chambers in Harare.

Residents of Zimbabwe who are holders of recognised foreign law degrees are required to pass examinations set by the Council of Legal Education before they can be admitted as legal practitioners. The Secretary of the Council of Legal Education is Mr CK Nyathi, c/o Secretary for Justice, Legal and Parliamentary Affairs, PO Box 1409, Harare, Zimbabwe.

A legal practitioner from a foreign jurisdiction may, upon application and on the recommendation of the Council, be granted authority to appear in a Zimbabwean court in a specific matter.

There are about 600 registered legal practitioners in Zimbabwe whose professional conduct is governed by a statutory body, the Law Society of Zimbabwe at PO Box 2596, Harare, Zimbabwe (Tel: +263 4 751000; Fax: +263 4 750327; email: lawsoc@primenetzw.com).

LAW REPORTS

- *Southern Rhodesia Law Reports* (SRLR) (1935–55)
- *Rhodesia and Nyasaland Law Reports* (R and N) (1956–64)
- *Rhodesia Law Reports* (RLR) (1964–79)
- *Zimbabwe Law Reports* (ZLR) (1980–date) (available from the Legal Resources Foundation – Fax: +263 4 728213; email: lrfhre@mail.pci.co.zw)
- Some cases are also reported in the *South African Law Reports* and *Law Reports of the Commonwealth*

LAW SCHOOL

UNIVERSITY OF ZIMBABWE

Faculty of Law, PO Box MP 167, Mount Pleasant, Harare, Zimbabwe
Tel: +263 4 303211 ext 1309; Fax: +263 4 333407; 335249
website: www.uz.ac.zw

Courses offered

LLB
LLM
MWL (Masters in Women's Law)
MPhil
PhD
Diploma in Women's Law

Centres

1   Legal Aid Clinic
    The Clinic's main objectives are:
    - To provide legal aid and legal representation in any court of law, tribunal or body before which a party may be represented by a legal practitioner for litigants or persons who are unable to obtain the services of legal practitioners on their own account due to insufficient means.
    - To establish, administer and assist legal clinics and other organisations which provide legal advice and assistance to the public to facilitate the optimal provision of legal services.
    - To assist in the practical training of law students through supervised provision of legal aid and legal representation.
2   Commercial Law Institute
3   Women's Law Centre (Fax: +263 4 304008; email: 243940@ecoweb.co.za; amyt@teko.zw)

Journals

1   *Zimbabwe Law Review*
2   *Women's Centre Newsletter*

SECTION 4
RESEARCH CENTRES AND
SPECIALIST JOURNALS

RESEARCH CENTRES AND SPECIALIST JOURNALS

RESEARCH CENTRES

This section provides a listing of legal research and other centres attached to Commonwealth law schools. Details of the work of research centres appear under the individual entry for each university in Section 3.

Administrative law and justice
Centre for Court Policy and Administration (University of Wollongong)
Centre for Law and Social Justice (Queensland University of Technology)
Centre for the Study of Administrative Justice (University of Bristol)
Institute of Judicial Administration (University of Birmingham)
Privatisation and Public Accountability Centre (Monash University)

Air and space law
Institute of Air and Space Law (McGill University)

Alternative dispute resolution
Alternate Dispute Resolution Centre (Pakistan College of Law)
Corrs Chambers, Westgarth Dispute Management Centre (University of Queensland)
Dispute Resolution Centre (Bond University)
Institute for Dispute Resolution (University of Victoria)
Unit for Dispute Resolution (University of Technology, Sydney)

Business law
See Commercial law

Charity law
Charity Law Unit (University of Liverpool)
Charity Law Research Unit (University of Dundee)

Children
Centre for Child and the Law (National Law School of India University)
Centre for the Study of the Child, the Family and the Law (University of Liverpool)
Centre for the Study of Law, the Child and the Family (Brunel University)
Child Studies Unit (King's College London)
National Children's and Youth Law Centre (University of Sydney)

Chinese law
Centre for Chinese and Comparative Law (City University of Hong Kong)

Civil law

Centre for Contemporary Civil Law Studies (Cardiff Law School)
Civil Law Centre (University of Aberdeen)

Civil rights

See Human rights

Commercial law

Bureau for Mercantile Law (University of Port Elizabeth)
Centre for Business Law and Practice (University of Leeds)
Centre for Commercial Laws (Australian National University)
Centre for Commercial and Property Law (Queensland University of Technology)
Centre for Commercial Law Studies (Queen Mary and Westfield College, University of London)
Centre for Consumer and Commercial Law Research (Brunel University)
Centre for Corporate and Commercial Law (University of Cambridge)
Centre for Corporate Governance and Financial Market Regulation (University of Newcastle, UK)
Centre de droit des affaires et du commerce international (Université de Montréal)
Centre for Instalment Credit Law (University of Wales, Swansea)
Centre for Law and Business (University of Manchester)
Centre for Transnational Business Law (Bond University)
Commercial Law Centre (Bond University)
Commercial Law Institute (University of Zimbabwe)
ESRC Centre for Business Research (University of Cambridge)
Financial Services Consumer Policy Centre (University of New South Wales)
Institute for Commercial Law Studies (University of Sheffield)
National Australia Bank's Banking Law Centre (Monash University)
National Centre for Corporate Law and Policy Research (University of Canberra)
Norton Rose Centre for Commercial and Banking Law (University of Bristol)

Communications law

Communications Law Centre (University of New South Wales)
Information Law and Technology Unit (University of Hull)

Comparative law

Australian Institute of Foreign and Comparative Law (University of Queensland)
Centre for Chinese and Comparative Law (City University of Hong Kong)
Centre for Comparative and Public Law (University of Hong Kong)
Centre for International, Comparative and European Law (University of Sheffield)
Comparative, International and European Law Unit (University of the West of England)
Institute of Comparative Law (McGill University)
Institute of European and Comparative Law (University of Oxford)
Institute of Foreign and Comparative Law (University of South Africa)

Competition law

Centre for Applied Legal Studies (Wits Law School, South Africa)

Conflict resolution

Asia Pacific Centre for Human Rights and the Prevention of Ethnic Conflict (Murdoch University)

Nametz International Centre for Conflict Resolution (University of British Columbia)

Constitutional law

Centre for Applied Legal Studies (Wits Law School, South Africa)

Centre for Constitutional Studies (University of Alberta)

Centre for Comparative Constitutional Studies (University of Melbourne)

Corporate law

See Commercial law

Criminal law

Coroners' Law Resource (King's College London)

International Centre for Criminal Law Reform and Criminal Justice Policy (University of British Columbia)

Nathanson Centre for the Study of Organised Crime and Corruption (York University, Canada)

Criminal justice studies and criminology

Cardiff Centre for Crime Law and Justice (Cardiff Law School)

Centre for Applied Socio-legal Studies (University of Teesside)

Centre for Capital Punishment Studies (University of Westminster)

Centre for Crime and Justice Studies (King's College London)

Centre for Criminal Justice Research (Brunel University)

Centre for Criminal Justice Research (University of Bristol)

Centre for Criminal Justice Studies (University of the West of England)

Centre for Criminal Justice Studies (University of Leeds)

Centre for Criminological and Legal Research (University of Sheffield)

Centre for Criminological Research (University of Oxford)

Centre for Sentencing Research (University of Strathclyde)

Crime Research Centre (University of Western Australia)

Criminal Justice Research Centre (Coventry University)

Criminal Justice Unit (University of Liverpool)

Institute of Criminology (University of Cambridge)

Institute of Criminology (University of Cape Town)

Institute of Criminology (University of Sydney)

International Centre for Criminal Law Reform and Criminal Justice Policy (University of British Columbia)

Institute of Criminology and Criminal Justice (Queen's University of Belfast)

Institute of Justice and Applied Legal Studies (University of the South Pacific)

Institute of Criminal Justice (University of Southampton)

International Centre for Prison Studies (King's College London)

Kent Criminal Justice Centre (University of Kent)

Customary law

Centre for International Indigenous Legal Studies
Native Law Centre of Canada (University of Saskatchewan)
Indigenous Law Centre (University of New South Wales)

Disabled, Law and the

Disablement Policy and Law Research Unit (Southampton Institute)

Economics, Law and

Centre for Law and Economics (Australian National University)
Centre for Legal and Economic Study of Institutions (University of Queensland)
David Hume Institute (University of Edinburgh)
Mandela Institute (Wits Law School, South Africa)

Elder law

Centre for Elder Law (University of Western Sydney)

Employment law

See Labour law

Energy/natural resources law

Canadian Institute of Resources Law (University of Calgary)
Centre for Energy, Petroleum and Mineral Law and Policy (University of Dundee)
Dr Andrew R Thompson Natural Resources Programme (University of British Columbia)
International Water Law Research Institute (University of Dundee)
Law Research Centre (Southampton Institute)

Environmental law

Australian Centre for Environmental Law (University of Sydney/Australian National University)
Centre for the Environment and Society (University of Essex)
Centre for Environmental Law, Education, Research and Advocacy (National Law School of India University)
Centre for Environmental Law (Macquarie University)
Centre for Environmental Law (University of Nottingham)
Centre for Environmental Law (University of Southampton)
Centre for Environmental Law and Policy (London School of Economics)
Centre for Law in Rural Areas (University of Wales)
Centre for Natural Resources Law and Policy (University of Wollongong)
Centre for Studies in Agriculture, Law and the Environment (University of Saskatchewan)
Environmental Law Institute (De Montfort University)
Environmental Law Unit (University of Cape Town)
Foundation for International Environmental Law and Development (University College, University of London)
Institute of Marine and Environmental Law (University of Cape Town)

Law Research Centre (Southampton Institute)
Marine and Environmental Law Programme (Dalhousie University)

Ethics, Law and

Centre For Health Law Ethics and Policy (University of Newcastle, Australia)
Centre for Law and Religion (Cardiff Law School)
Institute for Law, Ethics and Medicine (National Law School of India University)
Sheffield Institute for Biotechnological Law and Ethics (SIBLE) (University of Sheffield)

Ethnic minorities studies

Encountering Legal Cultures Research Group (University of East London)
Group for Ethnic Minority Studies (SOAS, University of London)
National Aboriginal Youth Law Centre (Flinders University/Northern Territory University)
Oliver Tambo Centre (University of Fort Hare)

European law

Centre of European Law (King's College London)
Centre for European Law and Integration (University of Leicester)
Centre for European Law and Practice (University of East Anglia)
Centre for European Legal Studies (University of Exeter)
Centre for European Legal Studies (University of Cambridge)
Centre for International, Comparative and European Law (University of Sheffield)
Centre for the Study of Law in Europe (University of Leeds)
Comparative, International and European Law Unit (University of the West of England)
Durham European Law Institute (University of Durham)
Edinburgh Europa Centre (University of Edinburgh)
European Law Centre (University of New South Wales)
Institute of European Law (University of Birmingham)
Institute of European and Comparative Law (University of Oxford)
Institute of European Public Law (University of Hull)
International and European Law Unit (University of Liverpool)
Pan European Institute (University of Essex)
Surrey European Law Centre (University of Surrey)

Family law

Canadian Research Institute for Law and the Family (University of Calgary)
Centre for Family Law and Family Policy (University of East Anglia)
Centre for Feminist Legal Studies (University of British Columbia)
Centre for International Family Law Studies (Cardiff Law School)
Centre for the Study of the Child, the Family and the Law (University of Liverpool)
Centre for the Study of the Family, Law and Social Policy (University of Staffordshire)
Centre for the Study of Law, the Child and the Family (Brunel University)
Community Law and Research Centre (University of Technology, Sydney)
Family Law Research Unit (Griffith University)
Newcastle Centre for Family Studies (University of Newcastle upon Tyne)

Feminist legal studies

Centre for Feminist Legal Studies (University of British Columbia)
Feminist Legal Research Unit (University of Liverpool)
Institute for Feminist Legal Studies (York University, Canada)
Women's Law Centre (University of Zimbabwe)
See also Gender law studies and women's law

First nations

Native Law Centre of Canada (University of Saskatchewan)
See also Customary law

Forensic studies

International Institute of Forensic Studies (Monash University)
Joseph Bell Centre for Forensic Statistics and Legal Reasoning (University of Edinburgh)

Gender issues

Centre for Applied Legal Studies (Wits Law School, South Africa)
Centre for Feminist Legal Studies (University of British Columbia)
Institute for Feminist Legal Studies (York University, Canada)

Health Law

See Medico-legal studies

Human rights

Alberta Civil Liberties Research Center (University of Alberta)
Asia Pacific Centre for Human Rights and the Prevention of Ethnic Conflict (Murdoch University)
Australian Human Rights Centre (University of New South Wales)
British Institute of Human Rights (King's College London)
Castan Centre for Human Rights Law (Monash University)
Centre of Human Rights (University Law College Peshawar)
Centre for the Study of Forced Migration (University of Dar es Salaam)
Civil Liberties Research Unit (King's College London)
Human Rights Act Research Unit (King's College London)
Human Rights Centre (Queen's University of Belfast)
Human Rights Center (Pakistan College of Law)
Human Rights Centre (University of Essex)
Human Rights Centre (University of Durham)
Human Rights Law Centre (University of Nottingham)
Human Rights Institute (University of Peshawar)
Human Rights and Peace Centre (HURIPEC) (Makerere University)
Human Rights Research and Education Centre (University of Ottawa)
Human Rights Research Unit (University of Leeds)
Human Rights Study Centre (University of Ghana)
Human Rights Unit (University of the West of England)
National Institute of Human Rights (National Law School of India University)

Indigenous law
See Customary law and First nations

Immigration law
Centre for the Study of Forced Migration (University of Dar es Salaam)

Intellectual property
Australian Centre for Intellectual Property in Agriculture (Australian National University)
Asia Pacific Intellectual Property Law Institute (Murdoch University)
Centre for Intellectual Property Law, Research and Advocacy (National Law School of India University)
Centre for Intellectual Property Research (Griffith University)
Intellectual Property Centre (University of Bristol)
Intellectual Property Unit (University of Cambridge)
Oxford Intellectual Property Centre (University of Oxford)
Shepherd and Wedderburn Centre for Research in Intellectual Property and Technology (University of Edinburgh)

International and comparative law
Centre for Asian Studies (University of British Columbia)
Centre for Chinese and Comparative Law (City University of Hong Kong)
Centre internationale de la common law en français (Université de Moncton)
Centre for International Law (University of Hertfordshire)
Centre for International, Comparative and European Law (University of Sheffield)
Centre for International and Public Law (Australian National University)
Institute of Comparative Law (McGill University)
Institute for European Studies (Université de Montréal)
International and European Law Unit (University of Liverpool)
Lauterpacht Research Centre for International Law (University of Cambridge)
Lockerbie Trial Briefing Site (University of Glasgow)
McCoubrey Centre for International Law (University of Hull)
Treaty Law (University of Nottingham)

International trade law
Centre for Applied Legal Studies (Wits Law School, South Africa)
Centre for Trade Policy and Law (University of Ottawa)
Estey Centre for Law and Economics in International Trade (University of Saskatchewan)
Institute of International Shipping and Trade Law (University of Wales)

Islamic law
Centre for Islamic and Middle East Law (SOAS, University of London)

Jurisprudence and legal philosophy
Centre de Traduction et de Terminologie Juridiques (Université de Moncton)
Joseph Bell Centre for Forensic Statistics and Legal Reasoning (University of Edinburgh)

Labour law

International Centre for Management, Law and Industrial Relations (University of Leicester)
Institute of Development and Labour Law (University of Cape Town)
Institute for Employment Law (Robert Gordon University)

Law and development

Institute of Development and Labour Law (University of Cape Town)
Mandela Institute (Wits Law School, South Africa)

Law and justice

See Social justice

Law and language

Centre for Plain Legal Language (University of Sydney)

Law and religion

Centre for Law and Religion (Cardiff University)

Land law/land rights

See Property law

Legal education and information

Australasian Legal Information Institute (University of Technology, Sydney)
Centre for Advanced Legal Studies and Research (University of Kerala)
Centre for Legal Education (University of Newcastle, Australia)
Commonwealth Legal Education Research Centre (University of Buea)
Legal Education and Professional Skills Research Unit (University of the West of England)
National Centre for Legal Education (University of Warwick)
South Asia Legal Education Consortium (SALEC) (Dhaka University/University of Rajshahi)
Zambian Legal Information Institute (University of Zambia)

Legal history

Centre of British and Constitutional Law and History (King's College London)

Legal process

Centre for the Study of State and Market (University of Toronto)
International Ombudsman Institute (University of Alberta)
Institute for Dispute Resolution (University of Victoria, Canada)

Legal research

Centre for Legal Research and Policy Studies (Oxford Brookes University)
Centre for Legal Research (Nottingham Trent University)

Centre for Legal Research (University of Middlesex)
Legal Research Centre (University of Peshawar)
Legal Research Institute (University of Warwick)
Legal Research Institute (University of Manitoba)
Justice Policy Research Centre (University of Newcastle, Australia)

Legislative drafting

Sir William Dale Centre for Legislative Studies (Institute of Advanced Legal Studies, University of London)

Marine law

See Environmental law

Maritime law

Centre for Maritime Law (University of Queensland)
Centre for Maritime Policy (University of Wollongong)
Institute of Maritime Law (University of Southampton)
See also Shipping law

Medico-legal studies

Behaviour Science and Law Network (University of Southampton)
Centre for Applied Legal Studies (Wits Law School, South Africa)
Centre For Health Law Ethics and Policy (University of Newcastle, Australia)
Centre of Medical Law and Ethics (King's College London)
Centre for Medico-Legal Studies (Cardiff Law School)
Centre for Health Law (University of Nottingham)
Health Law Group (University of Toronto)
Health Law Institute (University of Alberta)
Health Law Institute (Dalhousie University)
Institute of Law and Ethics in Medicine (University of Glasgow)
Institute for Law, Ethics and Medicine (National Law School of India University)
Institute for Law, Medicine and Bioethics (University of Manchester)
Institute of Medicine, Law and Bioethics (University of Liverpool)
Institute for the Study of Genetics, Biorisks and Society (University of Nottingham)
Sheffield Institute of Biotechnological Law and Ethics (University of Sheffield)
University of Toronto Joint Centre for Bioethics

Mercantile law

See Commercial law

Military law

Law Research Centre (Southampton Institute)

Natural resources

See Environmental law

Professional legal studies

Centre for Legal Practice (University of Exeter)
Centre for Professional Legal Studies (University of Strathclyde)
Institute for the Study of the Legal Profession (University of Sheffield)

Property law

Centre for Applied Legal Studies (Wits Law School, South Africa)
Centre for Commercial and Property Law (Queensland University of Technology)
Centre for Property Law (University of Reading)
Centre for Property Law (University of Aberdeen)
Centre for Property Studies (University of New Brunswick)

Public law/public policy

Centre for Comparative and Public Law (University of Hong Kong)
Centre for International and Public Law (Australian National University)
Centre for Politics, Law and Society (University College London)
Centre for Public Law (University of Cambridge)
Centre de Recherche en Droit Publique (Université de Montréal)
Gilbert and Tobin Centre of Public Law (University of New South Wales)
Institute of Governance, Public Policy and Social Research (Queen's University of Belfast)
Public Policy Group (University of Ulster)
Public Procurement Research Group (University of Nottingham)
York University Centre for Public Law and Public Policy (York University, Canada)

Regional legal studies

Asian Law Centre (University of Melbourne)
Caribbean Law Institute (University of the West Indies)
Centre of Asian and Pacific Law (University of Sydney)
Centre for Islamic and Middle East Law (SOAS, University of London)
Centre for Southeast Asian Law (Northern Territory University)
Centre for Welsh Legal Affairs (University of Wales, Aberystwyth)
East Asian Law Centre (SOAS, University of London)
Malaysian Legal Studies Group (SOAS, University of London)
South Asia Legal Education Consortium (SALEC) (Dhaka University/University of Rajshahi)

Shipping law

Institute of International Shipping and Trade Law (University of Wales)
London Shipping Law Centre (University College, London)

Social justice and welfare law/socio-legal studies

Centre for Law and Social Justice (Queensland University of Technology)
Centre for Law and Society (University of Edinburgh)
Centre for Social Welfare Law Research (Liverpool John Moores University)
Centre for Socio-Legal Research Law, Race and Gender Unit (University of Cape Town)
Centre for Socio-Legal Studies (University of Natal)

Centre for Socio-Legal Studies (University of Sheffield)
Centre for Socio-Legal Studies (University of Oxford)
Institute of Justice and Applied Legal Studies (University of the South Pacific)
Social-Legal Research Centre (Griffith University)

Technology and the law

Baker and McKenzie Cyberspace Law and Policy Centre (University of New South Wales)
Centre for Innovation Law and Policy (University of Toronto)
Centre for Law, Computers and Technology (University of Strathclyde)
Centre for Law and Computing (University of Durham)
Centre for Law in the Digital Economy (Monash University)
Centre for Technology Law (University of Queensland)
CTI Law Technology Centre (University of Warwick)
Cyberlaw Research Unit (University of Leeds)
Information Law and Technology Unit (University of Hull)
Law and Technology Institute (Dalhousie University)

Tourism law

Tourism Law Unit (University of Port Elizabeth)

Traditional law

See Customary law

Trusts and equity

Trust Law Committee (King's College London)

Women's law

Centre for Law and Gender (University of Bristol)
Centre for Woman and Law (National Law School of India University)
Women Law Centre (Pakistan College of Law)
Women's Law Centre (University of Zimbabwe)

LAW JOURNALS

This part provides details of specialist law journals published by Commonwealth law schools. Details of all law journals are included in the relevant law school entries in Section 3.

Access to justice

Windsor Yearbook of Access to Justice (University of Windsor)

Alternative dispute resolution

Bond Dispute Resolution News (Bond University)

Air and space law

Annuals of Air and Space Law (McGill University)

Business law

Australian Journal of Corporate Law (University of Canberra)
Caribbean Law and Business (University of West Indies)
Commercial Law Bulletin (University of Port Elizabeth)
Corporate and Business Law Journal (University of Adelaide)
Corporate and Business Law Journal (University of Canberra)
International Trade and Business Law Annual (University of Queensland)
Journal of International Commercial Law (University of Wales)
Juta's Business Law (University of South Africa)
SA Mercantile Law Journal (University of South Africa)

Civil law and justice

Civil Justice Quarterly (University of Birmingham)
Journal of Obligations and Remedies (University of Northumbria)

Commercial law

See Business law

Criminal justice

British Journal of Criminology (King's College London)
Current Issues in Criminal Justice (University of Sydney)

Elder law

Elder Law Journal (University of Western Sydney)

Environmental law

Antarctic and Southern Ocean Law and Policy Papers (University of Tasmania)
Australasian Journal of Natural Resources Law and Policy (University of Wollongong)
Centre for Energy, Petroleum and Mineral Law and Policy (CEPMLP) Internet Journal
  (University of Dundee)

Environmental Liability Journal (De Montfort University)
Marine and Environmental Law Programme (Dalhousie University)
New Zealand Journal of Environmental Law (University of Auckland)

European law
European Public Law Journal (University of Hull)

Evidence
International Commentary on Evidence (Queen's University of Belfast)

Family law
Canadian Journal of Family Law (University of British Columbia)

Federal law
Federal Law Review (Australian National University)

Health law
Journal of Mental Health Law (University of Northumbria)

Human rights
Asia Pacific Journal on Human Rights and the Law (Murdoch University)
Australian Journal of Human Rights (University of New South Wales)
Human Rights Defender (University of New South Wales)
Journal of Peace and Human Rights (Makerere University)
South African Journal on Human Rights (University of the Witwatersrand)

Indigenous law
Indigenous Law Bulletin (University of New South Wales)
Law Text Culture (University of Wollongong)
Native Law Reporter (University of Saskatchewan)

International law
Australian International Law Journal (University of Western Sydney)
Australian Yearbook of International Law (Australian National University)
Canadian Yearbook of International Law (University of Ottawa)
Comparative and International Law Journal of Southern Africa (CILSA)
Journal of Malaysian and Comparative Law (University of Malaya)
Melbourne Journal of International Law (University of Melbourne)
Singapore Journal of International and Comparative Law (National University of Singapore)
South African Yearbook of International Law (University of South Africa)
Sri Lanka Journal of International Law (University of Colombo)

International trade
International Trade and Business Law Annual (University of Queensland)

Intellectual property

Electronic Journal of Intellectual Property Rights (University of Oxford)

Jurisprudence

Canadian Journal of Law and Jurisprudence (University of Western Ontario)
Journal for Juridical Science (University of Orange Free State)

Labour law

Development and Labour Monographs (University of Cape Town)

Law and information science

Journal of Law and Information Science (University of Tasmania)

Law and justice

Law and Justice Journal (Queensland University of Technology)

Law and society

Australian Journal of Law and Society (Macquarie University)

Law reform

Flinders Journal of Law Reform (Flinders University)

Legal education

Alternative Law Journal (Monash University)
International Journal of Clinical Education (University of Northumbria)
Singapore Journal of Legal Studies (National University of Singapore)
National Centre for Legal Education Newsletter (University of Warwick)

Legal history

Australian Journal of Legal History (University of Adelaide)
Cambridge Studies in English Legal History (University of Cambridge)

Legal profession

The Advocate (University of Toronto)

Marine/maritime law

Ocean Yearbook (Dalhousie University)
Sea Changes (University of Cape Town)

Privacy law

Privacy Law and Policy Reporter (University of New South Wales)

Public law

Public Law (London School of Economics)

Revenue law

Revenue Law Journal (Bond University)

Regional studies

Australian Journal of Asian Law (University of Melbourne)
Asia Pacific Law Review (City University of Hong Kong)
Journal of African Law (School of Oriental and African Studies)
Journal of Malaysian and Comparative Law (University of Malaya)
Journal of South Pacific Law (USP)
Mediterranean Journal of Human Rights (University of Malta)
Oxford University Commonwealth Law Journal (University of Oxford)

Socio-legal studies

Alternative Law Journal (Monash University)
Journal of Law and Society (Cardiff Law School)
Windsor Review of Legal and Social Issues (University of Windsor)

Sports law

Journal of the British Association of Sport and the Law (Manchester Metropolitan University)

Tax law

See Revenue law

Technology and the law

CTI Law Technology Centre Newsletter (University of Warwick)
Canadian Journal of Law and Technology (Dalhousie University)
Digital Technology Law Journal (Murdoch University)
Electronic Journal of Law (Murdoch University)
Journal of Biotechnology and Law (NALSAR University of Law)
Journal of Information, Law and Technology (University of Warwick)
Journal of Law and Information Science (University of Tasmania)

Women and the law

Canadian Journal of Women and the Law (University of Ottawa)
Sister in Law (Murdoch University)
Women's Centre Newsletter (University of Zimbabwe)